Interpretive Reasoning

INTERPRETIVE REASONING

Laurent Stern

Cornell University Press

ITHACA AND LONDON

First published 2005 by Cornell University Press

Printed in the United States of America

Library of Congress Cataloging-in-Publication Data

Stern, Laurent.
  Interpretive reasoning / Laurent Stern.
  p. cm.
    Includes bibliographical refernces and index.
  ISBN 0-8014-4330-X (cloth : alk. paper)
  1. Hermeneutics. I. –Title.
    BD241.S825 2005
    121'.68–c22   2004018218

Cornell University Press strives to use environmentally responsible
suppliers and materials to the fullest extent possible in the publishing
of its books. Such materials include vegetable-based, low-VOC inks
and acid-free papers that are recycled, totally chlorine-free, or partly
composed of nonwood fibers. For further information, visit our website
at www.cornellpress.cornell.edu.

Cloth printing   10 9 8 7 6 5 4 3 2 1

"We demand that poets and critics give us new life-symbols, and that they imprint the forms of our questions on the still viable myths and legends. Isn't it a subtle and poignant irony that a great critic projects our longing unto early Florentine paintings or Greek torsi—thereby drawing for us out of them what we would have sought in vain everywhere else—when at the same time he speaks of new results of scientific research, new methods and new facts? Facts are always available, and they always contain everything. Yet, every era needs other Greeks, other Middle Ages, and another Renaissance. Succeeding generations create what they need, and only the immediate successors believe that their fathers' dreams were lies that must be opposed by their own new 'truths.' The history of poetry's reception follows the same course, and today's critics hardly touch the afterlife of their grandfathers' or remote ancestors' dreams. Thus, the different conceptions of the Renaissance can live together peacefully, just as a new poet's new Phaedra, new Siegfried, or new Tristan must always leave intact the Phaedra, Siegfried or Tristan of his predecessors."

—GEORG LUKÁCS, *Die Seele und die Formen,* 1911
 (Translated by Anna Bostock, revised.)

"What occupies me is how works of art are related to historical life. On this point what seems to me certain is that there is no such thing as a history of art. . . . Works of art are essentially ahistorical. . . . The explorations of the current history of art always end up only as a history of material or history of form, for which works of art serve only as examples, almost as models: of a history of works themselves there is absolutely no question. . . . Works of art are, in this respect, like philosophical systems, and the so-called 'history' of philosophy is either an uninteresting history of dogmas, or even a history of philosophers, or a history of problems, in which case it threatens to lose contact with the temporal extension and to change into timeless, intensive *interpretation.* The specific historicity of works of art is of a similar kind, which opens not into the history of art but only into interpretation. In the interpretation there arise connections between works of art which are timeless and yet not without historical importance."

—WALTER BENJAMIN, Letter to Christian Florens Rang, December 9, 1923
 (Translated by Charles Rosen, revised.)

Contents

———

Preface   xi

INTRODUCTION   1

1. TWO PRINCIPLES   5
   1. First Steps   5
   2. Natural Interpretation in the Indicative Mood   8
   3. Natural Interpretation in the Subjunctive Mood   11
   4. Deep Interpretation   15
   5. "You Must Change . . ."   18
   6. Whereof We May Remain Silent   21
   7. The Reasonable and the Knowledgeable   23

2. TWO KINDS OF BELIEFS   27
   1. Failure in Self-Understanding   27
   2. The Contents of Belief Box #1 and the Two Principles   34
   3. Do We Know the Contents of Our Belief Box #1?   35
   4. Conceive It Possible That You Are Mistaken!   37
   5. "*Hier steh' ich, ich kann nicht anders*"   39
   6. ". . . *Par ce que c'estoit luy; par ce que c'estoit moy*"   40
   7. What We Cannot Know   42

3. KINDS OF INTERPRETATIONS   45
   1. The Hereditary Property of Interpretations   45

2. Partially Mistaken or Insincere Interpretations *48*
3. Deep Interpretation *50*
4. Weakened Formulation of the Principles *51*
5. Alternatives to the Speaker's Self-Understanding *52*
6. The First-Person Perspective *54*
7. Natural and Deep Interpretations *56*
8. Grandeur and Misery of Deep Interpretation *58*
9. Interpretive Reports *62*

4. THE PRINCIPLES 66
1. The Appeal to the Principles *67*
2. Interpretive Goals *68*
3. Abusing the Principles *69*
4. The Hidden Authoritarianism of Universalizability *73*
5. The Appeal to the Restrictive Principle *76*
6. Can We Adopt a Weaker Form of the Principles? *78*
7. Do Numbers Count in Appealing to a Principle? *80*
8. Interpretive Traditions *83*
9. Universalizability within the Limits of
   Interpretive Goals *85*

5. CONTESTABLE INTERPRETATIONS:
   INTERPRETATIONS OF ARTWORKS 87
1. The Fragility of the Intentional Tie *88*
2. Intentionalism and Anti-Intentionalism *90*
3. The Interpreter's Perspective *91*
4. Levels of Understanding Artworks *93*
5. The Internal versus External Distinction *94*
6. On- and Off-the-Wall Interpretations *97*
7. Application *101*
8. Blurring Distinctions *102*
9. Art and Life *104*

6. ESSENTIALLY CONTESTABLE INTERPRETATIONS 106
1. On the Contents of Belief Box #1 *106*
2. Interminable Controversies *108*
3. Tolerance *110*
4. Interminable Controversies and Deep Interpretation *114*
5. Deep or Subjunctive Mood Interpretation *118*
6. Should We Appeal to Principles or to a Consensus? *121*
7. Conciliatory Remarks *123*

7. GRASPING, UNDERSTANDING, AND INTERPRETING   127
   1. Understanding and Translating   *127*
   2. Modes of Presentation   *133*
   3. Interpreting   *137*
   4. Paraphrases   *139*
   5. Deficient Understanding   *140*
   6. Are Interpretations Intralanguage Translations?   *143*
   7. Criteria of Adequacy   *145*

8. UNIVERSALIZABILITY AND SELF-DECEPTION   147
   1. Universalizability   *149*
   2. Kant   *150*
   3. Interpretive Choices and Aesthetic Judgments   *152*
   4. Two Kinds of Conflicts   *154*
   5. Internal Conflicts   *155*
   6. Negotiating Conflicting Judgments   *158*
   7. Facts and Interpretations   *159*
   8. Objections   *161*
   9. The Self-Deceiver's Mistake   *163*
   10. Tainted Interpretations   *165*

9. BEYOND THE PALE   167
   1. Relativism   *168*
   2. Reaching Beyond the Pale   *170*
   3. Psychological Limitations   *173*
   4. The Sincerity Condition   *179*
   5. The Shift of Focus in Interpreting   *180*
   6. Alternative Interpretive Goals   *183*
   7. Individual or Social Viewpoints   *185*

10. CRITIQUE OF INTERPRETIVE REASONING   187
   1. Principles   *187*
   2. Validity of the Principles   *191*
   3. Professional Interpreters   *196*
   4. The Voice of Professional Interpreters   *198*
   5. Consensus among Interpreters   *199*
   6. The Concept of Interpretation   *201*
   7. Alternatives   *205*
   8. Preparing the Ground for Others   *206*
   9. Envoy   *211*

Index   213

Preface

"*Je ne suis pas marxiste*," Marx once wrote. We would father this claim upon him, even if he had not written it. Respect for the seers and prophets within our tradition is often accompanied by contempt for their intellectual progeny. Since we do not want to visit upon the founders of a secular conviction or religious persuasion the discredited views of their defenders, we wish a disclaimer could be attributed to the founders. We argue that the founders would not find themselves at home with our contemporaries who are their defenders—regardless of whether their way of thinking is fundamentalist, liberal, conservative, orthodox, or nonconformist. We claim that Marx was not a Marxist, Freud not a Freudian, and Nietzsche not a Nietzschean. The point of such claims is to remain at a distance from the defenders' discredited views, while we reinterpret the founders' words in accordance with our beliefs, desires, and understanding.

What motivates our reinterpretations? Why do we insist on setting our concerns within traditional frames? Such questions motivate this study. What motivates a study is ordinarily hidden from view. The reader will find hardly a hint of these problems. For at an early stage of thinking about these questions it became obvious to me that prior to answering them, we must become clear about the interpreting activity.

This book was written at a time when problems about interpreting have been at the forefront of discussion in the social and human sciences. Since the 1980s an enormous number of books and articles have been written on this topic. I am not altogether innocent in this matter—I, too, have contributed to this ever-growing literature. My predicament was that by the time I saw my papers and reviews in print, I could also see that the problems I had discussed could get a more thorough treatment, if I would take into account related topics that were unclear to me at the time of writing. In writing a longer work on this topic, I could either take issue with the views that scholars in the field have defended or remain silent. I have chosen to write with few references to the work of others or to my own work. As a result, readers have a slim volume in their hands. I only regret that because of this choice, I could not show my appreciation for what I have learned from others in this field.

With few exceptions, the antecedents of the views defended here will be clear to readers. Among these exceptions are what I have learned from the work of Georg Lukács (especially his essays between 1908 and 1923) and Walter Benjamin. They have motivated my interest in interpreting since my student days in the early 1950s, and they have influenced my critical view of reinterpretations. The relevance of their work can be best seen in the opening epigraphs to this book. These quotations must be read both as an invitation to understand the scope of interpreting and as a critique of its limitations. Poetry has been alive and well since Lukács wrote these lines in the first decade of the twentieth century. (It has flourished beyond all expectations in Hungary.) Yet recent poetry is not about a "new Phaedra, Siegfried or Tristan." Great poetry finds its inspiration elsewhere.

Similarly, the best of contemporary philosophy is not a reinterpretation of traditional philosophical problems. Yet it has inspired a rethinking of these problems. More and better work has been done during the last third of the twentieth century on our predecessors' philosophical problems. However, the history of philosophy is only of marginal interest to philosophers engaged in discussing issues of contemporary philosophy. When Lukács and Benjamin wrote, concern with interpreting implied respect for tradition in poetry, art, and philosophy. They did their part in destroying that respect. But not even our contemporaries could offer a more radical critique of the history of philosophy and the history of art than what can be found in the lines quoted from Benjamin. After the interpretive turn, what is left of the history of philosophy and the history of art is the examination of well-defined problems and their available solutions. Interpreters always try to understand from their own viewpoint what is said or done. Having understood a given problem, they may even compare and contrast their own solution to that problem with other available solutions. But even if this yields a clearer understanding of a topic that worried Descartes or a better appreciation of a painting by Luca Signorelli, it will not yield elements of a narrative that can be called a history of philosophy or a history of art.

ONE reader's misidentification of the source of my views on make-believe in chapter 5 prompts a clarification. Kendall Walton's *Mimesis as Make-Believe* (1990) is certainly the most important contribution to the understanding of make-believe in the arts. Part Four of his book succeeded in solving philosophical problems that remained unresolved in the work of his predecessors. Still, the notion of make-believe in the arts appeared in a number of earlier discussions. Gilbert Ryle in *The Concept of Mind* and Monroe Beardsley in *Aesthetics* briefly mentioned the topic. I discussed it in two articles: "Fictional Characters, Places, and Events" and "On Make-Believe" (both in *Philosophy and Phenomenological Research* 26: 202–15, 1965, and 28: 24–38, 1967). These articles are the sources of my views on make-believe in chapter 5 and throughout this book.

Readers will easily recognize other sources for my views. Most important among them are Arthur Danto's views on deep interpretation (chapter 1, section 4); but I am not sure that Danto would agree with the connection that I suggest between deep interpretation and self-deception. I came to understand what I called the hereditary property of interpretation (chapter 3, section 1) after reading Tyler Burge's classic paper, "Content Preservation." Richard Wollheim was probably the first philosophical aesthetician to use the concept *seeing in* (chapter 5); I have learned about this concept from the lectures and writings of art historian Meyer Schapiro. Ágnes Erdélyi taught me about the properties I call the second model of translation (chapter 7, section 1). I became aware of Richard Holton's paper "What Is the Role of the Self in Self-Deception?" (*Proceedings of the Aristotelian Society*, 2001, pp. 53–69) after writing the first eight chapters of this book. Although I followed another path to this topic, our views converged concerning the self-deceiver's mistake (chapter 8, section 9). Finally, I must mention that J. L. Austin's analysis of the Hippolytus example at the end of Lecture I of *How to Do Things with Words* was most important in the development of my own views. Many difficult issues in theories of interpretation are variations on a theme Austin uncovered in the *Hippolytus*. What Hippolytus said in Austin's translation—"my tongue swore to, but my heart (or mind or other backstage artiste) did not"—resonates with what I maintain in this book about interpreters who speak with one voice from center stage and with another from backstage.

A remark about gender. As readers of chapter 7 will note, in my native language, Hungarian, personal and possessive pronouns make gender-neutral references to persons. My use of the English pronouns satisfies requirements of grammar and carries no implications about the gender of the persons imagined or denoted. Nonetheless, the availability of the two grammatical forms permitted my using in some chapters the masculine gender when referring to interpreters and the feminine when referring to their critics. In other chapters I use the masculine for amateurs and the feminine for professionals in a given field. A reader suggested that the feminine gender references reveal the more intelligent views and cogent arguments in this study. While this may be right, brevity in the exposition was my only goal.

I am very grateful to my friends and colleagues for discussing with me various topics of this study or for reading preliminary drafts of some chapters. First and foremost I owe an enormous debt to John Boler and Peter Kivy for their encouragement and criticism. They read and commented on my papers on interpreting and on earlier versions of parts of this book. Martin Bunzl, Seymour Feldman, Peter D. Klein, Amélie O. Rorty, and Frederic Schick read early drafts of several chapters. Their critical remarks and suggestions helped me to bring into focus the topics I wanted to discuss. Ágnes Erdélyi, Sándor Radnóti, and Susan Rubin Suleiman read early drafts of some parts of this book in both English and Hungarian. They were generous in offering their help and encouragement. On a personal level I am deeply grateful to Miriam Cohen for many helpful conversations on interpreting during the years I was working on this book. Without her moral support I could not have written this study.

Roger Haydon of Cornell University Press found ideal referees for *Interpretive Reasoning*. Philosophers working on theories and practices of interpreting often repeat Kant's claim that the reader must understand the author's views better than he understood them himself. Readers at Cornell and elsewhere succeeded admirably in this task. Without the referees' help I could not say about my work what they have said, and for this I am extremely grateful. I am indebted to Brin Stevens for her expert advice on matters of style. I am grateful to the copyeditor of this book, Karen Bosc, for recommending some changes, and the Senior Manuscript Editor, Teresa Jesionowski, for not insisting that I accept any recommendation. Hence only I am responsible for the remaining mistakes, unwarranted repetitions and infelicities of expression.

LAURENT STERN

New York City

Interpretive Reasoning

Introduction

This book is about the activity of interpreting. In interpreting, we talk about what was said or done; in talking about interpreting, we talk about that talk. What questions do we answer in interpreting? How do we improve the quality of interpretations? Excellent studies are available on these topics. My primary concern is with another matter: the structure of the interpretive process itself and the issues that arise within this process. Before writing this book, I expected that I would have to discuss the occasional insincerity of speakers and agents whose words and deeds are interpreted. But I was unprepared for the possibility that occasionally the interpreter himself is motivated to become insincere, when wanting to be tolerant of alternative interpretations, and when dealing with the insincerity of those he is interpreting. Moral issues arise during the interpreting process for those who are interpreted as well as for their interpreters. These topics are best discussed in the context of interpretive conflict. They seem to me important but oddly neglected issues in the literature about interpretation.

When we offer an interpretation, we are making a claim. And as with any sincere claim about a serious matter, we imply that we are familiar with the relevant facts and have provided a good account. Interpretations, however, are not susceptible to any sort of litmus test. So the implications of our claim have to be expressed in terms of what reasonable and well-informed interpreters will (or would, or even ought to) say in interpretive situations. I develop this formally under the heading of Universalizability Principle.

Interpretations are not (seriously) offered unless what is said or done either contains an unacknowledged component or is not immediately obvious. Explanations may range from the claim that the speaker simply misspoke (used the wrong word) to the charge of self-deception ("The lady doth protest too much, methinks."). But the basic structure of interpretation may not be clear until we consider the phenomenon of interpretive conflict, whether between two interpreters or between an interpreter and the original speaker or agent.

Such conflict, of course, puts a strain on the Universalizability Principle, in which case an interpreter may retreat to what I call the Restrictive Principle, claiming that at least those who agree with the proposed interpretation are qualified interpreters. Complications arise about this retreat, raising questions about the interpreter's sincerity. Is this a retreat in bad faith? Is the interpreter holding on to the Universalizability Principle in a backstage whisper while he loudly proclaims from center stage that he has retreated to a more modest position? I discuss the problems of this retreat and its relation to the Universalizability Principle.

As a practical matter, most interpretive disputes can be settled within the context of what I call surface or natural interpretation. The mark of such conflicts, however intense, prolonged, or embittered, is that the disputants focus on the data to be interpreted and the adequacy (and/or quality) of competing interpretations. Some of these disputes are interminable. Other interpretive conflicts can and do go a step further—to what I call essentially contestable or deep interpretation—where the charge, in effect, is self-deception and the focus of the dispute necessarily shifts to an assessment of the speaker or agent as self-interpreter, thus taking on a moral dimension.

These may seem—and in some sense are—familiar matters. In what follows, however, I try to show the need for more careful formulations to bring out the basic structure of interpretive reasoning. The goal of this work is to provide an explanatory and normative model of interpretive reasoning based on the two principles.

I start with the discussion of primitive manifestations of interpreting in chapter 1, use a heuristic device due to the work of Stephen Schiffer to distinguish two kinds of belief in chapter 2, and proceed to discuss the distinction between natural and deep interpretation in chapter 3. The principles of interpretation and ways in which they are abused are the topics of chapter 4. Problems of contestable interpretations in the context of artworks are discussed in chapter 5. Essentially contestable interpretations are the subject of chapter 6. Chapter 7 contains a comparison between interpreting and translating. Its burden is to show that contrary to common beliefs, the two activities have little in common. Chapters 8 and 9 discuss a model of the interpreting activity, personified by the solitary or professional interpreter and his critic. Chapter 10 binds the loose threads of what was introduced earlier into an account of interpretive reasoning.

CHAPTER ONE

Two Principles

---

1. First Steps

If we wish to understand the interpreting activity, we must try to reach it in its most primitive manifestations. We do not know what happened in those childhood days when we first succeeded in understanding others, but we can provide an account of what could have happened from an adult perspective. The account offered here is just one of many alternatives. All are acceptable if they explain how we come to understand others and ourselves on the kindergarten level that is consistent with our adult experiences.

"Do you understand me?" asks the adult. The child's affirmative answer and the adult's acknowledgement of that answer do not imply that either of them could provide an account of what is meant by understanding another person's words or deeds. Such an account is within the purview of professional psychologists and philosophers who often find it helpful to hide their account of understanding behind a veil of technical terms. No doubt, these terms have their uses, but we can at least try to describe what is meant by the child's affirmative answer without recourse to such terms. The vocabulary available for such a description prompts us to articulate our thoughts: are we talking about an activity or a state? Interpreting is an activity; its goal is understanding, a state.

At a very early age we became aware of sounds and pauses that we heard from adults and which we only tried to imitate: they were about events in our world. What the adult said was about what was happening; at the same time what was happening shed light on what he said. We moved around in a very small circle, but the continuous repetition taught us about the connection between words and things, between statements and facts. The adult's words referred to facts, and the facts shed light on his words. As long as we could speak about facts, we did not need the notion of truth. But very soon we needed the notion of falsity. However, this notion became available only after considerable training.

We played make-believe games: we played the roles of fathers, mothers, and other children, we played being doctors and their patients—all the while we knew quite well that we were not parents, doctors, or other children. In short, we were not those persons whose roles we played. Although the line separating make-believe and real is not as sharp in kindergarten as it is a few years later, and the very young child is—for short periods of time—caught up in the make-believe game, most of the time he knows he is playing. "Let us make-believe . . . ," says the child—at the same time he learns to differentiate between fiction and fact, between what is false and what is true. Kindergarten taught us what Vico called the convertibility of *verum* and *factum*, of what is true and what is a fact. The notion of truth became necessary only when we were thoroughly acquainted with the notion of falsity. Becoming aware of the notion of falsity required three steps. We reached the first step when we played make-believe games. The rules of these games were agreed on by the participants, and in playing them we did not wish to mislead anyone. We attained the second step when we learned that occasionally an adult or other child says what is not so, even outside of a commonly agreed upon game. He is lying. The game he is playing is no longer innocent: he is trying to mislead others. But it is also possible—and this is the third step—that the adult or other child neither participates in a make-believe game nor is trying to mislead: he is simply mistaken. He believes what he says; he believes that the facts correspond to his statements. The notion of falsity became available to us when we learned about these three steps. The third step led us to the notion of a false belief. We needed that notion in order to attribute to others a belief that does not correspond to the facts. We derived the notion of a belief or of a true belief—Davidson may have been the first philosopher to insist on this point—from the notion of a false belief.

We acquired the concept of falsity by learning about the uses of "Let us make-believe . . . ," "You are lying!" and "You are mistaken!" We learned at the same time that such phrases are used only in exceptional cases. Respect for authority—and especially authority of the stronger—was part of our training. Accusing anyone of lying was not only ill-mannered, but also may have had untoward consequences—especially if it was possible to account for that person's words and deeds in another way. And even if it was not possible, discretion in these matters was the better part of valor. Outside of make-believe games, adults and older children became indignant or vindictive when told that not even they believed what they were saying.

When we acquired the concepts of falsity and belief and learned about the advantages of respect for the authorities, we were ready for the next level of understanding. Thus far, in kindergarten the novice has learned to distinguish between two possibilities when understanding others: (1) if he were in their place in the current situation, he would say what they have said—in this case he interprets their words in the light of what he accepts as facts, and he accepts as facts what their words propose; (2) if he were in their place in the current situation, he would not say what they have said— in this case he also interprets their words in the light of what he accepts as facts, but he does not accept as facts what is proposed by their words. In the latter case, the novice understands what they propose as a lie or an error. There is no need to mention here a third possibility: the novice understands the words of others as part of a make-believe game. Regardless of whether he is right or wrong about the matter, this case can be understood within the limits of the first two possibilities.

The next level of understanding others is at loggerheads with what is taught in the classroom. It is more easily acquired while participating in extracurricular activities on street corners, playgrounds or at shopping malls. There, the novice discovers that in exceptional cases the two possibilities of understanding others are insufficient. Such cases arise when the words of others are not supported by facts, yet these others are not participating in a make-believe game and they don't seem to be lying. Are they mistaken? They are certainly mistaken, but that is not all there is to this matter. No doubt, they claim to believe what they are saying; moreover, they insist on that claim. But are they entitled to their beliefs? It seems odd that they accept as facts what they propose by their words: given the information at their disposal, they ought to know better.

So far, the novice has interpreted what others have said in the light of what he has accepted as facts. But the facts need not be at the center of his disagreement with those he is trying to understand. They may agree with him on the basic facts, and at the same time insist on holding beliefs that, in his judgment, are not right. Unfortunately, his vocabulary is insufficient for dealing with these cases—words suggesting that the others are victims of self-deception are not yet available. He either falls silent or he insists that those he tries to understand are not entitled to their beliefs. Both his silence and his insistence will have lasting consequences. In either case the adults may end the conversation: "When you become an adult, you will understand this as I do!" or "When you understand this as I do, you will become an adult!" Both conversation terminators insist on the adult's authority, and both are expressions of dogmatism—why one is more dogmatic and which one is more dogmatic requires further discussion. But as we shall see, the child's silence or either of the adult's conversation terminators will have consequences they do not presently realize.

2. Natural Interpretation in the Indicative Mood

The conversation between adult and child may continue at a later time. Meanwhile, the conversation terminators mark the end of the adult's effort in convincing the child to understand what is at issue, as he understands it. While the conversation lasted, the adult defended his views on the matter. Such defense is seldom needed. Most of the time, we understand the words and deeds of others as they want them to be understood; we interpret them in accordance with their wishes. Questions about matters of interpretation are raised only in exceptional cases.

The novice has already learned what he needs to know for interpreting what has been said or done. He understands the adults as they wish to be understood; and if he fails to do so, he expects to be told of his misunderstanding. Either immediately or after correction by those he is trying to understand, he interprets others in accordance with their self-interpretation. This agreement is dependent on what the interpreter accepts as facts. Interpretations that are inconsistent with what we accept as facts are subject to reexamination. As a result of such a reexamination, we either reject our interpretations, or reject what we previously believed about the facts. Note that our intuitions about the words and deeds of others function without question only as long as our interpretations are consistent with what we accept as facts. *Only* in these cases can we say that those we wish to understand are saying (doing) what we would be saying (doing) if we were in their place.

As soon as accepted facts no longer support our interpretations of what others are saying, we are sailing in uncharted waters. Our beliefs or our interpretations may be mistaken; those whom we are trying to understand may be mistaken about the facts or they may be lying. Suppose after examining these options, we settle for what we consider the most likely hypothesis. If the accepted hypothesis leads us back to an agreement with those we are trying to understand, our interpretive problem is solved. But if such agreement cannot be reached, our interpretations will raise further questions. Those we try to understand are not saying what we would be saying, if we were in their place; moreover, what they are saying is not supported by what we accept as facts—so, we believe, unless we are mistaken, they are mistaken or they are lying. But why are they mistaken, why are they lying?

The novice relies on few facts that he has accepted in support of his interpretations. He learns about the facts from what his caregivers tell him, and at the same time he must understand the caregivers' words by relying on the facts that he has accepted. The difficulty in understanding his caregivers' words is expressed by his often-repeated question: "Why?" As adults we face a similar difficulty if we cannot agree with a speaker's words. Relying on what we take to be facts, we ask: Is the speaker playing a make-believe game? Is he lying? Is he mistaken? Moreover, why is he saying/doing whatever he is saying/doing? We may not be able to answer these questions to our satisfaction, and in this case another question arises: can we understand the speaker if we do not agree with him? (Wittgenstein worried about this problem.) The answer to this question is not at all obvious. Regardless of how we answer this question, we will understand the speaker better if we can show why he is mistaken or why he is lying.

Occasionally the caregivers are unwilling or unable to answer the child's questions. On these occasions they dismiss the questions and use one of the conversation terminators. In some cases there is no important difference between the two conversation terminators. For example, when a caregiver instructs a child to look before crossing a busy intersection, and the child questions her instructions, then her choice between the two conversation terminators is irrelevant. The response "When you understand this matter the way I do (and look both ways before crossing the street), you will become an adult!" will do as well as "When you become an adult (and look both ways before crossing the street), you will understand this matter the way I do." Every reasonable person familiar with the circumstances will agree with both of these claims. It is literally true that the child's chances of becoming an adult are minimal if he does not learn to look before crossing a busy intersection. Nonetheless, both conversation terminators make important claims that must be taken seriously. From what premises or principles are they derived? Only one conversation terminator can be derived from what shall be called here the Universalizability Principle without the help of question-begging premises.

> Universalizability Principle: Every reasonable person who is familiar with the circumstances understands what is at issue the way I do.

Add to this principle the caregiver's expectation that as a grown-up the child will take his place among the reasonable persons (who are familiar

with the circumstances), and we can derive the first conversation terminator: "When you become an adult, you will understand this matter the
way I do!" Note, however, that we cannot derive from the Universalizability Principle the second conversation terminator. In order to derive
that conversation terminator, we need either an additional question-
begging premise or another principle, which shall be called here the
Restrictive Principle.

> Restrictive Principle: Only reasonable persons who are familiar with the
> circumstances understand what is at issue the way I do.

The Restrictive Principle is equivalent with "All persons who understand
what is at issue the way I do are reasonable and familiar with the circumstances." No question-begging premises are needed to derive from this
principle the second conversation terminator: "When you understand this
matter the way I do (and look both ways before crossing the street), you
will become an adult!"

Both principles are formulated as statements that are either true or
false. It is the burden of this study to establish conditions permitting an
appeal to one these statements as if it were a principle. (See especially
chapter 3 on the necessary and sufficient conditions for appealing to the
Universalizability Principle.) We appeal to principles only if we wish to
defend our interpretive choices. Our choices may be right even if we are
not guided by these principles. We may be guided by other principles, or
by no explicitly acknowledged principle. Two interpreters may agree on a
given interpretive choice, and if asked to defend that choice, one may
appeal to the Universalizability while the other appeals to the Restrictive
Principle. The implied restraint on dogmatism and authoritarianism may
counsel an appeal to one principle rather than another. To be sure, dogmatists and authoritarians can avoid that restraint, at least from their own
viewpoint. In their view the difference between the two principles is just a
matter of degree: confronted with disagreement, they can adopt either of
the two principles and argue that their opponents are either not reasonable or not familiar with what is at issue.

From the viewpoint of those opposed to dogmatism, the difference
between the two principles is of crucial importance. The opponents can
rely only on reasons and arguments to support their interpretive choices.
They must derive their choices from the conclusions of such arguments if
they wish to remain dogmatism's opponents. In presenting their reasons,
they solicit the agreement of all reasonable persons; hence, they are bound
to prefer the Universalizability rather than the Restrictive Principle. Even

a temporary retreat to the Restrictive Principle suggests that they could not abandon their interpretive choices although they failed to convince some reasonable persons. It is conceivable, for instance, that such a temporary retreat is necessary when a scientist tries to procure hearing for a new theory. But when a temporary retreat to the Restrictive Principle becomes a permanent feature of a given theory, then that theory becomes unacceptable for dogmatism's opponents.

3. Natural Interpretation in the Subjunctive Mood

While participating in extracurricular activities on the playground and street corner, the kindergarten graduate has learned to contest the claims of others. He knows that in exceptional cases his understanding of others seemed to be wanting. Their words were not supported by facts that he was taught, yet they were neither participating in a make-believe game nor were they lying nor is it sufficient to say that they were mistaken. They insisted on their sincerity in holding a certain belief, yet they did not seem to be entitled to that belief. Unless he received his first lessons in matters of cosmology or religion from physicists, theologians, or very intelligent laypersons, he noticed that all is not well with those sincere professions of belief. The conversation about the matter was terminated either by his exhaustion or by one of the two conversation terminators.

As children we were not so naïve, or so trusting, or so gullible as to believe all claims contained in conversation terminators, but the words and concepts required to formulate an answer were not yet available. We became silent. Much later, when professionals in a given field or self-appointed experts used similar conversation terminators in other contexts, we were a bit more articulate. They said: "When you become an expert in this field, you will understand this the way I do!" or "When you are rid of your neurosis, you will understand your story the way I do!" or "When the workers become class-conscious, they will understand their own situation the way I do!" No doubt, in some cases these conversation terminators can be supported by reasons and arguments. If they can be so supported, the persons in positions of authority deserve the respect of those who are so addressed. Adults relating to children, teachers responding to students, professionals arguing with dilettantes, self-appointed experts indoctrinating newcomers—all use these conversation terminators. Those who are so addressed often do not have the knowledge or experience required to respond, and in many cases even their vocabulary is insufficient for understanding the speaker's words as he understands them.

Adults, professionals, or experts are entitled to a conversation termina-tor if they can show that their interpretive choices are derived from the Universalizability Principle. Moreover, even if their interpretations dis-agree with the self-understanding of children, dilettantes, or newcomers—whose words or deeds they are interpreting—they are still engaged in natural interpretation; but their natural interpretations are no longer in the indicative mood. The disagreement shows that their natural interpre-tations are in the subjunctive mood. The conversation terminator claims that if the novice were in their place, he would understand his own words as they understand those words. One conversation terminator expresses the expectation that he will so understand his own words: "When you become an expert in this field, you will understand this the way I do!"

Interpreters are engaged in surface interpretation—i.e., natural inter-pretation in either mood—if their interpretive choices can be shown to have derived from the Universalizability Principle. If this cannot be shown, the conversation terminator will be understood as having been derived from the Restrictive Principle. The teacher may have said to his student, "When you become an expert in this field, you will understand this the way I do!" but his student might believe he has meant "When you understand this the way I do, you will become an expert in this field!" And this conver-sation terminator can be derived only from the Restrictive Principle: "Only reasonable persons who are familiar with the circumstances understand what is at issue the way I do." As mentioned previously, the Restrictive Prin-ciple is equivalent with "All persons who understand what is at issue the way I do are reasonable and familiar with the circumstances."

If we focus on the conversation terminator—"When you become an expert in this field, you will understand this the way I do!"—uttered by the teacher or the expert, we must distinguish between two cases. (1) The expert's audience does not contest his claim. No doubt, both expert and audience may be mistaken, and contrary to their beliefs, this conversation terminator cannot be derived from the Universalizability Principle. But regardless of whether both are right or both are mistaken, their agreement proves that even if they disagree about the topic of conversation, the con-versation terminator itself is understood by both of them in the same way. Both would agree—although both could be mistaken—that the conversa-tion terminator could be derived from the Universalizability Principle. (2) The expert's audience does contest his claim. The expert said: "When you become an expert in this field, you will understand this the way I do!" How-ever, he is understood by those who are so addressed to have meant "When you understand this the way I do, you will become an expert in this field!" No doubt, the claim that this is what the expert meant may be mistaken.

Yet even if the expert's audience is mistaken, it is a step in the direction of deep-level interpretation. This is a surprising claim. It suggests that we took this first step in the practice of deep-level interpretation long before our vocabulary was sufficient to understand the theories of deep-level interpretation. This claim requires detailed discussion.

Natural interpretations in both the indicative and subjunctive moods are surface-level interpretations. On this level the interpreter tries to understand the speaker's words as the speaker would understand them if he were in the interpreter's place. Disregarding the case that both of their interpretations are mistaken, a surface-level interpretation is considered successful and yields understanding of the speaker's words if it agrees with the speaker's self-interpretation, either in the indicative or the subjunctive mood. The interpreter leaves the limits of surface-level interpretation and takes a step in the direction of deep-level interpretation as soon as he substitutes an alternative to the speaker's self-interpretation that is no longer warranted by the Universalizability Principle. By substituting an alternative for the speaker's self-interpretation, he maintains that he knows what the speaker meant better than the speaker himself. For example, the speaker believes that every reasonable person who is familiar with the circumstances agrees with his understanding of what is at issue. Accordingly, he believes that he is entitled to "When you become an expert in this field, you will understand this the way I do!" His interpreter may concede only that every person who understands what is at issue the way the speaker does is reasonable and familiar with the circumstances. In this case, the speaker is only entitled to "When you understand this the way I do, you will be an expert in this field!" The speaker believes that the facts of what is at issue support his reliance on the Universalizability Principle; his interpreter believes that the facts support only the speaker's reliance on the Restrictive Principle and not on the Universalizability Principle. Since we disregarded the case that both of them are mistaken, we can conclude that in such a debate the speaker's view, that he is relying on the Universalizability Principle, is mistaken. Why is this so?

His interpreter can easily falsify the speaker's belief about his reliance on the Universalizability Principle in support of his views. After all, the mere fact that a qualified interpreter—i.e., a reasonable person who is familiar with the issues—believes that the speaker's understanding of what is at issue is mistaken, is sufficient for defeating the speaker's contradictory claim that every reasonable person familiar with the circumstances agrees with his understanding. Moreover, there is no need for the interpreter to rely overtly on the Universalizability Principle in support of the claim that the speaker's understanding of what is at issue is mistaken; in his debate with the speaker it is sufficient for the interpreter to rely on the Restrictive Principle. Hence, it is easier to defeat than to establish the claim that a given interpretive choice can be derived from the Universalizability Principle. A case in point is the following—not purely fictional—example.

An art historian-connoisseur of established reputation attributes a certain painting to X; his younger colleagues and admirers doubt the attribution, and are willing to concede only that the painting may have been produced in X's studio. When the older connoisseur wishes to terminate the discussion by reference to the Universalizability Principle and tries to silence his younger colleagues by saying, "When you become an expert in this field, you will understand this the way I do!" the latter insist on continuing the discussion. The younger colleagues neither doubt the expertise nor the sincerity of the older connoisseur; in fact, they would not want to continue the conversation if they doubted one or the other. But they know that the older connoisseur receives routinely a percentage of the price of the paintings sold with his attributions. Could it not be that the older connoisseur's self-interest plays an intangible role in the attribution? So, they tell their older colleague: "We don't believe this painting can be attributed to X. Of course, you may continue to believe that your attribution is supported by the Universalizability Principle; but if you continue to hold that belief, you can neither count us nor anyone who disagrees with you among the reasonable persons who are familiar with the circumstances. Hence, unless you are willing to consider all those who disagree with you either unreasonable or unfamiliar with the circumstances, you can only believe that your attribution is supported by the Restrictive Principle. Finally, we would be glad to agree that your attribution is supported by the Restrictive Principle, for this only commits us to the claim that all those who agree with you are reasonable and familiar with the circumstances." Of course, the younger art historians could avoid all complications connected with discussions of self-deception by claiming that the older expert was mistaken. No doubt, he was mistaken—but we would seriously underdescribe the example, if we would merely say that he was mistaken. It is important to add that he was not entitled to this mistake. Given the speaker's level of knowledge or expertise, the mistake could have been avoided.

Deep-level interpretation is at work in this story. Prompted by self-interest, the older connoisseur could be lying; or his attribution could be based on an honest mistake. In these cases there is no need for deep-level interpretation. What we learned when we were children is sufficient for understanding lies and honest mistakes. Deep-level interpretation is needed only if all of the following conditions apply:

1. In the interpreter's judgment it is at least questionable whether the facts or the speaker's understanding of the facts support what the speaker believes.
2. The interpreter is convinced that the speaker sincerely believes what he claims to believe.
3. The speaker's knowledge of the facts—in our example, his expertise—is incompatible with the claim that his belief is based on an honest mistake.
4. The speaker can be blamed for failing to avoid the mistake.
5. By failing to avoid the mistake, the speaker prepared grounds for his interpreter's substitution of an alternative to his self-interpretation.
6. By substituting an alternative for the speaker's self-interpretation, the interpreter suggests that he knows what the speaker meant better than the speaker himself.
7. The interpreter relies on a set of interconnected beliefs about human nature—an overt or covert rudimentary theory—supporting the claim that he knows what the speaker meant better than the speaker himself.

4. Deep Interpretation

"The lady doth protest too much, methinks" (*Hamlet*, III.ii.242) would be a concise expression of a first step in deep-level interpretation, if it were said in an ordinary context rather than in a play. (At issue here is not the correct interpretation of Shakespeare's line.) In using such expressions, the interpreter does not accuse a certain lady of lying. He indicates merely that her very protestations convict her: she does not believe what she claims to believe. The interpreter's judgment overrides her own judgment. No doubt, his judgment must be defended by reason and argument, but it will not be defeated by her disagreement. It is not lost even on children that her very protests argue against their accepting her self-interpretation. They may not be able to formulate the notion of self-deception or provide adequate descriptions of cases of self-deception, and they certainly cannot suggest even the most rudimentary theory about human nature—supporting the claim that they know better what the speaker meant than she herself did. Yet they are quite successful in judging words that are contradicted by actions or qualified by the way they are spoken. Their understanding of deep-level interpretation did not begin with reading Shakespeare or studying Marx, Nietzsche, or Freud. They were led to deep-level interpretation by their own experiences.

Deep-level interpretation is often triggered by the suspicion that all is not well with the self-understanding of those we wish to understand. The suspicion is reinforced by the interpreter's judgment that the speaker is not entitled to hold the belief he claims to hold. This judgment need not be based on the interpreter's superior knowledge of what is at issue. Children who are taught by confused elders about matters of cosmology or religion do not have adequate information about what is at issue. Their judgment that those they wish to understand are not entitled to their beliefs is based primarily on the way these beliefs are presented. Children are offered instruction about topics in cosmology or religion; their elders' confidence in their own claims is insisted upon—yet this very insistence casts doubt on their confidence and raises questions about their claims. Their elders seem to believe what they ought to reject by their own lights: given the information at their disposal, they ought to know better. In other cases, the interpreters rely on some of the same facts as the speaker but doubt whether these facts support the speaker's beliefs. In my example of the art historians, the younger historians were aware of the same facts as their more established colleague. Yet in their understanding, the available evidence supported only the attribution of the painting to the studio of a given painter and not to that painter.

Children lack the required maturity to ask certain questions in these conversations with the adult caregiver, and they either accept their caregiver's views or fall silent. The younger art historians have two additional alternatives. Citing the available evidence, they can maintain their own view and argue that it is grounded on the Universalizability Principle. In this case they must be prepared to dismiss the judgment of their more established colleague as not sufficiently knowledgeable about the issues. In dismissing his judgment, they tell him that if he were more reasonable and knowledgeable about this matter, he would agree with them. In other words, their understanding of his view is grounded on the Universalizability Principle in the subjunctive mood. Or, they can ground their own view on the Restrictive Principle and opt for continuing the debate with their colleague. This final alternative makes sense only if they wish to continue the debate.

The adult caregiver is in at least as good a position to know the facts at issue as his charges; the established art historian-connoisseur is at least as well-informed as his younger colleagues—why do they believe what they ought to reject? In supporting their questionable beliefs they appeal to the Universalizability Principle. If a qualified interpreter does not share their understanding of that topic, then his disagreement falsifies their belief that the Universalizability Principle supports their understanding. So why do they try to support their understanding with the Universalizability Principle?

A more detailed discussion of the debate between the more established connoisseur and his critics provides answers to this question.

In supporting his attribution of a given painting to X, the more established connoisseur must appeal to some form of Universalizability. He can clear himself of the suspicion that his attribution was ever so slightly motivated by self-interest if he can demonstrate that anyone who had his eye for noticing characteristic traits in paintings, his prodigious memory, and his vast knowledge of art history would agree with his judgment. He is convinced that any reasonable person would agree with his attribution if that person could match his qualifications as a connoisseur. The Restrictive Principle is of no help in arguing against his critics, for it falls short of shielding him against accusations that he was biased. In responding to his claims, his critics could agree that he was indeed a highly qualified connoisseur, but their own expertise and contradictory judgment was sufficient for falsifying his belief that every connoisseur would agree with his claims. He is vulnerable to the charge of being biased only if his critics succeed in depriving him of the support provided by the Universalizability Principle.

Suppose his colleagues defeat the established connoisseur's appeal to Universalizability. (To save words, I will write "appeal to Universalizability" instead of "appeal to the Universalizability Principle.") They will now claim that his attribution of the painting to X was mistaken. If they believe that given his expertise he was not entitled to this mistake, and they wish to blame him for failing to avoid it, then they may even add that the mere fact that he attributed the painting to X provides evidence that self-interest predisposed him in favor of authentication. The reader may object: since they have claimed that the attribution was mistaken, the additional remark that bias supported the attribution merely adds insult to injury. Indeed, the additional remark is not needed, provided that there is room for such a remark, when they argue against his belief that Universalizability supports authentication. Nothing short of self-deception can explain that the established connoisseur thought he could exclude all those who disagreed with him from among the reasonable persons who are familiar with the circumstances of what is at issue. If his colleagues merely claim that his belief was mistaken and do not add that his understanding was biased or that his belief that Universalizability supported his understanding was due to self-deception, they blunt the moral edge of their senior colleague's assessment. Charges of deficient self-understanding or self-deception always have a moral dimension.

Caution is required at this stage: it would be a mistake to overvalue the appeal to Universalizability. In some cases, such an appeal may be unchallenged or considered successful by other interpreters. Yet even in these cases the successful appeal does not transform an interpretation into a good interpretation. Moreover, an interpretation that cannot be supported by Universalizability need not be judged a bad interpretation. For example, at one time, bloodletting with leeches was the favored treatment for pneumonia. Early-nineteenth-century physicians could support such a treatment with an appeal to Universalizability. Such an appeal did not transform the interpretation of the available data into a good interpretation. Conversely, controversial treatments in present-day medical practice that cannot be supported by an appeal to Universalizability may turn out to be based on a good interpretation of the available data.

5. "You Must Change . . ."

Should we allege self-deception when disagreeing with another person's belief, or his understanding, or both his belief and understanding? The moral edge of the charge of self-deception is crucial in answering this question. Although beliefs and background knowledge often decisively influence the interpretation of texts or paintings, we cannot assume that this is always the case. And even if there is evidence that previously accepted beliefs determined an interpretation, it would be inappropriate to tell another person that he is deceiving himself unless accompanied by an overt or covert call for change. (Hitherto only empiricist considerations guided the dying patient, but now he turns to spiritualism for help; his empiricist friends consider him a victim of self-deception—wouldn't it be cruel to tell him that?)

To be sure, the suspicion about a connoisseur's belief that a painting is authentic need not extend to his interpretation or understanding of significant traits in the painting. The suspicion that both his belief and understanding are biased as a result of self-deception is appropriate only if we are willing to blame him not only for authenticating the painting in the service of unacknowledged self-interest, but also for understanding significant features in the painting prompted by unavowed self-interest. Even if we claim that his beliefs contaminated his understanding, we need not charge him with self-deception in the context of understanding, just because this was our charge in the context of belief. In other cases, we may charge him with self-deception in the context of understanding, without such a charge in the context of belief, even if his understanding influenced his belief.

In charging another person with self-deception, we cannot just claim that he happens to be mistaken, or that he is lying; we must first take into account his knowledge and sincerity. No doubt, he is mistaken: from the interpreter's viewpoint the difference between false belief and self-deception is often irrelevant. The difference becomes relevant if the interpreter wishes to blame the speaker or agent for the mistake, while admitting that he is not lying. In responding to a charge of self-deception, he must choose among four alternatives: ignoring the charge, disagreeing with the charge, agreeing with a slightly modified charge, or charging his interpreter with deception. (The last alternative is discussed in chapter 3.)

In the large majority of cases, he will either ignore or disagree with our charge. After all, not much logical acumen is needed for noticing that he is on firm ground in either of these two cases. If he would admit that he is here and now deceiving himself, then that admission would be self-defeating. Since we know quite well that he cannot agree with our charge without modifying it, our charge can be supported only by the Restrictive Principle and not by the Universalizability Principle. In charging self-deception we imply that as interpreters we understand his words or deeds better than he understands them; moreover, we blame him for failing to understand them; finally, in telling him that he is deceiving himself, we issue a call for change.

In a very few cases he will agree with a slightly modified charge. Having heeded the call for change, he will claim that presently he is not deceiving himself, and at the same time admit that in the past he was deceiving himself. Assured of his agreement, we can now support our charge with the Universalizability Principle; our reliance on the Restrictive Principle becomes superfluous. As a result of his agreement, surface-level interpretation replaces deep-level interpretation.

"*Du mußt Dein Leben ändern!*"—"You must change your life!"—wrote Rilke. Our telling another person that he is deceiving himself would be incomprehensible without such a call for change. It would be easier to dismiss his beliefs or interpretations as false beliefs or misinterpretations. And this can be achieved by appealing to Universalizability in the subjunctive mood. Charges of self-deception arise only if we wish to provide reasons for his false belief or his mistaken understanding, and blame him for the mistake. If he either ignored or rejected these charges, his interpreter will claim: (1) the charge of self-deception is supported only by the Restrictive Principle, a weak but not unimportant principle; it supports the claim that all persons who understand what is at issue the way the interpreter does are reasonable and familiar with the circumstances; (2) after changing their lives, those who are charged with self-deception will confirm that they deceived themselves. At that time, all who are reasonable and familiar with the circumstances will concur with the interpreter's understanding of what is at issue. At that time, the Universalizability Principle will support the interpreter's claims.

Surface-level interpretation speaks with a universal voice; a deep-level interpretation speaks with a prophetic voice. Herein lies the grandeur and misery of both deep-level interpretations and deep-level interpretation theories. When discussing topics of common sense or the sciences, surface-level interpreters will boldly claim the agreement of all reasonable persons who are knowledgeable about the issues. We claim their agreement until we are shown that we are mistaken. The escape clause about the possibility of being mistaken merely acknowledges that a reconsideration of what is at issue will be forthcoming, if it turns out that we were mistaken. For instance, the astronomer's calculations concerning the future position of a comet are supported by a well-tested theory; if his predictions turn out to be wrong, he will revise the calculation; if a sufficient number of predictions by many astronomers turn out to be wrong, we will revise the theory. There are no such escape clauses available to those who speak with the prophetic voice of deep-level interpretations.

Since in the large majority of cases deep-level interpretations are either ignored or contradicted by the speakers or agents who are so interpreted, their response does not motivate a revision of the interpretation. The interpreter can derive support only from the claim that all those who agree with him are reasonable and knowledgeable about what is at issue. The Restrictive Principle seems weak when compared with the Universalizability Principle, but as soon as we focus on the principle itself rather than the comparison, it turns out to be sufficiently strong for supporting deep-level interpretations. Moreover, the rudimentary or fully worked out theories supporting deep-level interpretations do not contain an escape clause about the possibility of being mistaken. The disconfirmation of deep-level interpretations does not yield their revision or the revision of the theory supporting such interpretations. Suppose, however, that the deep-level interpreter's predictions turn out to be true, and at a later time those who were so interpreted agree with his interpretations. Moreover, a given deep-level interpretation theory becomes accepted by all reasonable persons who are knowledgeable about what is at issue. As soon as such a theory speaks with a universal voice, it becomes a commonsense view or a scientific theory and the interpretations it supports become surface-level interpretations. It is the confirmation rather than the disconfirmation of deep-level interpretations that contributes to their demise as deep-level interpretations, and it is the confirmation of deep-level interpretation theories that contributes to their failure as deep-level interpretation theories.

The great textbooks on deep-level interpretation—written by Marx, Nietzsche, Freud—originally sought to explain why reasonable persons, with at least as much information at their disposal about a given topic as their critics, accepted false beliefs. In their critics' judgment, deficient self-understanding or self-deception was at work, if reasonable persons accepted these beliefs. The deep-level interpreter's prophetic voice becomes messianic in at least some deep-level interpretation theories. Yet the future of these theories and the interpretations they support is not bright. There are but three possibilities: (1) They become accepted by all reasonable persons, and the universal voice of surface-level interpretation and scientific theories replaces the prophetic voice of deep-level interpretation and its supporting theories. (2) They become rejected and join the ranks of the discredited and quaint theories of deep-level interpretation that are ready to be resurrected by a changing intellectual fashion. (3) They continue to be subjects of an endless debate.

If success changes deep-level into surface-level interpretation and its supporting theory into a commonsense view or scientific theory, then deep-level interpretation together with its supporting theory must be understood in the context of failure. Astronomers are discredited if they do not avail themselves of the escape clause when their predictions or theories turn out to be mistaken. Those who speak with the prophetic voice of deep-level interpretation are not discredited, even if their interpretations are wide of the mark. Their prophetic voice will be heard only as long as they did not succeed. "*Wo Es war, soll Ich werden,*" wrote Freud.[*] (In *The Standard Edition* this is translated as "Where id was, there ego shall be."[†] If this is what Freud wanted to say, he would have written "*wird Ich werden,*" instead of "*soll Ich werden.*" The translation "Where id was, let there be ego!" better captures what is said in the German sentence.) If this ever happens, it will spell the end of psychoanalysis as a deep-level interpretation theory. In a world that is free of want and exploitation, Marx's views understood as a deep-level interpretation theory will become obsolete. Meanwhile, Marx's and Freud's advocates always point to the future, when their views will be validated. At that time, if their views will be useful, then they will be useful only for the understanding of the history of men or women and of mankind. It is, of course, also possible that at that time, the theories of Freud and Marx will turn out to be less useful than the competing theories for understanding the past.

6. Whereof We May Remain Silent

The rudimentary account of surface- and deep-level interpretation sketched here is silent on the speaker's or agent's thoughts or internal states before, during, and after he communicated his words or performed his

[*] Sigmund Freud, *Neue Vorlesungen 31* (1932).
[†] Sigmund Freud, *Standard Edition*, vol. 22 (London: Hogarth Press, 1964), 80.

actions. In the case of surface-level interpretation, the interpreter is guided by what he accepts as facts in trying to understand another person's words and deeds as that speaker or agent understands them (in case of a natural interpretation in the indicative mood) or as he would understand them (in case of a natural interpretation in the subjunctive mood) if he were in the interpreter's place. In the most favorable case the speaker and his interpreter agree about the facts and in their understanding of what was said. In less favorable cases they disagree, and the question arises whether the speaker is mistaken, or lying, or a victim of self-deception. In the debate about their disagreement, the speaker can raise the same questions about his interpreter as the interpreter raised about him. Are there any additional facts they could appeal to in support of their interpretations?

The object of understanding is commonly called "meaning"; our talk about self-deception implies that there is a phenomenon designated by using words to the effect that others are—or we were—victims of self-deception. But just as the notion of understanding does not become clearer by claiming that meaning is its object, our talk about self-deception does not become clearer by supposing that there is such a phenomenon. Our notions of understanding and our talk about self-deception cannot be explained by reference to an object called "meaning" or a phenomenon called "self-deception." For all we know, there may—or may not—be such an object or phenomenon. But we can afford to remain silent about such matters. After all, when we discuss understanding, lack of self-understanding, or self-deception, we speak about what the interpreter, speaker, or agent accepts as facts, how his understanding of one topic is shaped by his understanding of a wide variety of other topics, how he supports some beliefs with other beliefs. Interpretations are always supported not only by facts but also by other interpretations—attention to our talk about facts and interpretations will be more illuminating than a futile search for an object or a phenomenon that is supposedly at the center of our talk.

In favorable cases, we understand others as they understand themselves, if we were in their place. We support our claim for understanding them with the Universalizability Principle. In less favorable cases our appeal to the Universalizability Principle is a bit more complicated: we attempt to place those we wish to understand in our place, and suggest that if they were in our place they would understand themselves as we understand them. For example, the caregiver may not think that the child in her charge can now be counted among the reasonable persons who are familiar with what is at issue; but in the near future he will take his place among them, and at that time he will agree with his caregiver's and all other reasonable persons' understanding of his words or deeds.

In the least favorable case, we deliberately disregard the self-understanding of others, and replace their self-understanding with our understanding of their words or deeds. In some cases the replacement is prompted by our suspicion of a mild deficiency in self-understanding, in others by our belief that we are facing a full-blooded case of self-deception. If we focus on interpreting what other persons have said or done—and disregard cases of self-interpretation (discussed in later chapters)—we need to support our interpretations with the Restrictive Principle, but only if we suspect a case of deficiency in self-understanding or a case of self-deception. An orderly redescription of interpreting or understanding someone's words or deeds must start from the interpreter's viewpoint. Suppose, however, that the interpreter and the person whose words are interpreted are the same person. In this case the interpreter will not be able to validate his own interpretation by claiming that he understands the speaker as the speaker understands himself; nor will he be able to replace the speaker's understanding of his own words with his interpretation of those words. To be sure, if it can be argued that he is no longer the same person as he was when he spoke those words, then his present interpretation can either validate or discredit the understanding of those words by his former self. But given insufficient distance, how do we support our claim of adequate self-understanding? The Universalizability Principle will be of further use in this context.

7. The Reasonable and the Knowledgeable

By the time we became adults, we were already experts in interpreting what had been said or done. Readers of a study on interpreting need not be told what interpreting is. It would be pointless to insist that interpreters must be told what they know anyhow, so that they should know it very well. (Ordinary language philosophers suggested at one time that their task was to let others know very well what they know without such help.) But some aspects of the interpreting activity may have escaped notice. Interpreters must occasionally defend a given interpretation, but they are seldom urged to defend the general principles supporting their interpretive choices. Even experts in interpreting are sailing in uncharted waters when trying to explain the principles invoked in defending contested interpretations.

Most of the time we understand what was said or done without any interpretation. Failure in understanding others triggers the interpreting activity only occasionally. Still, once we settle on an interpretive hypothesis, we come to rest. At least until we are challenged, the claim that we understood what was said or that we have chosen the best interpretive hypothesis leading to our understanding is self-confirming. Since most of the time we remain unchallenged, we do not get much practice in defending the principles supporting our interpretive choices.

A comparison with reasoning in other contexts will be helpful. A reasoner may come to a conclusion on the grounds of premises that he accepts. When challenged, he may reply that his conclusion is a logical consequence of the accepted premises. Even if he is mistaken, and his conclusion cannot be derived from those premises, he may be right in defending that conclusion. For example, logic will not sanction deriving the conclusion "p" from the two premises "if p then q" and "q." Yet the reasoner may be right in believing "p," even if he mistakenly believes that the derivation of the conclusion is sanctioned by logic. He may be right in his belief, even if he does not know the grounds for it. His being right cannot be impeached, whether he tells us that his belief is based on a guess or on what he calls "a gut feeling." Similarly, an interpreter may not be able to tell us why he has chosen a given interpretive hypothesis, yet he may have been right in choosing that particular hypothesis over any other. When called to defend his hypothesis, he may tell us that he just picked one from a number of available hypotheses. If the hypothesis seems right, we will not continue the conversation; yet if it seems contestable, then at least on some occasions we will raise questions. Is it reasonable to accept the "gut-feeling" hypothesis? Are those who accept it knowledgeable about what is at issue? What is the consensus of interpreters about this interpretive hypothesis?

In raising questions about the consensus of interpreters, we become aware that often it is useless to search for statistical evidence about other interpreters' opinions. Before counting their opinions we must be certain that their opinions count. And their opinions count only if they are both reasonable interpreters and knowledgeable about what is at issue. The prior decision on counting only those interpreters whose opinions count may be supported by further statistical evidence, but in the last analysis the solitary interpreter must decide whether he accepts the available statistical evidence. Interpreters who are neither reasonable nor knowledgeable about the issues may support the majority opinion. The solitary interpreter may still endorse that opinion, but surely not because interpreters holding it were deficient. On the other side, he will be motivated to endorse the consensus of interpreters if he believes that they were both reasonable and knowledgeable. Conformism to established interpretive choices can be defended, but we cannot always rely on the availability of a conformist choice. The solitary interpreter cannot hide behind a conformist choice in accepting a given conformist interpretation. In accepting (or rejecting) it, he shows himself endowed with an individual voice. One of the burdens of this study is to show that in using his own individual voice, he is sometimes speaking with a universal voice (see chapter 8). He is speaking with a universal voice only if he is both reasonable and knowledgeable about what is at issue.

Theories of interpretation relying on a consensus of interpreters are incomplete at best. They cannot account for the solitary interpreter's interpretive hypotheses. Such an interpreter is often required to rely only on himself in formulating an interpretation. For example, professionals in a given field are expected to speak with their own individual voices. To the extent that they repeat what they have learned from their teachers, gurus, friends, or students, they merely give voice to the opinions of others. They are professionals to the extent that they rely only on themselves in formulating their interpretive hypotheses. They contribute to their field of interest by formulating their interpretations.

The aim of this study is to understand interpreting from the viewpoint of a solitary interpreter. No doubt, we often depart from the solitary interpreter's viewpoint, and we become concerned about other interpreters' opinions. In such cases our reliance on a consensus can be defended, but such a defense will not illuminate the solitary interpreter's ways of reaching and defending interpretive hypotheses.

Yet a consensus of interpreters is also important for the solitary interpreter. He does not want to follow a consensus; his goal is rather that others follow his interpretation. A consensus formed around his interpretation will provide for its acceptance by all who follow a consensus of other interpreters' opinions. We may want to claim that either we follow a consensus or we want to create a new consensus, but for many reasons this is not an exclusive alternative. For example, unbeknownst to the solitary interpreter, another interpreter has offered the same interpretive hypothesis; or, other interpreters reject his interpretation because they do not consider him either reasonable or knowledgeable about the issues. In the court of public opinion, the solitary interpreter may not be able to create a new consensus. His failure to create a new consensus around his interpretation may prompt him to adopt one of three responses. He may choose to abandon his interpretive hypothesis, or maintain it and abandon only its public defense, or maintain it and continue its public defense. The first two alternatives are of no great interest. The last alternative deserves further discussion.

In maintaining and publicly defending an interpretive hypothesis that is contested by a consensus of other interpreters' opinions, the solitary interpreter risks being judged unreasonable or told he lacks sufficient

knowledge about what is at issue. The issues between the solitary interpreter who wishes to create a new consensus around his interpretive
hypothesis and other interpreters who follow a consensus could find a
quick resolution if we had evidence independent of the contesting parties
about objective criteria for being reasonable and knowledgeable. Unfortunately, no such criteria are available. Knowledgeable persons among our
remote ancestors considered beliefs based on Stone Age physics or theology reasonable. What is reasonable among knowledgeable persons at one
time is quite unreasonable at another time. Opinions about what is reasonable and knowledgeable are at a variance even within a given time and
place. The very notions of reasonable and knowledgeable are themselves
subject to interpretation. Although they are subject to interpretation, they
also regulate our interpreting activity.

In offering an interpreting hypothesis, the solitary interpreter *demands*
of others that they adopt his interpretation. On what grounds does he issue
such a demand? Guidance on this matter is already contained in the two
principles introduced in this chapter. The import of these principles and
their connection to the philosophical tradition will become clearer in the
course of this study. Meanwhile, we must remember that only if a new consensus is formed around the solitary interpreter's interpretive hypothesis
can we judge it to be a successful interpretation. Of course, his demand
may be ignored, rejected, or responded to somewhere in between. (For
example, an interpreter belonging to one religious denomination may
ignore, or pay insufficient attention to, or reject an interpretation originating in another religious denomination.) But the outright rejection of an
interpretive hypothesis often implies that the interpreter offering that
hypothesis has been found wanting. By calling into question the interpreter's qualifications, we change our focus from what is interpreted, to
the interpreter's beliefs.

Two Kinds of Beliefs

1. Failure in Self-Understanding

As speakers and agents, we are in a very good position to know how our own words or deeds must be understood. Guidance by external authorities and reliance on observation are seldom needed after our initial education in kindergarten, on the playground, and at the shopping mall. But there is a large gap between what we *can* know about our own words and deeds and what we *do* know. Without that gap, there would be no room for natural interpretation in the subjunctive mood, or deep-level interpretations or deep-level interpretation theories. In trying to bridge that gap with a natural interpretation in the subjunctive mood, our critic claims that we could in principle know what in fact we do not know. In attempting to join what we know to what we can know with a deep interpretation, our critic suggests that if we were not self-deceived, then we would know what we do not know; moreover, we deserve to be blamed for not knowing what our critic knows about our own words and deeds.

Praise or blame is primarily appropriate in contexts where we could have done other than what we have done. Failure in self-understanding, on the other hand, is not always blameworthy. Stupidity and many cases of ignorance are not blameworthy. Our remote ancestors cannot be blamed for believing in Stone Age physics or theology; however, our contemporaries may be questioned if they hold such eccentric beliefs. Admittedly, we do blame another person for holding a certain belief. The question arises: can we blame him for his way of understanding what he considers to be a fact? Is it fair to blame him for seeing what he considers to be a fact in a certain way?

As we have seen, what we consider facts guide our interpretations. Hence, our understanding of what we consider facts is crucial for our interpretations. Since we have learned at an early age about the convertibility of what is true and what is a fact, it would be easy but quite imprudent to define facts in terms of true beliefs. If we wish to differentiate between beliefs that are subject to the moral edge of another person's criticism and beliefs that are impervious to such criticism, we must hold on to the difference between facts and beliefs. How do we establish what we consider to be facts? Juries in criminal proceedings, for example, are specifically charged to determine the facts in a given case that must be adjudicated. How do they establish what they consider to be facts?

Two kinds of claims are heard during the deliberations. One juror finds the case for or against the defendant compelling. He did not deliberate on the matter and he did not examine the merits of the arguments presented. When pressed for his reasons, he either invents a response that accords with his judgment or he offers another juror's previously suggested reasons. When his fellow jurors are dissatisfied and insist on a better answer, he suggests: "I find for (or against) the defendant because he is innocent (or guilty)." The answer is uninformative in all cases and inarticulate in some cases; but it is often the only answer that he can give. Must we always reject such an answer? If we reject this answer, our alternative is a natural interpretation in the subjunctive mood, or a deep interpretation of this juror's words together with an appeal to some theory of deep interpretation. But at least in some cases, the claim that the facts of the matter are such that he could not do otherwise must be taken seriously and literally. Have we not all made important decisions in our lives without being able to provide cogent reasons for our choices? Could we all provide cogent reasons for our choice of a profession, a spouse, or a friend? The best response to inquiries on such matters may be no more informative than Montaigne's remark about his friendship with Étienne de la Boétie: "If I were pressed to say why I loved him, I feel that my only reply could be: 'because it was he, because it was I.' "

In contrast to the first juror, the second juror is aware of having weighed the available evidence; he is aware of having deliberated. He found the arguments conclusive: he decided on the guilt or innocence of the defendant. The second juror may use the same words as the first—"I find for (or against) the defendant because he is innocent (or guilty)." Even if their votes happen to contradict each other, each may claim that his vote was based on facts and not on beliefs. Yet there is a crucial difference between (1) becoming aware or finding that we hold a certain belief to be a fact and (2) considering that belief to be a fact as a result of deliberation or the examination of arguments.

We could say that at times we become aware of holding a certain belief to be a fact, at other times we deliberate and examine the available arguments for a given belief and hold that belief to be a fact as a result of our examination. Let us focus on a few facts that we would be unwilling to doubt, except in the context of radical skepticism. I shall call such facts "privileged facts." For example, I have a brain, I am now looking at a computer screen, I am now in a book-lined study, some words in my native language hook up with some items in the world in which we live, and I knew my biological parents. For ease of exposition, I shall speak in the first-person singular about three groups of privileged facts and their contrast with firmly held beliefs.

(1) Some facts are as evident as any premise of an argument that I could offer in support of my claims about these facts. I *found*—this word in italics signals a change in attitude—these privileged facts to be so evident, so deeply entrenched, and so compelling that I am so bold as to claim that no reasonable persons who are familiar with the circumstances would disagree with my understanding of these facts. Moreover, if they disagree with me about one of these facts, I will not change my understanding of that fact; instead I will focus on the reasons for their disagreement. Are they talking seriously? Are they trying to make a philosophical point? Why don't they see what is so clear to me and to all those who agree with me? I would be seriously underdescribing my situation concerning these few privileged facts if I would merely say that they are the contents of true beliefs. My attitude toward the privileged facts is different from my attitude toward the content of true beliefs. In some cases, I would dismiss those who doubt these facts; in others, I would shift the focus of my attention from these facts to those who doubt them or to the reasons offered for doubting them. Concerning my understanding of these privileged facts, I will not change my mind, at least as long as I am the same person as I am right now—no matter what happens. (I do not intend to raise the philosophical problem of personal identity. "The same person" is meant here in its colloquial sense: I am not the same person as I was in my remote past, and it can be expected that I will not remain the same person in the indefinite future.)

(2) I am not consciously aware of other privileged facts at this time, but I could become aware of them at any time in the future. Friends, advisors, amateur or professional psychologists, and even strangers could make me aware of some of these facts at any time. If, with their help, a privileged fact

of this group is *found*, it will join the ranks of the privileged facts of the first group. At the present time, I could not offer arguments in support of the first two groups of privileged facts.

(3) Without examining the available evidence, I *found* the facts belonging to the first group to be evident, deeply entrenched, and compelling. On the other side of the ledger, there is the third group. I examine the evidence, the reasons, and the arguments, and come to the conclusion that the facts in this group are as evident, deeply entrenched, and compelling as the facts of the first group. How could I come to that conclusion? In order to answer this question, we must first discuss firmly held beliefs.

I have beliefs that are less deeply entrenched. I hold them to be true, but about these I can merely say that I will reexamine them only if some reasonable persons familiar with the circumstances disagree with me. In the past, I have been mistaken, and I would welcome others to show me the error of my ways. Beliefs function as intermediaries between the facts and me: I hold them to be true as long as they are representative of the facts; I reject them as soon as they are discredited by the facts. Concerning privileged facts, I have no need of such intermediaries. I understand these facts immediately and directly, and as long as I am the same person I am now, I will not even entertain the possibility of error—provided that no philosophical considerations concerning these privileged facts are at issue.

Let us first examine Universalizability with respect to the privileged facts of the first and third groups and all my firmly held beliefs. Disagreement with my understanding of the privileged facts I would dismiss: anyone who does not agree with my understanding of these facts is either not serious or unreasonable or unfamiliar with what is at issue. The Restrictive Principle, on the other hand, would guide me: only reasonable persons who are familiar with the circumstances understand the topic the way I do. As mentioned earlier, this is not a very strong claim, for it says merely than all persons who understand the topic the way I do are reasonable and familiar with the circumstances. If accused of dogmatism, I would accept the charge and repeat Luther's words: "Here I stand, I cannot do otherwise."

Disagreement with my firmly held beliefs would trigger a reexamination of these beliefs, unless I am willing to dismiss the disagreement in accordance with the Universalizability Principle: every reasonable person who is familiar with the circumstances understands what is at issue the way I do. (Since I do not have an infinite amount of time and energy at my disposal, the reexamination of my most firmly held beliefs will remain an empty promissory note. In these cases, the objectors' complaint that I dismissed their views deserves to be taken seriously.) It will be admitted that often I am ignorant of what is implied by the privileged facts for my firmly held beliefs, or the other way around. Moreover, I may be unconscious of some firmly held beliefs, just as I am unconscious of some beliefs that I hold to be privileged facts. Finally, at times I may defend what I consider to be a privileged fact as if it were a firmly held belief, or the other way around. For example, advocates of various proofs for the existence of God often consider God's existence to be a privileged fact, yet they wish to offer a proof in accordance with the Universalizability rather than the Restrictive Principle. Or, advocates of a new scientific hypothesis may temporarily prefer to support their hypothesis with the Restrictive rather than the Universalizability Principle.

The reader will ask: if, in considering privileged facts, we cannot do better than to rely on the rather weak Restrictive Principle, why must we support our firmly held beliefs with the much stronger Universalizability Principle? The answer is that Universalizability is built into the very notions of adequate evidence, good reasons, and acceptable arguments; whenever we argue for a given belief, we cannot be satisfied with anything less than Universalizability. On the other hand, neither the Universalizability nor the Restrictive Principle will provide adequate support for any matter of fact to be considered privileged (see chapter 2, section 2). I have distinguished between beliefs that I have *found* to be privileged facts (facts in the first group), and beliefs about which I have concluded after weighing the evidence, the reasons, and the arguments that are privileged facts (facts in the third group). Strictly speaking, I can prove only that Universalizability supports certain firmly held beliefs. When I conclude that some of these beliefs are privileged facts (of the third group), I can no longer rely on Universalizability. In saying that they are just as privileged as the facts of the first group, I say no more than that I *found* these facts to be privileged facts. Accordingly, the third group of privileged facts can be understood as containing firmly held beliefs that were at one time supported by Universalizability that I *found* to be privileged facts. Since the second group of privileged facts contains only facts that will be joined to the first group of privileged facts as soon as they are *found*, we need not worry about different groups of privileged facts. What remains is the contrast between privileged facts and firmly held beliefs.

Now, it would be easy to bury the distinction between privileged facts and firmly held beliefs underneath an avalanche of objections drawn from current philosophical literature. After all, it has been claimed that there are no facts, that there are only beliefs, that there are neither facts nor beliefs, that there are only propositions we hold to be true, that the very notion of a proposition is unclear, and so on. These views are not necessarily incompatible with the distinction between privileged facts and firmly held beliefs. Those who hold some of these views will be able to translate what I have said into their preferred idiom. The following may be useful for facilitating such a translation.

Let us dispense with the talk about facts and suggest instead a distinction between two kinds of beliefs. I assume that everyone who has beliefs has at least one belief box in his head. (The heuristic device of a belief box has been invented by Stephen Schiffer.)* Let us assume that belief box #1 contains all my beliefs that are so deeply entrenched and so compelling that I am prepared to hold on to them, no matter what happens. Should I ever abandon them, I would no longer be the same person I am now. Belief box #2 contains all my beliefs that I am willing to revise. Concerning the contents of box #1, the Universalizability Principle is ineffectual. I am prepared to hold on to these beliefs against any majority, no matter how compact or how large. Concerning the contents of box #2, the Universalizability Principle is highly effective. The contents of both boxes will vary from one person to the next. Some prefer desert landscapes to oriental bazaars, others jungles to formal gardens. Similarly, some will keep in belief box #1 very few items and argue for placing what others keep in that box in belief box #2. Some will keep in belief box #1 what they know about physics; others will keep in that box what they have learned in the course of their religious instruction. Some will claim that they keep their religious—or antireligious—beliefs in box #2, but after some probing it may turn out that in fact they keep them in box #1, or vice versa.

We are now in the position of distinguishing clearly between beliefs that are subject to the moral edge of another person's criticism and beliefs that are impervious to such criticism. Remember that in talking about the contents of a person's belief box #1, I used only another way of talking about what that person considers to be evident, deeply entrenched, and compelling facts. These privileged facts define the way he understands the world, the way he sees the world, the way he interprets the world. If we take his claim seriously that as long as he is the same person he is now, he could not even entertain the possibility of error in these facts, we must add that what he considers to be privileged facts are the foundation and core of his self-understanding.

Suppose we agree with him that he placed a certain belief in a given box, but we disagree with him about that belief. (We hold that belief to be false [or true], while he holds it to be true [or false].) As long as we agree with the belief he placed in box #2, we can argue with him about that belief. In

---

* Stephen Schiffer, "Truth and the Theory of Content," in *Meaning and Understanding*, ed. H. Parret and J. Bouveresse (Berlin: Walter de Gruyter, 1981).

the course of the argument, one of two things will happen: either of us will convince the other, or we will come to agree that we disagree. As long as each of us is willing to revise his beliefs, if they are discredited by the facts or unsupported by the Universalizability Principle, we have no reason to blame each other for holding a given belief. Certainly, we cannot charge each other with self-deception for holding that belief. Such a charge is appropriate only about a belief that has been placed in someone's box #1. Even about these beliefs, however, there is a surprise in store.

Suppose we agree with him that he placed a given belief in box #1—he considers the content of that belief a privileged fact—but we disagree with him about that belief. In other words, what he understands to be a privileged fact, we accept only as a belief; moreover, we claim that it is a false belief. We may tell him that he is mistaken about his belief; we may even tell him that he is demonstrating his limited understanding, his stupidity, or his ignorance by placing that belief in box #1. But if we agree with him that the belief in question is indeed placed in box #1, we cannot blame him for having placed it in that belief box. If we agree that he did place it in box #1, then blaming him would be tantamount to blaming someone for not having perfect pitch or for being partially color-blind. By placing that belief in box #1 he became impervious to the moral edge of our criticism.

"Preposterous!" objects the reader. The penultimate sentence contains a convenient escape hatch for anyone guilty of self-deception. Anyone so accused can easily dismiss the charge raised against him by claiming that he placed the beliefs disputed by his critics in box #1. The answer is that we need not worry about such a possibility, for the objector has overlooked a critical point. Our supposition was that we agreed with another person that he placed a given belief in box #1. Under this supposition we cannot accuse him of self-deception, for we agreed that he understands the world in a certain way. In our judgment, his understanding is deficient, and it is this deficiency that made him impervious to the charge of self-deception.

But let us drop the supposition that we agree with him that he placed a given belief in box #1. If we hold that belief to be false, we can either suggest that he is mistaken or that he is insincere in holding that belief. Three cases must be distinguished: (1) He claims that the belief in question is in box #2. After repeated probing we become convinced that the arguments aimed at proving that they are in box #1 do not reach him. We conclude that no matter what he says, he placed that belief in box #1. (2) He does not even suggest that he considers the belief in question a privileged fact, but in the course of our discussion we become convinced that he did place that belief in box #1. (3) He claims that the belief is in box #1. Our examination of his claim yields the result that the belief itself is in box #2, but unbeknownst to him, his belief that his belief is in box #1 is itself in box #1.

These cases have in common that another person considers a false belief as a privileged fact, without admitting that he holds that belief in box #1. We blame him, and in the right circumstances we charge him with self-deception for holding a false belief in box #1.

2. The Contents of Belief Box #1 and the Two Principles

In appealing to one of the two principles, the solitary interpreter claims that all or some competent interpreters agree with his understanding of what is at issue. He may draw attention to objective features of what is interpreted and stipulate that all who count agree with him. While appealing to Universalizability, the solitary interpreter is in the background, and any other interpreter who counts in that situation could replace him. His understanding of the issues is not determined by his unique characteristics, but is available to any arbitrarily selected interpreter from among those who count. On another occasion, he may focus on the interpreters and claim that all who agree with him are qualified. An appeal to the Restrictive Principle moves the interpreters who count in that situation into the foreground. They can no longer be replaced by anyone who is reasonable and knowledgeable about what is at issue; they can be replaced only by those who agree with a given interpretation. The focus is now on interpreters who happen to agree with a given interpretation. A subjective feature of the interpreting situation is now in the foreground.

As mentioned before, the solitary interpreter and his critic need not consider the alternative between the two principles as an exclusive alternative. They may not even agree as to the principle that has been appealed to by the interpreter. Yet it may be useful to answer questions about the foreground and background of a given interpretation. Are objective features of what is interpreted in the foreground? Could arbitrarily selected interpreters among those who count reach the same interpretation? Alternatively, are the subjective qualifications of the interpreters themselves in the foreground? It may be helpful to the reader to be reminded of a Kantian distinction (discussed in chapter 8). As an interpreter, I may claim that a given object is beautiful; on other occasions I may suggest that I like a certain object. The objective features of what is interpreted are in the foreground in one case; in the other case the interpreter occupies the foreground. These are not exclusive alternatives: ordinarily I like what I find beautiful, and occasionally I find beautiful what I like. But only one of these claims must be defended; the other need not be justified.

It should be noted that both principles are insufficient for transforming a solitary interpreter's understanding of a belief about a matter of fact into a belief about a privileged matter of fact. It is easier to discuss this topic in the idiom of the two belief boxes.

Suppose "p" is a belief about a matter of fact, and it is in an interpreter's belief box #2. For a long time he has been in the habit of supporting "p" by appealing to Universalizability. Even if his belief continues to be unchallenged, he cannot claim that just because it remains unchallenged, it must be considered part of the content of his belief box #1. It could be in that belief box, but this depends on his attitude toward that belief rather than on the ways he supported it. He—or his critic—could claim that he will not change his mind about "p," no matter what happens. In this case there may be good reasons for believing that "p" is indeed in his belief box #1. His attitude toward "p" determined that it could be *found* there, regardless of the ways it became such a deeply entrenched belief.

3. Do We Know the Contents of Our Belief Box #1?

It bears repeating that we can always know and we ordinarily do know what we believe. When in doubt, especially about whether a given belief is a firmly held belief or considered a fact, we can easily devise the same test others are using to determine our beliefs. They suggest imaginary circumstances and ask what we would say or how we would behave in those circumstances. Given enough time, energy, and imagination, we could in principle devise these tests without the help of others. No doubt, we would not be able to shed light on our blind spots without the help of friends, advisors, psychotherapists, or others. For instance, those who are vain are notoriously among the last to know that they are vain; those suffering from anorexia or bulimia are among the last to discover that they have a distorted body-image. But outside of these blind spots, the tests prepared by others while probing for clarity about our beliefs are primarily helpful in reaching speedily and without detour the goal of knowing what we believe in other than ordinary circumstances. Our success in ordinary circumstances supports the expectation that we would know what we believe, and in what belief box we have placed, or would place, a given belief, even in the context of our blind spots, extraordinary circumstances, or extreme situations. This expectation is often disappointed.

To be sure, even in these cases we can know what we believe; but do we know it? Can we know whether a given belief that in ordinary circumstances is understood to be a privileged fact will remain a privileged fact in extreme situations? Can we know whether a firmly held belief in ordinary circumstances will remain such a belief in extreme situations? Could it not be that because of the change from ordinary circumstances to extreme situations—or the other way around—some of our beliefs currently in box #2 will be rejected, while others will be preserved in box #2, and still some of our beliefs will be moved to box #1? Could it not be that such a radical change in our circumstances—from the ordinary to the extreme or the extreme to the ordinary—would bring about a radical change in what we believe and what we understand to be a privileged fact?

Popular wisdom or moral philosophy is not very helpful in answering these questions. For example, it was the received wisdom after World War I that there were no atheists in the foxholes. Speculation about the religious beliefs of front-line soldiers or concentration camp inmates after World War II was less frequent. In both world wars, the tales about nonbelievers who turned to religious consolation in extreme situations must be balanced against the stories of believers who lost their faith in these situations. Extreme situations bring about radical changes, and it is important to remember that those who experienced such situations are no longer the same persons they were before their experiences. Hence, it is not surprising that those who experienced extreme situations reject as a false belief what they once accepted as a privileged fact.

Moral philosophers often speculate about the behavior of agents in extreme situations. But it is not always the case that what we know about the beliefs and desires of a person in ordinary circumstances will be helpful in understanding his behavior in extreme situations, and vice versa. Soldiers in battle, for instance, are often ordered to do what they ordinarily find abhorrent. Knowing their behavior in ordinary circumstances, can we predict what they will do, if given such an order? Another example: can there be a "perfect" Nazi who is willing to kill all Jews who are in his power to kill, for this is what he considers to be his duty? There are reasons to believe that there cannot be such a person. Suppose he discovers one day that he is a Jew. He can either commit suicide in the line of duty or give up the notion that he must kill in the line of duty. Regardless, his being a "perfect" Nazi will not survive his discovery.

"Improbable story" objects the reader. Perhaps the story is improbable, but is it impossible? Here is a contemporary version of this story. (The story was broadcast by a war correspondent from the former Yugoslavia in 1994;

I have borrowed the part about the mirrors from the autobiographical account of a contemporary Hungarian novelist, Péter Nádas.)

> Two young men from the same neighborhood in the outskirts of Sarajevo take up arms to join the forces of their different ethnic groups. One understands himself to be a Serb, and swears to kill the first Croat he encounters on the next day; the other understands himself to be a Croat, and swears to kill the first Serb he encounters on the next day. They meet for a last time to mark the end of their friendship. Their mothers are horrified; they decide to reveal their common secret. Both of them bring to the meeting place of their sons a bundle of old letters and a mirror. The letters prove beyond a reasonable doubt that the one who thinks himself to be a Serb is a Croat, and the one who thinks himself to be a Croat is a Serb. Each mother presents a mirror to her son: "So, you think that you are a Croat (Serb) and hate the Serbs (Croats) so much that you want to kill the first one you meet tomorrow. Look into the mirror before going on a killing rampage!"

There are some basic facts that we ordinarily know about ourselves. We understand these to be privileged facts; they include information about our parents or caregivers in our childhood and about our ethnic or religious origin. The so-called "perfect" Nazi and the two young men from the former Yugoslavia have something in common. Before the discovery of their origin, they literally did not know who they were. Their stories are not more improbable than the story of their literary archetype, Oedipus Rex. Their stories show that we can be hurt by what we don't know about ourselves. We could be mistaken about what we consider to be privileged facts. We consider these stories improbable because we expect that each of us is right about the basic facts about ourselves. But the improbability of these stories—including the story of Oedipus—is irrelevant, for these stories merely hold up a mirror to our faces, wherein we must examine whether the content of our belief box #1 agrees with the facts.

4. Conceive It Possible That You Are Mistaken!

Learning from the sad fate of those who were mistaken about who they were, we could try to avoid that fate by stipulating that henceforth all our consciously held beliefs will be placed in our box #2. What we once accepted as facts and as supported by the Restrictive Principle will henceforth be judged as firmly held beliefs on the grounds of the Universalizability Principle. Will all these firmly held beliefs survive once we judge them by appealing to the Universalizability Principle? Even if some will be rejected, this project will not keep us from harming others or ourselves. Moreover, it will keep us from reaping some of the benefits of considering certain beliefs to be privileged facts. I shall first discuss the failure of this project to keep us from harm's way.

To begin with, not all of our beliefs are held consciously. We become aware of some of our most firmly held beliefs when we examine our doubts about a given belief and ask ourselves what we would say or do in circumstances that we imagine. Beliefs that we do not hold consciously, we cannot judge in accordance with the Universalizability Principle. Secondly, even concerning beliefs we hold consciously, we may be mistaken: will we hold on to that belief if our situation changes radically? Will we hold on to that belief in extreme situations? Thirdly, are we aware of all other beliefs that we rejected so that we should be able to hold on to a given belief? Finally, we may believe that we have succeeded in placing our consciously held beliefs in our box #2, but unbeknown to us, we consider the belief that we hold a given belief, a privileged fact. In other words, unbeknown to us, the belief that we hold a certain belief is itself in our box #1, which undermines the project of placing all beliefs in our box #2.

If the "perfect" Nazi, the Serb, or the Croat harms his enemy or himself, we will, of course, condemn him as a criminal or a fool. In addition to condemning him for his deeds, we will also blame him for his mistaken understanding. In his understanding, considerations of racial or ethnic "purity" warranted his harming fellow human beings—these considerations overruled his understanding of his obligations to them and many of his other beliefs. In our understanding, his reasoning proves that he knew what he was doing when he harmed them. He believes that his understanding of the circumstances is mitigating, when in fact it is aggravating the offense. His reasoning proves that while committing his deeds, he was not merely a tool in the hands of others; he was a willing executioner of his victims. Given his mistaken understanding, he would not have been prevented from acting as a willing executioner just by placing the ideas of racial or ethnic "purity" in box #2. As mentioned earlier, authoritarians or dogmatists can always reject a dissenting view by claiming that their opponents are either not reasonable or not familiar with what is at issue.

On the other side of the ledger, it is advantageous to hold certain beliefs to be privileged facts. When action is required on the grounds of a given belief, the delay while considering the possibility that our beliefs are mistaken is often contrary to the best interests of others or ourselves. No doubt, we must value any delay or procrastination that prevents our harming them or us. Yet inaction cannot be sanctioned when we could produce good effects while conceiving the possibility of being mistaken. If the resolve to act on behalf of others or ourselves requires that we hold certain beliefs to be privileged facts, then conceiving of the possibility that we are mistaken ought not distract us.

5. *"Hier steh' ich, ich kann nicht anders"*

Luther's words, "Here I stand, I cannot do otherwise," give an accurate description of anyone who finds himself to be holding a given belief in box #1. His finding himself in a certain state must be understood literally, and not as a metaphor. The question arises: in what contexts do we ordinarily discover that we hold certain beliefs to be privileged facts?

Often we become aware of strongly held beliefs in situations involving intense fear or love. Some of these strongly held beliefs might even turn out to be in our box #1. For example, the agnostic airplane traveler finds himself to be praying for supernatural intervention in cases of severe turbulence. When this happens for the first time, he dismisses his experience as the result of a temporary instability, induced by intense fear. At first, he tries to avoid airplane travel. When he can no longer do so, and he can no longer dismiss the experience of praying, he finds himself to be a believer in supernatural powers. Other examples, these from the domain of love, are stereotypes of world literature: as a result of experiencing a great love, the novel's protagonist rejects as false beliefs what hitherto he considered to be privileged facts; or the other way around, what hitherto he considered to be a false belief, or a firmly held belief, he now considers to be a privileged fact.

Suppose I tried to support with the Universalizability Principle a given belief that I found to be a privileged fact. I would be saying that every reasonable person who is familiar with the circumstances understands what is at issue the way I do. It would be useless to argue that before my discovery I was either not reasonable or not familiar with the circumstances of what is at issue. After all, those who now disagree with me are in the same situation as I was before my discovery. My credentials as a reasonable person are not bolstered by the admission that at one time I was unreasonable, nor is it quite right that before my discovery I was unfamiliar with the circumstances of what is at issue. The belief that I now hold to be a privileged fact did not just suddenly appear from nowhere. Before my discovery I was at least partially familiar with what is at issue—otherwise, it would be incomprehensible how the belief in question suddenly appeared in my box #1. The best support I can offer for the belief I found to be a privileged fact is the claim that all persons who understand what is at issue the way I do are reasonable and familiar with the circumstances. And this just says more ponderously what popular wisdom teaches the religious person to say after he has lost his faith: "I only lost my faith, not my mind." The religious person who suddenly lost his faith or the agnostic who unexpectedly found himself to be religious will make good use of the Restrictive Principle in explaining to himself and to others his sudden change of fundamental beliefs.

Some beliefs that are presently in our box #1 were originally firmly held beliefs in our box #2. They became firmly held beliefs as a result of the examination of available evidence, reasons, or arguments. Because of a change in our attitude toward them, they are now *found* in our box #1. Nonetheless, we could aim to defend these beliefs with the Universalizability Principle, as if they were still firmly held beliefs in our box #2. If it turns out that the evidence and the arguments that we found persuasive in the course of our deliberations cannot convince others, then we must choose among three alternatives: (1) We could reject the arguments for our belief together with that belief as not well-founded. (2) We could reject the arguments for our belief, while maintaining that belief. This time we could claim that we *found* that belief in our box #1. (3) We could claim that all those we could not convince are unreasonable or insufficiently familiar with the circumstances at issue. This last choice is intolerant, but it may be the only choice available for interpreters who wish to reconcile the beliefs they *found* in their box #1 with the need to provide sound arguments in support of these beliefs.

6. ". . . *Par ce que c'estoit luy; par ce que c'estoit moy*"

Montaigne first wrote on his friendship with Étienne de la Boétie: "because it was he." According to the editors of the scholarly edition *Essays*, he added on a later occasion: "because it was I." He may have discovered in the interim that his explanation did not make sense without an explicit reference to himself.

We always provide autobiographical information for our audience when we speak about our beliefs. But such information is often merely an accidental part of talking. When we speak about a belief that we *found* in our box #1, however, the autobiographical information becomes an essential part of our talk. It is the autobiographical information that provides a license for supporting that belief with the Restrictive rather than the Universalizability Principle. Without the autobiographical information that we *found* a given belief in our box #1, the support of that belief with the Restrictive Principle would be found wanting—why didn't we support it with the much stronger Universalizability Principle? The answer has been explained earlier: Universalizability will not provide support for any matter of fact to be a privileged matter of fact. And it is fortunate that there is no such support. We would be waiting in vain for support from the Universalizability Principle to justify our religious—or irreligious—beliefs, or the beliefs leading to the choice of a profession, a spouse, or a friend.

As we shall see, conflicting ways of understanding or interpreting the same words or deeds can be adjudicated in a number of ways. If we have exhausted all other available possibilities, we may try to trace the conflicting ways of understanding to different beliefs that each of two interpreters (or one interpreter at two different times) *found* in box #1. In the large majority of cases it would be useless to suggest such an explanation: we would succeed only in shifting the focus of attention from the object of the interpretation to the interpreter.

The content of belief box #1 is different for each interpreter. Moreover, if our interpretations are guided by what we consider to be facts (i.e., our firmly held beliefs or the content of our belief box #2), the interpretations are certainly guided by what we hold to be privileged facts (i.e., the content of our belief box #1). Accordingly, every interpretation can be traced to either the interpreter's belief box #1 or #2. Even if an interpretation is guided only by the contents of the interpreter's belief box #2, some connection—no matter how tenuous—can always be established between the contents of the interpreter's two belief boxes. Now, if every interpretation can be shown to be connected to the interpreter's belief box #1, that connection cannot, without further support, provide an explanation of any given interpretation. For example, we could claim that (1) the connection between a given interpretation and the interpreter's belief box #1 provides a better explanation of that interpretation than all alternative explanations; and argue that (2) our claim is supported by the Universalizability Principle. Our suggestion· may fail as an explanation, since the standards for adequate explanations are quite high. Interpretations have lower standards than explanations; hence, the connection to the belief box #1 may succeed as an interpretation, even if it fails as an explanation. However, if we wish to credit the connection as an interpretation of a given interpretation, we must be on guard against a common illusion. Two examples will illustrate the matter.

(1) Exodus 4:24 relates the following about Moses: "And it came to pass by the way in the inn, that the Lord met him, and thought to kill him." As long as the interpretation's application in religious practice was predominant, the interpreters asked: what sin provoked God when He thought to kill his first prophet at a roadside inn? Motivated by a radically different

application, Russell asked: what kind of a god is this who thought to kill his first prophet at a roadside inn?

(2) During an urban riot, a guardsman noticed a child, about twelve years old, aiming a machine gun at a group of people facing him. The guardsman could have shot the child; but he hesitated, and lowered his gun. The child did not hesitate; he fired his machine gun into the crowd. Some were killed; others were severely wounded. Afterward, the guardsman tried to explain his hesitation: "I could not shoot: I saw a child!" His commander replied that he would have used his gun: "You saw a young criminal; he was a danger to others and to himself!"*

We may side with either Russell or the traditional Bible interpreter, with either the guardsman or his commander. Either way, we will not illuminate a given interpretation by tracing it to one of the interpreter's belief boxes. We may have the illusion that we said something important about an interpretation by providing a connection to the contents of the interpreter's belief boxes; but what we said is informative only about the interpreter and not about the object of the interpretation. The reader may judge the two examples differently. He may find it informative about Russell that his antireligious beliefs prompted a radically new interpretation of a biblical text. In the second example, what we would like to know is whether the guardsman or his commander saw the situation correctly. An account of what prompted one to see a child and the other to claim that he would have seen a criminal is quite uninformative.

7. What We Cannot Know

Did the guardsman or his commander see the situation correctly? The shortest answer is that we do not know; we can also show that we cannot know the answer to that question. First, we must discredit a number of ways that could be used to find out how such a question could be answered.

To begin with, a misunderstanding of Wittgenstein's views on interpreting must be discredited. What the guardsman saw and what his commander would have seen in the same situation cannot be accounted for in terms of the "seeing as" locution. A duck picture in the company of rabbit pictures can be seen as a rabbit picture, but seeing someone as a child or as a dangerous criminal would not have been sufficient to motivate the guardsman or his commander to lower or to use his gun. The claim that one acted on what he saw and that the other would have acted on what he would have seen in that situation must be understood literally.

* Frederic Schick discusses similar examples in *Understanding Action* (Cambridge: Cambridge University Press, 1991), 1–3.

Secondly, a favorite Hegelian device to let history decide between two equally plausible interpretations would not be useful here. Where foresight and hindsight are in conflict, the Hegelian will side with success in history. For example, last year's investment was deemed to be prudent by the majority of an estate's trustees; hindsight identifies it as reckless. Another example: the political decisions leading to war seemed to be correct to the majority of voting participants; hindsight identifies them as irresponsible. Could the participants who decided on these matters have had the foresight necessary to avoid failure? Such issues are settled by a judgment of the courts or of history. Note, however, that the verdict obliterates the difference between hindsight and foresight. The participants are found innocent or guilty because they did or did not have the foresight expected of agents in their circumstances. The cynic may claim that success or failure decides such matters. If this were the case, the verdict of the courts or of history would be an empty gesture.

Finally, it would be useless to suggest that we try to imagine what each of us would do if we were in the guardsman's circumstances. Popular wisdom encourages such an exercise of the imagination. While the exercise may be useful for the development of our imagination, it will not provide an answer to our question. While living in ordinary circumstances, I do not know how I or anyone else will act in an extreme situation. In fact, although I may know how another person will act, and he can know how I will act in an ordinary situation, ultimately our concepts of options and choices exclude each of us from knowing how he will actually act. Gilbert Ryle indicated the problem:

> . . . [W]hen I consider what I thought and did yesterday, there seems to be no absurdity in supposing that that could have been forecast, before I did it. It is only while I am actually trying to predict my own next move that the task feels like that of a swimmer trying to overtake the waves that he sends ahead of himself.*

But his proof relies on the claim that a prediction of an action must overlook at least one of the data relevant to the prediction: the agent's state of mind just before acting. A proof that relies only on conceptual issues is due to Frederic Schick's analysis:

> We can know how others will choose, and others can know how we will. But we can't know how *we* will be choosing (not even if we are told by the others!). We can't foreknow our own choices, not because they will be capricious or because we lack the right data but because our concepts exclude it, our concepts of options and choices. We can't because we cannot choose where

* Gilbert Ryle, *The Concept of Mind* (New York: Barnes & Noble, 1949) 187–88.

we face no issue, and because we face no issue where there is no uncertainty for us—and there *would* be no uncertainty if we knew our choice beforehand. We can't foreknow our choices, because they then wouldn't be choices.[*]

We cannot know whether the guardsman or his commander saw the situation correctly. If either tried to support what he saw with the Universalizability Principle, the other could argue that this is an abuse of the principle. The fact that there are two incompatible ways of seeing the same situation and both ways are reasonable shows that an appeal to this principle will not decide the issue between the two contestants. It is, of course, easy to misuse or abuse this or any other principle. In case of an abuse of the Universalizability Principle, the focus of attention shifts from what is at issue to those who abuse the principle. Are they authoritarians, or dogmatists; is their intelligence limited; do they have a blind spot about what is at issue; or are they victims of self-deception? By appealing at least overtly to the Restrictive Principle, each contestant defends those who agree with his interpretive choice. At the same time, the contestants admit the continuation of the debate. (As we shall see in chapter 3, "overtly" carries a heavy burden.)

The reader will remember the debate between the art historian-connoisseur of established reputation and his younger colleagues about the attribution of a certain painting to X or to X's studio in chapter 1. In that case, as in the case of the debate between the guardsman and his commander, the Restrictive Principle is the best support that is available to all parties in the debate. In both cases each contestant could claim that what he saw was decisive in his acting as he did (or in claiming that he would have acted in accordance with what he saw). Charges of self-deception were mentioned in one case, and not in another. If we knew more about the guardsman and his commander, such charges could also arise in this case.

So far I have insisted that we can know and we ordinarily do know what we believe and how our own words and deeds must be understood. At the same time, I admit that in some cases our knowledge about these matters is quite limited. It must be shown why our knowledge about our own beliefs and understandings of our words and deeds is so important. In addition, the Universalizability Principle must be defended against its critics.

---

[*] Frederic Schick, *Making Choices* (Cambridge: Cambridge University Press, 1997), 80.

CHAPTER THREE

Kinds of Interpretations

In the large majority of cases there is no need for an interpretation; we understand what is at issue immediately and without further inquiry. I have suggested that our vocabulary prompts us to distinguish clearly between the state of understanding and the activity of interpreting. The reader may object: there is no clear distinction between understanding and interpreting, and we interpret even if the need for an interpretation does not arise. The answer is that even if the reader believes what is said in the objection, it is useful to focus first on cases where the need for an interpretation arises naturally. We shall see that as soon as such a need arises, the interpreter must evaluate the speaker's or agent's self-understanding and his knowledge about the facts at issue.

1. The Hereditary Property of Interpretations

If the flow of information directed at an audience is interrupted for lack of understanding, the questions raised can be answered either by an exact quotation, or by a report in indirect speech on the content of what was said. The quotation merely reiterates what was just said, and—except in extraordinary circumstances—is useful only if failure to understand is due to a perceptual problem. The report provides the audience with understanding of what was said. Quoting does not presuppose the understanding of what is quoted. But a report in indirect speech presupposes at least an attempt at understanding. Such reports are often, but not always, interpretations. For example, they are not interpretations if they contain neither more nor less than the content of what was said earlier.

"Interpreting" and "interpretations" have been used in a wide variety of contexts. At this stage we must set aside natural contexts (e.g., "spots mean measles" or "clouds mean rain") and nonverbal contexts (e.g., an actor's interpretation of his role or a conductor's interpretation of a score). We shall discuss only interpretations that are reports in indirect speech of what was said or done.

In understanding the words and deeds of others, ordinarily our goal is to understand them as they understood themselves when they communicated their words or performed their actions. The need for an interpretation arises if we believe we have failed in reaching an accurate understanding. The speaker's words or the agent's deeds are the subjects of our inquiry. We ask: What did he say? What did he do? Let us first assume that the speaker's or agent's understanding of his own words and deeds is both sincere and in accordance with independently known facts. As mentioned earlier, interpretations that aim at understanding the speaker or agent as he understands himself are *natural* interpretations in the indicative mood. Such an interpretation is successful if the interpreter's understanding of the speaker's words agrees with the latter's self-understanding. The interpreter's understanding of a speaker's or agent's words or deeds is transmitted to his listeners or readers, who can then transmit it to their audiences, if the need arises. The speaker's or agent's understanding of his own words and deeds becomes thereby a hereditary property of a successful series of natural interpretations. This hereditary property, when successful, connects the speaker or agent with his most remote interpreter.

Natural interpretations are steered by the speaker's or agent's self-understanding as long as the interpreter judges by his own lights that his assumptions are warranted: the speaker's self-understanding is sincere and it agrees with the facts. If these assumption are not warranted, the interpreter must shift from the indicative to the subjunctive mood. Instead of understanding the speaker or agent as he understands himself, the interpreter must now *try* to understand him as he would understand himself, in a way that is both sincere and knowledgeable about the facts. Common to natural interpretations in the indicative and the subjunctive moods is that they are both supported by the Universalizability Principle.

Natural interpretations in both moods take for granted that the speaker or agent would agree in principle, if not in fact, with the proposed interpretation. The Universalizability Principle supports the proposed interpretation only if the interpreter can attribute agreement with the interpretation to the speaker, at least in principle. The need for a *deep* interpretation arises if the interpreter can no longer attribute to the speaker agreement with the proposed interpretation. For example, a speaker will contest an interpretation triggered by his choice of words, tone of voice, or behavior, if it does not agree with his self-understanding. Only the Restrictive Principle can support deep interpretations. Deep interpretation is the only alternative to natural interpretation that is even in principle unacceptable to the speaker. Accordingly, as long as this does not lead to misunderstanding, when speaking about interpretations, "natural" will thenceforward be omitted.

We accept a given interpretation as long as it agrees with facts that are known independently of that interpretation. In case of a disagreement with independently known facts, we dismiss a proposed interpretation and replace it with another. The replacement need not be on a different level from the original interpretation. In the large majority of cases, we take it for granted that speakers and agents are aware of what they have said or done: they have at least psychological access to their own words and deeds. Hence, it is quite right that we should accept their understanding of what they have said or done. We reject their interpretations only if psychological access to their own words and deeds did not entail epistemic access. For example, if a child complains, "I have a pain in my hair," we cannot expect to understand him as he understands himself. The self-understanding of the speaker or agent may be insufficient, his vocabulary limited, his judgment clouded. In these cases we set aside the speaker's self-understanding, and we substitute an interpretation of his words that accords with facts known to the interpreter. In diagnosing the ailments of an inarticulate or unbalanced patient, the physician routinely substitutes her understanding of the patient's complaints for his own. The replacement of the child's understanding by his caregiver's or the patient's understanding by his physician's is supported by the Universalizability Principle. In substituting an alternative, the caregiver and the physician do not propose a deep interpretation. They argue that if the child and the patient were in the place of the caregiver or the physician, they would agree with the proposed alternative—because all reasonable persons who are knowledgeable about what is at issue agree with that alternative. The alternative interpretation can be defeated only if it is no longer supported by the Universalizability Principle.

We also substitute an alternative interpretation for the speaker's self-understanding if his sincerity is questioned. Those who go back on their word, break their promise, or welsh on their bets will not be forgiven if they claim that they did not mean what they said. In giving their word they relied on a convention that discharges what they said from what they meant. The

Universalizability Principle also supports our alternative interpretation in these cases.

The relatively unproblematic substitution of the interpreter's understanding of what is at issue for the child's or the patient's self-understanding shows that we cannot always attribute self-understanding to others. Self-awareness does not always yield self-understanding. Concerning the child's complaint about a pain located where no pain can be felt, we concede that he is aware of discomfort or pain, yet we do not attribute to him an understanding of his own words. It would be futile to argue that we understand the words he has uttered as he understands them, and we merely claim that he is mistaken about the location of his pain. Since we cannot understand him as he understands himself, what grounds do we have for claiming that he understands himself? Granted, sometimes we have evidence that another person is understood by some of his interpreters, even if we don't understand him. Their conversation suggests that they understand him, and some even agree with him. But if no other person can understand him as he understands himself, do we have reasons to believe that he understands himself? Of course, it is sometimes useful to suggest that we understand another person whose self-understanding implies a wildly false belief. We could not register our disagreement unless it was grounded on our common understanding. Note, however, that we always have a choice between two alternative claims: (1) we understand him as he understands himself, although he has a mistaken belief, and (2) we don't understand him as he understands himself, and yet we have no grounds to claim that he does understand himself. If we have didactic goals, we may insist that we understand the other as he understands himself, and that he has a mistaken belief; if our primary purpose is to provide help, we need not argue with him about his lack of self-understanding.

2. Partially Mistaken or Insincere Interpretations

For lack of a better understanding of the speaker's words or the agent's deeds, even partially mistaken or insincere interpretations can be accepted as long as there is no better interpretation that would serve our purposes. However, our tolerance for mistaken or insincere interpretations has limits. Interpretations have a normative character: they are presented as the best available to an interpreter for a given purpose. While interpretations serving different purposes don't even compete, among alternative interpretations serving the same purpose only the best available is considered to be acceptable. There is a convergence to the best interpretation, only if the interpretations are competing with each other; and they are competing with each other only if they serve the same purpose.

Interpretations may be completely mistaken or insincere in attributing a given self-understanding to the speaker or agent; such interpretations are not even misinterpretations of the speaker's words or the agent's deeds. They are merely stories about what the interpreters claim to have interpreted; at best, they are off-the-wall interpretations or no interpretation at all of what was actually said or done. In contrast with off-the-wall interpretations, partially mistaken or insincere interpretations can be considered misinterpretations as soon as a better interpretation becomes available. However, even a misinterpretation must at least partially contain the hereditary property of successful interpretations.

Let us take stock. An interpretation need not be labeled true or false, but it must be consistent with the facts as the interpreter knows them. An interpretation is acceptable only if it is the best available for a given purpose. These two constraints—the factual and the normative—permit us to override the speaker's self-understanding. We rely on the Universalizability Principle in replacing the speaker's or agent's self-understanding with an alternative interpretation that agrees with the facts and—from the viewpoint of our goals—provides for a better understanding of his words or deeds. Even if our alternative interpretation no longer contains the hereditary property of successful natural interpretations, it will be judged a *natural* interpretation as long as it is supported by the Universalizability Principle. Partially insincere self-interpretations do not present additional problems; the factual and the normative constraints on interpretations permit us to replace the speaker's insincere self-understanding with an alternative interpretation.

We are now in the position to establish a connection between the two constraints on interpreting and the Universalizability Principle.

> Interpreters are entitled to appeal to the Universalizability Principle for a given interpretation if and only if they believe they have satisfied the two constraints for that interpretation.

If interpreters are challenged about the claim that every qualified interpreter agrees with a given interpretation, their best response is to show that the interpretation has satisfied both factual and normative constraints. They may be confronted by opponents who agree with their interpretive goals yet continue to disagree with their interpretation. When interpreters answer such a challenge, the answer will fall between two extremes. The intolerant will claim that their opponents are either not reasonable or not knowledgeable about the issues. The more tolerant interpreters will suggest that the Universalizability Principle must be understood as a *demand* that all qualified interpreters agree with their interpretations. (The fast retreat from the statement that "All qualified interpreters agree with me" to the recommendation "All qualified interpreters *ought* to agree with me" is quite common. It is effective when interpreters are accused of intolerance. After all, they cannot be faulted for recommending interpretations that have satisfied both constraints on interpreting.) To be sure, interpreters eager to continue a debate with their opponents about an interpretation are well advised to refrain from appealing to Universalizability, even if they are entitled to such an appeal. Also, the fact that they did not appeal to Universalizability does not imply that they have not satisfied both constraints. But the connection between the two constraints and the Universalizability Principle creates a problem in the context of deep interpretation.

3. Deep Interpretation

Sometimes we don't understand what another person has said or done, and we don't have evidence that he understands himself. The rules of etiquette require that even in these cases we refrain from faulting that person. The charge that he does not understand what he is saying is considered to be only slightly less insulting than the claim that he is lying. Politeness finds an ally in caution: maybe there is an interpreter who understands him better than we understand him, and maybe he is understood by this interpreter as he understands himself. But the natural interpretation provided by his interpreter—or by the speaker or agent—does not satisfy the factual or normative constraint on interpreting. At this stage we have a choice.

(1) We dismiss the natural interpretation as grounded on a mistaken belief and provide an alternative interpretation. As long as we support our alternative with the Universalizability Principle, we appeal to the speaker or agent to understand what is at issue as we interpret it. We claim that he would agree with us if he were both reasonable in judgment and knowledgeable about the facts; based on our claim we demand that he agree with us. The proposed alternative falls within the limits of natural interpretations as long as the speaker can at least in principle, if not in fact, agree with the interpretation.

(2) We provide an alternative interpretation that we can support only with the Restrictive Principle. We no longer claim that all reasonable persons who are knowledgeable about what is at issue agree with us. What is more important, we do not expect the speaker or agent to agree with us either

in fact or in principle. If he will agree with us in the future, he will no longer be the same person he is now. (Occasionally, we even issue a call that he change, so that he will come to agree with us.) The best support for our interpretation at this time is the weak claim that all those who agree with us are reasonable and knowledgeable of what is at issue. We expect disagreement with our alternative interpretation not only from the speaker, but also from all others who will want to submit yet another alternative. We propose a *deep* interpretation that is essentially contestable. Others who propose another alternative may claim that they have offered a natural interpretation or another deep-interpretation alternative.

4. Weakened Formulation of the Principles

So far I have suggested that in appealing to the Restrictive Principle the interpreter claims that *all* who agree with him are reasonable and knowledgeable about what is at issue. The reader may object: couldn't this admittedly weak principle be further weakened by replacing in its formulation "all" with "some"? As we shall see in section 5, the replacement is indeed useful in at least one context; in others this would be at loggerheads with important features of defending interpretations. What is the difference between the two formulations?

In its universal form the Restrictive Principle has a feature in common with the Universalizability Principle. As a solitary interpreter I cannot offer empirical evidence for the claim that all reasonable and knowledgeable persons agree with me or that all who agree with me are reasonable and knowledgeable. Although unsupported by empirical evidence, these claims are vulnerable only to counterexamples. Both claims are used to indicate an interpreter's assumptions. What is the function of these claims? In appealing to Universalizability, the interpreter *demands* the agreement of other interpreters about what is interpreted; in calling on the Restrictive Principle, the interpreter *defends* all interpreters who agree on a given interpretation. His demand and defense come (logically) prior to any empirical investigation about the facts of the matter. It may be the case that not all who agree with him are reasonable and knowledgeable or that not all who are reasonable and knowledgeable agree with him. As soon as counterexamples arise, they must be addressed. Meanwhile, he is appealing to principles on the basis of his assumptions. As soon as he replaces "all" with "some" in the formulations of these principles, he not only weakens these claims, but also collapses the two different claims into one, ultimately undermining them.

The weakened form of the Restrictive Principle, "Some persons who understand what is at issue the way I do are reasonable and familiar with the circumstances," is equivalent to the weakened form of the Universalizability Principle, "Some reasonable persons who are familiar with the circumstances understand what is at issue the way I do." Accordingly, if we weaken both principles, we also collapse the two into one. Moreover, if we weaken either principle, we remove the linchpin supporting our understanding of interpreting by the solitary interpreter.

We must assume that each interpreter agrees with his own interpretation. Accordingly, if there is only one interpreter who agrees with that interpretation, then—in this quite uninteresting case—both principles are satisfied. The claims appealing to either of the two principles are vulnerable to counterexamples only as long as they are formulated as universal claims. If one of the principles is formulated in its weakened form, we must assume that more than one person satisfies the claim used by the interpreter in appealing to a principle. But if we replace "all" with "more than one" or "most," then the question arises: how many? Since the interpreter's claims are no longer vulnerable to falsification by counterexamples, he can no longer assume that there is more than one or that there are many persons who satisfy the conditions specified in a given claim. Only an empirical investigation can answer the "how many?" question. But in order to launch an empirical investigation, the interpreter must answer a prior question that arose when we discussed problems concerning the consensus of interpreters (chapter 1, section 7): before counting the opinions of others, he must be certain that their opinions count. Moreover, if the point of his empirical investigation is to *demand* support for his interpretation or to *defend* interpreters who agree with his interpretation, then he can rely only on other interpreters who agree with his interpretation. Accordingly, he must offer an interpretation prior to counting interpreters who agree with him and whose opinions matter. With an exception, to be addressed in section 5, an appeal to a weakened form of either principle becomes thereby a futile exercise. If our goal is to understand interpreting from the viewpoint of a single individual, we must formulate both principles in their universal form.

5. Alternatives to the Speaker's Self-Understanding

Unless we believe that another person's self-understanding violates either the factual or the normative constraint on interpreting, we not only accept his self-understanding as the best available interpretation of his words or deeds, but (in case of need) also pass it on to others. However, if we believe that his self-understanding violates one of the two constraints on interpreting, we have a choice. We can claim to understand him as he understands himself and add that his self-understanding is based on a mistaken belief. Or we can substitute our interpretation of what he has said or done for his self-understanding. In substituting an alternative that no longer contains the hereditary property of successful natural interpretations, we imply that his self-understanding is deficient. We either propose a natural interpretation in the subjunctive mood, or we propose a deep interpretation. In the former case, the deficiency is so obvious that we expect agreement from all reasonable persons who are knowledgeable about what is at issue. In the latter case, the deficiency is at least partially hidden and we only aspire to be considered reasonable and knowledgeable about what is at issue together with those who agree with our alternative interpretation.

As long as the content of self-understanding is indeed a hereditary property of an unbroken chain of interpretations, the interpreting activity has a conservative—at times even authoritarian—bias. In such a chain, the authority is vested in the speaker, writer, or agent whose words and deeds are subject to interpretation. The interpreter challenges this authority by claiming that the speaker's self-understanding violates the factual or normative constraint on interpreting. If the interpreter successfully overrides this authority, an alternative interpretation is substituted for the speaker's self-understanding. This alternative interpretation will be the beginning of another unbroken chain of interpretations.

We must avoid confusion. Ordinarily, speakers or agents are expected to understand their own words or deeds. We not only expect them to know what they say, but also what they mean. In this sense they have interpretive authority over what they say or do. A critic who has questioned the notion of interpretive authority used here prompts my insistence on this point.[*] Interpretive authority must not be confused with the right understanding of what has been said or done. Agents of ethnic cleansing or terror understand what they are saying or doing in planning their activities, and in that sense they have interpretive authority. But such an authority does not yield authority concerning a right understanding of what they were saying or doing. Right understanding does not depend on any authority.

---

[*] Laurent Stern, "Are There Definitive Interpretations?" in *Is There a Single Right Interpretation?* ed. Michael Krausz (University Park: Pennsylvania State University Press, 2001), 86–89.

An appeal to the weakened form of one of the two principles has a limited use in debates about the right understanding of what has been said or done. In defending an eccentric interpretation, the interpreter may claim, "Some persons who understand what is at issue the way I do are reasonable and familiar with the circumstances." For example, a terrorist may specifically appeal to this claim in order to show that more than one interpreter shares his understanding of the issues. He could not reach this goal by appealing to the Restrictive Principle as originally formulated, for this principle defends all who happen to agree with him, but does not require empirical evidence that there are persons sharing his views. The assumption that there are such persons is sufficient for appealing to this principle. But he wants to show more: he wants to show that there is empirical evidence that others share his views. He needs such evidence to help persuade others, to show that his views cannot be easily dismissed as irrational. And this evidence is available only through an appeal to a weakened form of one of the principles. To be sure, typically such evidence persuades other interpreters only when they are in desperate straits, but occasionally it is successful when better support is needed for eccentric interpretations.

6. The First-Person Perspective

Self-understanding is quite limited when compared with our understanding of others. When regarding another speaker or agent, I can distinguish between psychological access and epistemic access to his own words and deeds. If by my own lights he violates the factual or normative constraint on interpreting, I substitute my alternative interpretation for his self-understanding. Concerning myself, are my own lights sufficient for distinguishing between psychological and epistemic access? Can I judge whether in trying to understand myself (here and now) I violate one or the other constraint on interpreting? Others would not knowingly violate a constraint, provided they are sincere. My situation is certainly not worse than theirs: I would not knowingly violate a constraint; moreover, most of the time—although not always—I know that I am sincere. So why is my self-understanding more limited than my understanding of others?

One answer is that confusion between psychological and epistemic access is more easily detected in and attributed to others than to oneself. In drawing attention to another speaker's confusion, a critic may be in a good position to rely only on her own judgment. But my own judgment is surely insufficient whenever I try to play the critic's role concerning my self-understanding; I must rely on support from the Universalizability or the

Restrictive Principle. Occasionally I rely on evidence that my self-understanding agrees with another person's—my critic's—interpretation of my words and deeds. Granted, unless I consider my critic both reasonable and knowledgeable about what is at issue, I would not seek her help. Hence, the agreement between her interpretation of my words and my self-understanding supports my self-understanding at least within the limits of the Restrictive Principle; her disagreement excludes support of my self-understanding by the Universalizability Principle.

My critic's intervention is sometimes useful and at other times necessary whenever I violate the factual or normative constraint in my self-understanding. Whenever my self-understanding is based on a mistaken belief, a limited vocabulary, or a confused judgment, my self-understanding is only factually mistaken. Once the mistake is pointed out, I revise my self-understanding. The revision proves that in principle I am capable of understanding my words as my critic interprets them. For example, a patient complains, "My pancreas hurts," but he will withdraw to safer grounds as soon as his physician points out that he is mistaken about the location of his pancreas. On the other hand, if I make a remark to my spiritual advisor, and he charges me with self-deception, I must reject the charge. Our concepts are such that in the first-person perspective I have no choice but to reject it. It would be self-defeating to admit that I am deceiving myself here and now.

I can admit that in the past I have deceived myself—claims about my past are associated with third-person claims. I can say about myself that when overwhelmed by fear, guilt, shame, or some other emotion I have deceived myself. About others I can make the same claim. But about myself I cannot claim that I am here and now deceiving myself. There are two reasons why I cannot make such a claim. First, "I am here and now deceiving myself" is just as self-defeating as Moore's paradoxical statement, "p, but I don't believe that p." Second, and more important, if I am indeed deceiving myself, then the fact (if it is a fact) of my self-deception must be part of my self-deception. If I were not self-deceived about deceiving myself, I could not deceive myself. Hence, I cannot admit to self-deception when I am subject to self-deception. Note that the self-defeating character of my claim, that I am deceiving myself, is independent of the peculiarities of first-person claims. The claim is self-defeating, even if rephrased in the third person: "S believes that he is here and now deceiving himself."

It may be objected that this shows that we do not know enough about self-deception (if there is such a phenomenon) for a serious discussion. The answer is that even if the reader believes what is said in the objection, it must be admitted that the very charge of self-deception removes an important anchor for the understanding of another person. Ordinarily we wish to understand another as he understands himself. If his self-understanding is factually deficient, we try to understand him in accordance with the Universalizability Principle. We expect that sooner or later he will join all reasonable persons in understanding himself as they understand him. But if his self-understanding is in principle deficient—for he is here and now deceiving himself—we cannot rely on his self-understanding to anchor our understanding of his words or deeds in his self-understanding. As long as he is indeed deceiving himself, and as long as he is the same person that he is now, we cannot expect that he will join all reasonable persons in understanding himself as they understand him. For want of an anchor, the claim that we understand him becomes quite unstable.

If we judge another person to be unreasonable or uninformed about what is at issue, we could—relying on the Universalizability Principle—override his self-understanding with our interpretation of his words or deeds. We could even add that sooner or later we expect him to agree with us. Of course, the sincerity of our expectation can be doubted, for even if our expectation started out sincere, with the passage of time we would find it more and more surprising if he did come to agree with us. When we can no longer sincerely sustain our expectation that he will come to agree with us, we must withdraw to unstable ground. We must override his self-understanding with our interpretation of his words or deeds, admit that he cannot agree with us, and support this shaky claim with the Restrictive Principle.

He cannot agree with us because he is deceiving himself. This charge, whether done in an overt or covert manner, is a necessary condition for deep interpretation. As long as he is not overtly charged with self-deception, we can continue to express the (more or less sincere) expectation that he will come to agree with us. If he comes to agree with us, our reliance on the Universalizability Principle will have been justified. But as soon as he is openly charged with self-deception, we have lost him as an anchor of our interpretation and we can no longer rely on the Universalizability Principle. Deep interpretation is our interpretive strategy for dealing with the self-deception of others. Is it a successful strategy? It is not. As we have seen (chapter 1, section 4), deep interpretations and their supporting theories thrive on failure.

7. Natural and Deep Interpretations

Let us now turn to the discussion of the distinction between understanding and interpreting that had been postponed while we focused on cases of natural interpretation. Suppose that the need for an interpretation does not arise naturally. In this case, is there a distinction between understanding and interpreting? It has been mentioned that understanding is a state and that interpreting is an activity. Moreover, our goal in interpreting is the understanding of what is at issue, and we attain our goal in interpreting when we reach understanding. But the distinction is not very useful. If we don't question our understanding, we don't care whether it was preceded by interpreting; and if we question our understanding, we question only the activity leading to understanding—that is, interpreting. We could argue that interpreting always precedes understanding, but in unproblematic cases we are unaware of the interpreting process. Or, we could argue that unless we wish to postulate an unconscious interpreting activity prior to understanding, we must admit that in many cases we reach understanding without any prior interpreting. Philosophers endorsing either side of this debate will find themselves in very good company. Arguments leading to a sharp distinction between understanding and interpreting can be traced to Wittgenstein's views on interpreting; arguments leading to the collapse of the two notions can be traced to Heidegger's views on understanding. What is said here about the interpreting activity can be adjusted to agree with either side of this debate.

If we again focus on cases where the need for an interpretation arises naturally, we notice a continuous line extending from interpretation in the indicative mood to deep interpretation. A way station on that line is interpretation in the subjunctive mood. Interpreters move forward or backward on that line in accordance with their needs and purposes. While they move, concerns about being mistaken or insincere arise. Since interpretation in both the indicative and subjunctive moods requires support from the Universalizability Principle, interpreters can be mistaken about the agreement between their interpretation of another person's words or deeds and his self-understanding. They may believe that his self-understanding agrees with their interpretation, while this agreement is merely attributed to him in accordance with the Universalizability Principle: interpreting in the subjunctive mood is mistaken for interpreting in the indicative mood. Or, they may believe they have only attributed to him a given interpretation in accordance with the Universalizability Principle, while in fact his self-understanding agrees with their interpretation: interpreting in the indicative mood is mistaken for interpreting in the subjunctive mood. Finally, they may believe that the Universalizability Principle supports their interpretation, when in fact only the Restrictive Principle can support it, or the other way around.

Interpreters are insincere if they pretend that an interpretation in the subjunctive mood is in the indicative mood, or vice versa. More important, they are insincere if they pretend that a deep interpretation is an interpretation in the subjunctive or the indicative mood, or the other way around. For example, unsavory politicians or unscrupulous ideologues often recommend a deep interpretation as if it were a natural interpretation in one of the two moods. Religious or political fanatics often exemplify both error and insincerity. After first persuading themselves that the Universalizability Principle supports their sectarian views, they recommend their deep interpretations as if they were interpretations in the indicative mood.

Moreover, methods of deep interpretation sometimes lead to the interpreters' self-deception in judging their own interpreting activity. Many theoreticians of Marxist or Freudian persuasion exemplify self-deception in addition to error and insincerity. They may have started by persuading themselves that their interpretations of social reality or individual behavior are nothing but interpretations in the subjunctive mood that are supported by the Universalizability Principle. Unchallenged within a given coterie, they become convinced that only the benighted disagree with their doctrines, interpretive methods, and interpretations. Marxists and Freudians offer doctrines that provide methods for the analysis of the self-deception of others—false consciousness in the Marxist, and neurotic behavior in the Freudian vocabulary. When the doctrines become dogmas, many advanced practitioners of these much-advertised methods become benighted victims of self-deception.

8. Grandeur and Misery of Deep Interpretation

Deep interpretation is grounded on the failure of natural interpretation. We propose a deep interpretation when the guideposts of natural interpretation no longer help us to understand another person's words or deeds. Ordinarily, a speaker's or agent's beliefs, desires, and self-understanding provide these guideposts. Natural interpretation—even in the subjunctive mood—is useless, however, if his self-understanding is deficient not only in fact but also in principle. How could we steer by his understanding of his own words if at the same time we believe that he is deceiving himself? How can we attribute to him agreement with a given interpretation grounded on the Universalizability Principle if at the same time we know that he not only does not accept but further cannot accept that interpretation? However, if he did not deceive himself in the first place, the need for a deep interpretation would not arise. If such a need does arise, interpreters ordinarily resort to a deep interpretation with rhetorical questions: What other choices do they have? What else could they do?

Rhetorical questions are bad substitutes for arguments. Moreover, "what else . . ." premises do not provide firm support for allowing an interpreter to produce a successful interpretation. At best, they shift the burden of providing viable alternatives from the speaker to his audience. The case for deep interpretation is indeed weak; its weakness is evident by the words we use to explain or justify it. Its weakness becomes obvious when we examine our standards of correctness for deep interpretation.

Since deep interpretation is our strategy for dealing with self-deception, we cannot solicit the speaker's or agent's agreement with a proposed deep interpretation of his words or deeds. Since his deceiving himself about his self-deception is part of his self-deception, his disagreement serves to reinforce the need for a proposed deep interpretation. This proposal is further supported either by empirical generalizations about human nature or by theories of deep interpretation. Finally, if we need to, we can appeal to an admittedly weak principle, and *only* to an admittedly weak principle, the Restrictive Principle, in support of a proposed deep interpretation.

Prompted by the weakness of the case for deep interpretation, advocates of a given deep interpretation theory often try to defend it as a science. This defense is misguided. Deep interpretations are best understood as extensions of natural interpretations. Neither natural nor deep interpretations need scientific support, nor do successful or unsuccessful interpretations, for it is questionable whether there could be a science of understanding or interpreting at all. If there were such a science, would we need a second science for understanding or interpreting the first science? Or, could we understand or interpret the first science without the help of a second science? Assent to the first alternative implies the threat of infinite regress; agreement with the second alternative defeats the claim that understanding or interpreting requires a science. Deep interpretations are not supported by a science, or by the person whose words or deeds we are interpreting, or by the Universalizability Principle. They seem to be hanging in the air.

Yet the case for deep interpretations can be strengthened. The case could be at least as strong as the case for (natural) interpretation in the subjunctive mood if the interpreter could convince the speaker or agent that she provided an interpretation of his words or deeds that can be supported by the Universalizability Principle. Admittedly, he does not *now* agree with her interpretation, because he is deceiving himself; but he would agree if he didn't deceive himself. Clearly, it is not enough for her to tell him that he should not deceive himself. The founding parents of deep interpretation never suggested that their textbooks' readers would recognize their own self-deception just by being told about the matter. Advocates of deep interpretation theories never suggested that reading

Freud could cure patients in psychoanalysis or that reading Marx was a universal remedy for false consciousness.

However, defenders of deep interpretation theories offer helpful techniques. As a reminder of Michel Foucault's work, they will be called here techniques of the confessional. Examinations of free associations, dream narratives, mistaken performances—in short, all techniques associated with the Freudian confessional serve an overarching purpose: to convince the patient that he has been deceiving himself. If he can be so convinced, the truth shall make him free, and in Freud's words, "*Wo es war, soll Ich werden.*"

We never experienced state terror based on degraded Freudian principles. We were not so lucky with Marxist principles. The Marxist confessional—consisting of frequent criticism and self-criticism—was invented long before it was abused in the service of states based on perverted Marxist principles. The goal of this confessional was to persuade Marxism's most faithful followers that they had been deceiving themselves. They may have believed that they served their cause; while in reality their "false consciousness" hindered it. (A case in point is the pretentious nonsense in Marxist literature, contrasting what is "subjectively revolutionary" and "objectively counterrevolutionary.") Only by the admission of past mistakes can the faithful discard their false consciousness and participate as free agents in mankind's liberation.

No doubt, Freudian and Marxist confessionals testified initially to lofty ideals. The confessionals not only provided support for deep interpretations, but also endorsed a central claim entered by these two theories of deep interpretation. Those who now deceive themselves will at some time admit that they have deceived themselves. At that time they will agree with their interpreters, thereby providing retroactively the needed support for the interpretation. What is now a deep interpretation will at that time be a natural interpretation. If this central claim is admitted, then deep interpretations together with deep interpretation theories of the Freudian or Marxist variety can be as securely supported as natural interpretations.

A modest amount of skepticism about such promissory notes is justifiable: what will happen *at that time* when deep interpretations are retroactively validated? Prophetic voices urging the acceptance of deep interpretations together with theories supporting such interpretations should be resisted. Yet their outright rejection is unwarranted. Remember, entry to the confessional of deep interpretation—at least initially—is entirely voluntary. Practitioners of deep interpretation do not pursue those who could use their services; they are in demand by those who need their help. The legitimacy of deep interpretations together with deep interpretation theories can be provided only by those who freely endorse the expectation of retroactive validation.

Interpretive authority is ordinarily vested in the speaker or agent whose words or deeds are interpreted. Practitioners of deep interpretation replace, at least partially, the speaker's authority with their own interpretive authority. They can either assume the prophetic voice of retroactive validation or the universal voice of interpretation in the subjunctive mood. Although the first choice may be considered more honest than the second, it suggests religious persuasion. The second choice, on the other hand, suggests scientific conviction. Neither suggestion is now welcome to the practitioners of deep interpretation. Theoreticians of deep interpretation have been charged, at different times, with having either religious or scientific pretensions. Faced with such opposition, considerable courage and hard work are required for defending the theories and practices of deep interpretation. Practitioners of deep interpretation may try to avoid the task to defend their views. They can succeed only by pretending to others or convincing themselves that their deep interpretations are in fact natural interpretations in the subjunctive mood.

We can avoid deep interpretations and reject deep interpretation theories. The price of such a choice is too high: the moral dimension of the interpreting activity becomes lost to sight. This dimension is the most neglected aspect of deep interpretations and their supporting theories. No doubt, the views of Marx, Nietzsche, and Freud have been found wanting. But even if most of their contributions to philosophical speculation have become or will be discredited, the moral aspect of their thinking deserves to be preserved. Amateur readers unconcerned with Marx's views on the philosophy of history, Nietzsche's understanding of the philosophy of literature, or Freud's contribution to the philosophy of mind hear their call for change better than many professional critics of these theories. What amateur readers hear are Rilke's words, "You must change your life!" Are the fundamental claims of deep interpretation theories worth preserving if they are removed from such admonition? It could be argued that deep interpretations together with their supporting theories deserve to be discredited if their moral import is discarded.

But the price of admitting deep interpretations and their supporting theories is also high. Suppose an interpretation is defended by showing that it satisfies the factual and normative constraints on interpreting. The interpreter proposing such an interpretation is entitled to appeal to Universalizability. Suppose also that it is an essentially contestable or deep interpretation. He cannot defend it from center stage by appealing to Universalizability; he is forced to appeal to the Restrictive Principle and to proclaim that all who agree with him are qualified interpreters. This seems to leave the door open to claiming that those who disagree with him are also qualified interpreters. He must leave that door open, for he believes that the speaker whose words he is interpreting is also a qualified interpreter. (It would not make sense to argue with him and to try to convince him if he were not a qualified interpreter.) But while he proclaims from center stage that he appeals to the Restrictive Principle, he must also hold that his interpretation has satisfied the two constraints on interpreting; hence, he is entitled to appeal to Universalizability. In a whisper and from the backstage area he appeals to one principle, while from the center stage he proclaims to appeal to the other. He must believe not only that all who agree with him are qualified interpreters (in accordance with his center stage voice), but also that all qualified interpreters agree with him (in line with his backstage voice). However, his belief in agreement with his backstage voice is contradicted by the speaker whom he has admitted among the qualified interpreters but who disagrees with his interpretation.

Earlier I suggested various strategies for responding to a charge of self-deception (chapter 1). One alternative was to charge the interpreter with deception. We can now spell out the basis of such a charge. The charge of deception or self-deception can be returned against an interpreter who charges others with self-deception. The targets of deep interpretation can respond to their interpreters: they could not assert their deep interpretations unless they satisfied both constraints on interpreting; hence, they are entitled to appeal to Universalizability; their appeal to the Restrictive Principle is hypocrisy. Its avowed goal is to defend those who agree with a given deep interpretation; its hidden agenda is to continue the debate with the targets of deep interpretation. So, if they are aware of their hypocrisy, they are deceiving others; and if they are unaware of their hypocrisy, they are deceiving themselves. (The younger art historians—in my earlier example—would not maintain their competing interpretation unless they could appeal to Universalizability; hence, their appeal to the Restrictive Principle amounts to either deception or self-deception.) To be sure, the interpreters who are charged with deception or self-deception can return the same charges against those interpreters who criticized them.

9. Interpretive Reports

The reasons and arguments supporting a deep interpretation deserve considerable scrutiny. Since deep interpretations can be easily misidentified as natural interpretation, and since the misidentification can be further supported by unscrupulous practitioners, a demarcation line must be found for separating deep interpretations from interpretations in the subjunctive mood. Earlier I suggested that deep interpretations can be supported only by the Restrictive Principle, and that natural interpretations in both the indicative and the subjunctive moods can be supported by the Universalizability Principle. Did I find or did I create this demarcation line? Before answering—in the next chapter—in the context of an extended discussion of the Universalizability and the Restrictive Principles, I must discuss the content of interpretive reports.

Interpretations are solicited in a wide variety of situations. Given their variety, we cannot expect to find necessary conditions that have to be satisfied for a report to be considered an interpretation. Earlier I suggested that quotations are replications of what has been said, and do not ordinarily serve as interpretations. Even this suggestion can be rejected if it is reformulated as a necessary condition for interpretations. The recitation of poetry may not be a quotation or a replication, but it can serve as an interpretation. After hearing Rilke's first recitation of the *Duino Elegies*—one of the most interpreted poems of the last century—his audience became convinced that this poem was so marvelously simple that it did not need or admit interpretation. Contrary to my suggestion, the reading aloud of a written text can be considered both a replication and an interpretation.

A discussion of the content of interpretive reports must avoid two mistakes: casting our net on a field that is too wide or too narrow. In the first case, we notice characteristics that seem to be vacuous; in the second, we notice what appears only in a small group of interpretive reports. One characteristic of many reports must be mentioned, even if it is considered to be trivial by most readers. In offering an interpretation, the interpreter ordinarily provides a context for what has been said or done. In providing a context, she expects to illuminate what is at issue. The speaker's or agent's beliefs, desires, understanding of what has been said or done are part of what the interpreter provides as the context of the speaker's or agent's words or deeds. If the interpreter's report does not satisfy the factual or normative constraints on interpreting, the report must be discredited. If the interpreter's report satisfies both constraints, three cases must be distinguished.

1. The interpreter's understanding of the speaker's words *agrees* with the speaker's self-understanding. The interpretive report will contain a natural interpretation in the indicative mood.
2. The interpreter's understanding of the speaker's words *disagrees* with the speaker's self-understanding, and the speaker does not satisfy the

factual or normative constraints on interpreting. This case calls for a natural interpretation in the subjunctive mood or

3. a deep interpretation.

The context provided by the interpreter will be decisive in her choice between a natural interpretation in the subjunctive mood and a deep interpretation.

The first case is unproblematic; in the two other cases the interpreter's choice and interpretive report must be defended. If asked, the interpreter must articulate her response to demands that are at cross-purposes. While arguing for her understanding of the words or deeds of others, she must claim—in accordance with the normative constraint on interpreting—that her interpretation is the best among the available alternatives for a given purpose. Since her interpretation of the speaker's or agent's words or deeds disagrees with his self-understanding, she must also defend her interpretation against the charge that she usurped his authority over his own words or deeds. In arguing for her interpretive authority, she must claim that she knows the speaker or agent better than he knows himself. At the same time, she must admit that there is no convergence to the best interpretation, regardless of whether she opts for an interpretation in the subjunctive mood or a deep interpretation. Other interpreters pursuing other purposes may propose alternatives that do not compete with her interpretation.

In arguing for her understanding of what has been said or done, the interpreter expects to convince all reasonable persons. Those she cannot convince must be unreasonable, mistaken, or disingenuous. Trying to escape from these unattractive alternatives, she may argue that if other interpreters disagree with her, this merely indicates that they pursue other purposes, and that is the reason they have proposed alternative interpretations. Tolerance for the alternatives seems preferable to their dismissal. Yet if her arguments are only good enough to convince those who have the same understanding of what is at issue as she has, then her arguments could carry conviction only with the converted. If she cannot persuade the unconverted, if she cannot expect the agreement of all reasonable persons, why does she argue for her interpretations? And, if she insists on arguing for her interpretations, why does she admit the lack of convergence to the best interpretation?

Given the wide variety of interpretations, we cannot expect to provide the same answer to these questions concerning all interpretive situations. Different answers are appropriate to each situation. For our purposes the questions are more important than the available answers. The questions arise about both interpretation in the subjunctive mood and deep interpretation. We cannot escape the subtleties of deep interpretation by restricting our purview to natural interpretation, for natural interpretation in the subjunctive mood must confront the same questions and problems as deep interpretation. Moreover, we cannot avoid interpretations in the subjunctive mood—they are the cornerstones of our social and human sciences.

As mentioned before, the context of a given interpretation is decisive in choosing between an interpretation in the subjunctive mood and a deep interpretation. In the first case, we attribute agreement with our interpretation to those we interpret and support the interpretation with the Universalizability Principle. In the second case, we expect the disagreement of those we interpret and support the interpretation with the Restrictive Principle. Interpretations supported by the Universalizability Principle are not derived from a survey of a given population; they are not formulated as a result of counting the number of persons in agreement with a given interpretation. In speaking with a universal voice, we demand agreement with that interpretation. The demand is addressed to all who are reasonable and knowledgeable about what is at issue. In issuing such a demand, we are not at liberty to include all those who *by our own lights* are not reasonable or not knowledgeable about what is at issue. In speaking with a universal voice, we are prepared to dismiss them from the population considered relevant. These are strong claims. Yet at least since Kant, they have supported the Universalizability Principle. If we strengthen these claims, they become vacuous; if we weaken them, they become useless.

In comparing the two principles, it may seem that although Universalizability is stronger than the Restrictive Principle, the Restrictive Principle lends itself more easily to abuse by dogmatists and authoritarians. This is a mistake. The magnitude of the mistake does not become clear unless we reformulate the two principles and provide reasons for the initial mistake.

CHAPTER FOUR

The Principles

———

Some of your opinions and beliefs are different from your interpreter's. You believe that life is like a fountain and that the glass is half full; he believes that the well is dry and that the glass is half empty. In some cases you don't consider his views sufficiently important to discuss them. In other cases they are more important to you, but you are tolerant of alternatives. Ordinarily, we consider what we tolerate second-class, but we often accept without discussion that others hold opinions contrary to our views. Suppose, however, that some of your opinions solidify and become persuasions, and some of your beliefs harden and become convictions. You become more insistent about your convictions and accept popular wisdom's challenge to "put your money where your mouth is." (Not surprisingly, philosophers agree with this challenge. The *locus classicus* is in the *Critique of Pure Reason*, A824, B852.) You are willing to wager a fairly large amount of money on a hardened conviction, but you are still tolerant of others who hold contrary convictions. No doubt, tolerance has a limit. Accustomed to speaking about intolerance in the context of racial or ethnic persuasions, political or religious convictions, we must remember that intolerance reared its head in many contexts. Some of our remote ancestors became intolerant with the messenger who told them about irrational numbers, less distant ancestors with mathematicians who speculated about non-Euclidean geometries. There is evidence about intolerance concerning philosophical views: the *odium philosophicum* seems to rival the *odium theologicum* of bygone years. You may wish to defend your convictions, regardless of your tolerance or intolerance of alternative views. Thus, an appeal to principle is often your opening move in defending your convictions.

1. The Appeal to the Principles

In appealing to the Universalizability or the Restrictive Principle we cannot dispense with critical judgment. These principles are not mechanical procedures at our disposal that can be put to work when we need a decision in matters of interpretation. If we decide to support an appeal to Universalizability with a second appeal to the same principle, ultimately it is within the purview of our critical judgment whether it is right or proper to appeal to that principle. We may be mistaken that all reasonable and knowledgeable persons agree with our understanding of what is at issue; also, we may be mistaken that all reasonable persons agree with our appeal to Universalizability. Our critical judgment will be faulted in both cases. The principles can be abused, but they cannot be faulted.

How did we learn about the Universalizability and the Restrictive Principles? We need not agree on how we acquired these principles. Some may claim that we learned about them in our childhood, in response to our incessant "why?" questions. Our elders may have answered some of those questions by saying, "Everyone understands this as I do" or "Not everyone, but all members of *our* group understand this as I do." Others may claim that each of us discovered these principles independently of what we have been taught. We may have acquired or created them; or we may have inherited these principles from our remote ancestors—but we all use them, and occasionally we abuse them. They are the foundation when we understand and evaluate what others have said or done, and occasionally we appeal to them in the context of our self-understanding. We all use (or abuse) these principles not only as subjects to whom they apply, but also as subjects to whom they uniquely apply. Although we can abuse these principles, we cannot—in the long run—rebel against them. We can rebel against what is imposed on us, but we cannot rebel against what we impose on ourselves. Accordingly, we have good reasons for treating these principles as if they had been given by each of us. As legislators of these principles, we distinguish between what is binding for all reasonable persons and what is valid only for members of a group sharing significant and important characteristics.

In appealing to Universalizability, we claim that all reasonable and knowledgeable persons agree with our understanding of what is at issue. Accordingly, we are entitled to *demand* that our present listeners or hearers also agree with that understanding. If some disagree, we have two choices: (1) We stand firm, continue to support our interpretation with the Universalizability Principle, and claim that the dissenters pursue goals that are different from ours, or are not reasonable, or not sufficiently knowledgeable, or did not satisfy the factual and normative constraints on interpreting. (2) We retreat to the safer ground of interpreting in the subjunctive mood, and claim that the dissenters would agree with our understanding if they were reasonable and knowledgeable about the facts.

When interpreting others, a further retreat to the Restrictive Principle is open to us only in case of a deep interpretation. The speaker or agent whose words or deeds are being interpreted is self-deceived, and for this reason he cannot agree with us. His disagreement grounded on self-deception is decisive in our choice between a natural and a deep interpretation. We need not solicit the judgment of other interpreters—our interpretations are neither strengthened nor weakened by their agreement or disagreement. In the course of negotiating our disagreement, other interpreters may, of course, convince us that our interpretations were mistaken. In accordance with the Universalizability Principle, we must rally behind their views when their interpretive goals are the same as ours and their candidate for an interpretation satisfies the two constraints on interpreting. We are not following the consensus among interpreters in agreeing with an interpretation. We accept it because it satisfies both constraints, while our competing candidate for an interpretation fails this test.

2. Interpretive Goals

Archaeologists and aestheticians have different goals when reading the Homeric poems. Some read the Bible as a religious document, others as a literary artwork. This does not imply that the Homeric poems have independent archaeological and aesthetic layers or that the Bible has literary and religious strands. The survival of the Homeric poems and Biblical texts is in part due to the interweaving of multifarious layers and strands. Yet when we try to understand these texts, we are guided by our own purposes and goals. Given our specific goals, we emphasize one strand of a given text and neglect others. For example, Bible interpreters always acknowledged that the literary qualities of Biblical texts serve their religious content, yet before the 1950s they were indifferent to the distinction between prose and poetry in these texts.

Our understanding of what others have said or done is guided by its application to a given purpose. Interpretations are application-driven. In appealing to Universalizability we demand agreement with our interpretations only from interpreters who share our interpretive goals. The archaeologists' and the aestheticians' application-driven interpretations of the same text do not compete with one another. Each may recommend an interpretation that seems to contradict the other; but the apparent contradiction vanishes as soon as each interpretation is seen within its own framework.

The limitation of our demand for agreement with our interpretation to interpreters who share our interpretive goals is not an appeal to the Restrictive Principle. As mentioned before, an appeal to this principle when interpreting others is available only in the context of deep interpretation. The limitation merely draws attention to an ever-present feature of interpreting. Two interpreters may share similar goals and aim at the same application for their interpretations, but given their different viewpoints, they recommend contrary interpretations of the same text. For example, interpreters of Biblical texts belonging to different religious communities may recommend interpretations that seem to contradict each other. Both agree on the application of their interpretations for religious practices; both have similar goals. Their interpretive traditions are different. Each demands agreement with his interpretation only of interpreters who share a specific interpretive tradition. Occasionally, one may wish to convert the other to his own tradition. Suppose he suggests that his appeal to Universalizability is not limited to members of his own religious community, but literally to all who share his goal of applying his interpretation for religious practice. Is his suggestion legitimate? Is his appeal to Universalizability fraudulent? Is he self-deceived about the legitimacy of his suggestion? In the interest of leaving these questions open, the example here is deliberately underdescribed.

3. Abusing the Principles

All principles can be abused, and the abuse always has a point—this much is trivially true. Dogmatists and authoritarians can abuse either the Universalizability or the Restrictive Principle. Which of the two principles lends itself more readily to abuse? Which principle can be considered more dogmatic than the other? The answers to *these* questions are not at all trivial. Our strategy is to discuss each of the two principles within the context of interpretive disagreements. In appealing to each of the two principles, we must distinguish between two viewpoints that are in conflict in many interpretive disagreements: the perspective of the interpreter who is appealing to a principle, and the perspective of his opponent, against whom a principle is invoked. Let us start with the second group of conversation terminators (mentioned in the first chapter):

> "When you understand this as I do, you will become an adult!" or

> "When you understand this the way I do, you will become an expert in this field!"

It will be understood that these conversation terminators leave the door open for becoming an adult or an expert in a given field without agreeing with the interpreter's understanding. It will also be understood that these conversation terminators can be derived without question-begging premises from the Restrictive Principle. Nonetheless, persons so addressed seem to disregard the door left open by the interpreter using these conversation terminators: there may be other ways of becoming an adult or an expert in addition to the one way he advocates. They understand them as if he had said, "You will become an adult *only* when you understand this as I do!" or "You will become an expert in this field *only* when you understand this as I do!" These claims cannot be supported by good reasons or adequate arguments; they are expressions of authoritarianism or dogmatism. It must be admitted that this misunderstanding of the second group of conversation terminators is not an off-the-wall interpretation of what was said. The interpreter insisted that others would become experts in his field, provided they follow in his footsteps. Why would he insist on this matter, if he did not mean to imply that this is the only way they would become experts in his field?

If we agree with this misinterpretation of the second group of conversation terminators, the first group of conversation terminators seems less threatening as an expression of dogmatism and authoritarianism. If we falsely believe we were told that the only way of gaining expertise is by following the speaker's beaten path, then the first group of conversation terminators—

> "When you become an adult, you will understand this matter the way I do!" or

> "When you become an expert in this field, you will understand this the way I do!"

—appears considerably less dogmatic than the misinterpreted second group of conversation terminators. If we now add that the first group of conversation terminators can be derived from the Universalizability Principle without additional question-begging premises, then the (mistaken) claim that this group of conversation terminators is relatively undogmatic becomes understandable. No doubt, in appealing to Universalizability an expert makes a stronger claim than in defending his views with the Restrictive Principle; presumably he is better equipped with reasons and arguments than if he defended his views with the Restrictive Principle. After all, he is entitled to appeal to Universalizability if and only if his interpretation has satisfied both constraints on interpreting. Finally, the appeal to the Restrictive Principle seems to share guilt by association with deep interpretation and theories of deep interpretation. The conversation terminators—

> "When you are rid of your neurosis, you will understand your story the way I do!" or

> "When the workers become class-conscious, they will understand their own situation the way I do!"

—seem to share guilt by association with dogmatic or authoritarian Freudian or Marxist interpreters.

Judging from the perspective of those opposed to an interpretation, it seems that the Restrictive Principle lends itself more easily to abuse and is more dogmatic than the Universalizability Principle. Remember that this judgment is in part due to a misinterpretation of the second group of conversation terminators. The facts of the matter seem different when examined from the viewpoint of the interpreter who appeals to one of the two principles.

From the interpreter's perspective the Universalizability Principle demands the consent of all reasonable and knowledgeable persons for a given interpretation, and the interpreter is entitled to appeal to this principle if and only if that interpretation has satisfied both constraints on interpreting. Only the Restrictive Principle admits disagreement of reasonable and knowledgeable persons. The first group of conversation terminators—

> "When you become an adult, you will understand this matter the way I do!" or

> "When you become an expert in this field, you will understand this the way I do!"

—contains a threatening prediction: the person so addressed will not become an adult or an expert in a given field unless he comes to agree with the interpreter. Moreover, these conversation terminators are not misinterpreted if they are understood as foreclosing on becoming an adult or an expert in case of disagreement with the interpreter. Finally, remember that the first group of conversation terminators can be derived from the Universalizability Principle. So, in appealing to this principle and in using a conversation terminator that can be derived from it, the interpreter asserts a very strong claim: if you disagree with him, you are either not reasonable or not knowledgeable. Isn't this more dogmatic and more authoritarian than an appeal to the Restrictive Principle?

From the interpreter's perspective, an appeal to Universalizability is more dogmatic than an appeal to the Restrictive Principle. From his opponent's perspective, the Restrictive Principle—because of a misinterpretation—seems more dogmatic than Universalizability. Who is right? Before discussing this question, we must remember the trivially true claim: dogmatists and authoritarians can abuse both principles. We must take it for granted in our discussion that dogmatism or authoritarianism do not motivate the interpreter in appealing to one of the two principles.

Two preliminary remarks: (1) According to the account defended here, the interpreter can appeal to the Restrictive Principle when interpreting others only if some form of self-deception confronts him and he therefore recommends a deep interpretation. This requirement, together with the common assumption about the interpreter's sincerity, effectively undermines any useful comparison between the two principles. For the purposes of this comparison, I shall liberalize the requirement for an appeal to the Restrictive Principle, and assume that the interpreter is free to appeal to either of the two principles. (2) To be brief, I shall use the notion of an unimpeachable interpretation: interpretations are unimpeachable if and only if they satisfy the factual and normative constraints on interpreting.

The interpreter is entitled to appeal to Universalizability if and only if to the best of his knowledge the interpretation he recommends is unimpeachable. Assume that he expects, imagines, or conceives of a disagreement with his interpretation that is based on an unimpeachable interpretation. To avoid a confrontation with his opponents, he intends to appeal to the Restrictive rather than the Universalizability Principle. Given our common assumption about the interpreter's sincerity, he cannot do this. Either there is an unimpeachable alternative to his interpretation, and in this case his interpretation is no longer unimpeachable; or there is no such unimpeachable alternative, and in this case his is the only unimpeachable interpretation. He can remain silent and avoid recommending his interpretation. But if he wants to get a hearing for his interpretation and at the same time vindicate his sincerity, he must appeal to Universalizability. (Earlier I suggested that for strategic reasons a temporary retreat from the Universalizability to the Restrictive Principle may be necessary—for instance, when a scientist tries to procure hearing for a new theory. Are such temporary retreats ever sincere?) Accordingly, even if from his perspective the appeal to Universalizability is more dogmatic than an appeal to the Restrictive Principle, the appeal to the former is forced on him. Moreover, if he is forced to retreat from an interpretation in the indicative mood to an interpretation in the subjunctive mood, his interpretation will seem to him even more dogmatic. Finally, if he further retreats to a deep interpretation and now appeals to the Restrictive Principle, it may seem to him that this appeal is less dogmatic than an appeal to Universalizability—but is this really the case? After all, in defending a deep interpretation, he must at least do the following: (1) defend his claims against the charge that he usurped the interpretive authority of those he is interpreting; (2) claim that his interpretation is the best among the available alternatives; (3) maintain that he knows those he is interpreting better than they know themselves. Granted, from his perspective the appeal to the Restrictive Principle seems less dogmatic than the appeal to Universalizability. But isn't the undogmatic and nonauthoritarian character of such an appeal vitiated by the practice of deep interpretation?

If we ask again, which principle can be considered more dogmatic and authoritarian than the other, we will receive an answer that is distorted by the interpretive situation. Free of distortion, the interpreter and his opponent would agree that the Universalizability Principle is more dogmatic than the Restrictive Principle. But within the interpretive situation, the practice of deep interpretation reveals to the interpreter the authoritarian character of the Restrictive Principle; for his opponent, the same practice leads to a misinterpretation of the second group of conversation terminators and to the misunderstanding of the Universalizability Principle as less dogmatic than the Restrictive Principle. Because of the distortion, the interpreter and his opponent are both mistaken, but the mistake has a salutary effect. It alerts them to the dangers of deep interpretation.

4. The Hidden Authoritarianism of Universalizability

Children know more about authoritarianism than their caregivers and teachers. The newcomer in any field, as well as the alienated or the disadvantaged of any society, knows more about dogmatism than the expert or the elite member of that society. It takes children, the newcomers, and the alienated to discover the hidden authoritarianism of the Universalizability Principle. At one time, each one of us experienced its force—why did we forget what we once knew? Our (partial) amnesia about this matter should be of interest to psychologists. Here, only the authoritarian character of Universalizability is important.

The expert appeals to the Universalizability Principle—but what are his grounds for claiming that all reasonable persons agree with his understanding of what is at issue? How does he know what they would say or do in the situation at hand? What gives him the authority to demand agreement with his understanding? These are just some of the questions that arise when the newcomer becomes suspicious. The disadvantaged become radicals, and come to believe that Universalizability is but another "gentleman's agreement" of a liberal Establishment specifically designed to bar outsiders from the ranks of the elect or chosen.

Elementary logical inference rules are ordinarily the most innocuous paradigms of the appeal to Universalizability. For the alienated even these rules have become suspect as instruments of oppression and domination. The rhetoric accompanying such suspicions is either dismissed or countered with derision by members of the liberal Establishment. Liberals are grievously mistaken on two counts. They miss discovering an authoritarian strand in their own thinking. They fail in supporting their appeal to Universalizability with the best defense: appealing to a rule is one matter, but enforcing a rule is quite another. Experts are not enforcers; teachers are not police officers. Liberals can dismiss the suspicions of the alienated who become radicals only by taking unfair advantage of their common confusion between appealing to a rule and enforcing that rule.

The Kantian origins of the appeal to Universalizability will be obvious to the reader. (For a more detailed discussion, see chapter 8.) The strand of authoritarianism that can be traced to Kant and his followers in the German interpretive tradition may be less obvious. At the risk of providing a *déjà lu* experience for some readers, I cannot do better than to retrace the steps along what I have elsewhere called "the road from Königsberg to Siberia."

According to Kant, judgments of the beautiful are uttered with a universal voice: in saying that a given object is beautiful, I assert that all other reasonable persons would judge as I do; a judgment that agrees with mine is imputed to them. A question arises for us that Kant did not raise: what should I do if others disagree with my judgment? In this case, there are only three alternatives: (1) I revise my judgment. (2) I retreat to a judgment of the agreeable. Such a retreat—"it is pleasant to *me*" is one of Kant's examples; "*I* like it" would be my example—effectively removes the judgment from further discussion. (3) I hold on to my judgment of the beautiful, despite all disagreement.

Only the last alternative is of interest here. Notwithstanding the contrary judgment of others, I hold on to my judgment claiming universal validity. Regardless of how I formulate my judgment—"When they become reasonable, they will agree with me" or "When they will agree with me, they will become reasonable"—I speak not only with a universal voice, but also a prophetic voice. I not only claim to know what they do not know, but I also claim to know what—from the viewpoint of my critics—I cannot now know. As mentioned before, within the idiom of prophetic voices, escape clauses about the possibility of being mistaken are unavailable. (Even the Book of Jonah agrees on this point; see Jonah 3:4–4:11.) Of course, there are slight differences between the two formulations. Provided that I am reasonable, I may be able to suggest reasons and to offer arguments proving that others will agree with me when they become reasonable. On the other hand, even if others come to agree with me, they may not become reasonable. "When they will agree with me, they will become reasonable" is compatible with agreement on unreasonable and highly sectarian views. Although both formulations are of a piece with Kant's text, the second seems more dogmatic than the first.

Both formulations express my views: the judgment of others is mistaken, for it is based on what they praise and not on what they need. The fundamental distinction between what others praise and what they need was introduced into the German interpretive tradition of the *Third Critique* by Schiller's *Letters on the Aesthetic Education of Mankind* (1794–95). This distinction dominated the discussion of Kant's views in the German-speaking world. "Render to your contemporaries what they need, not what they praise" was Schiller's advice to the ideal artist. As a critic or aesthetician, I merely follow in the artist's footsteps: I arrogate to myself knowledge of aesthetic value, and I claim to know what others need, regardless of their views about the matter.

As long as critics and aestheticians do not have the power to enforce their views, and as long as their activities are restricted to aesthetic matters, their views are harmless. According to Kant, the logical quantity of the pure judgment of taste is singular: "This painting is beautiful." If you disagree, I may try to convince you, but there are no sanctions at my disposal to enforce my views. Given these conditions, judgments of the beautiful require considerable courage. Had I only offered a judgment of the agreeable and said that I like this painting instead of saying that it is beautiful, I could have saved time and effort in discussing matters with you and trying to convince you. Yet, had I not tried to convince you, I could not have argued on behalf of values responding to needs rather than to wishes. Only in arguing for a judgment of the beautiful can critics and aestheticians issue an invitation to share values credited to needs rather than to wishes. Judgments of the agreeable do not argue on behalf of such values. Critics and aestheticians may have spoken with a universal voice, and they may have claimed that all reasonable persons ought to agree with them, but they spoke for a minority. They repeated their claims in spite of disagreement by a majority—a majority they knew they could not convince. We may even admire their courage for advancing their arguments in the face of certain failure—but our admiration is primarily due to their moral and historical luck. If they had power and used it to enforce their claims about what others needed, our judgment about them would change. Those who deserved our admiration would be perceived as petty tyrants.

Schiller wanted to convince his contemporaries that they should read Goethe rather than Klopstock. This was the received wisdom accepted by successive generations of German teachers, literary critics, and historians of literature. His understanding of the *Third Critique* in the light of the distinction between what others praise and what they need became the standard interpretation within the German tradition. We have to reach outside of that tradition to notice the authoritarian character of the appeal to Universalizability. In telling their audiences what they need, without asking them, critics and aestheticians are in effect legislating for their audiences. Their legislating is harmless only as long as the critics remain powerless to enforce their views. Should they become powerful, the teachers within an intellectual tradition can easily become the enforcers of that tradition.

5. The Appeal to the Restrictive Principle

Seen in the light of deep interpretation, the undogmatic character of the appeal to the Restrictive Principle appears to be vitiated. Moreover, because of a misunderstanding, subjects of deep interpretations seem to consider the appeal to the Restrictive Principle more authoritarian than the appeal to Universalizability. In order to compare the two principles, I have liberalized the requirements for appealing to the Restrictive Principle and have assumed that the interpreter is free to appeal to either principle. Since, independently of an interpreter's judgment, there are no cases that necessitate an appeal to the Restrictive Principle, the requirements could be liberalized. The question arises: who or what decides whether an appeal to the Restrictive Principle is appropriate? The short answer is that—in the last analysis—the interpreter is free to decide on the appropriateness. The longer answer must remind the reader of a number of features of the interpreting situation.

Interpretive decisions are always subject to the factual and normative constraints on interpreting. Accordingly, the interpreter must always be prepared to defend his choice as unimpeachable. On the assumption that he is sincere, he will not support an interpretation with an appeal to the Restrictive Principle when an appeal to Universalizability is available. (Interpreters speaking in one voice from center stage and another from the backstage area do not satisfy the sincerity assumption. See chapter 3.) After all, an interpretation that can be supported with an appeal to Universalizability satisfies the normative constraint on interpreting better than an appeal to the Restrictive Principle that ordinarily supports only essentially contestable interpretations. Deep interpretations are certainly essentially contestable interpretations, and an appeal to the Restrictive Principle is appropriate if the interpreter recommends a deep interpretation. Two possibilities must be discussed. (1) Suppose an interpreter does not wish to recommend a deep interpretation, under any circumstances: he believes that another person's self-understanding is deficient only in fact but never in principle. (2) Suppose two interpreters disagree: one judges that the self-understanding of the person whose words are interpreted is only factually deficient, while the other argues that it is in principle deficient (because he is deceiving himself); one recommends an interpretation in the subjunctive mood, while the other recommends a deep interpretation.

There are no criteria at our disposal that distinguish between cases in which only interpretations in the subjunctive mood are appropriate from cases in which only deep interpretations are appropriate. The interpreter must decide whether he wishes to recommend an interpretation that requires support by an appeal to the Universalizability or the Restrictive Principle. The question arises: why couldn't we also appeal to the Restrictive Principle in case of a natural interpretation in the subjunctive mood?

When recommending an interpretation in the subjunctive mood, we rely either on a well-established commonsense view or on a theory in the human or social sciences for supporting that interpretation. We demand agreement from all reasonable persons who are knowledgeable about the issues, and support our demand with the claim that our interpretation is unimpeachable. Were we appealing only to the Restrictive Principle, we would be merely saying that all persons who agree with our interpretation are reasonable and knowledgeable about the issues. An appeal to the Restrictive Principle may be sufficient for essentially contestable interpretations—such as deep interpretations—but such an appeal is useless in trying to convince others that our interpretation is supported by well-established views. On the other hand, we cannot support an essentially contestable or a deep interpretation by appealing to the Universalizability Principle. The best we can say about such an interpretation is that all who agree with it are reasonable and knowledgeable about the issues—and this is not more than an appeal to the Restrictive Principle.

All deep interpretations are essentially contestable interpretations, but are all essentially contestable interpretations deep interpretations? This is a highly controversial topic. Although I defend—in chapter 6—the rather surprising view that only deep interpretations are essentially contestable, I also show how the account presented here must be adjusted in order to admit essentially contestable interpretations that are not deep interpretations.

6. Can We Adopt a Weaker Form of the Principles?

We must not confuse a defense of interpreters with a defense of their interpretations. Interpretations can be defended only by showing that they satisfy the factual and normative constraints on interpreting. Nonetheless, the Universalizability Principle is at least one step closer to the defense of interpretations than the Restrictive Principle. By appealing to Universalizability we imply that the two constraints on interpreting have been satisfied. An appeal to the Restrictive Principle defends primarily the interpreters who happen to agree with a given interpretation. By appealing to the Restrictive Principle, we expect to secure a hearing for a given interpretation. After securing such a hearing, we must defend that interpretation by showing to what extent it satisfies the two constraints. On one end we will find interpretations that have fully satisfied these constraints. Interpreters offering such interpretations are entitled to appeal to Universalizability. If they fail to do so, they are deceiving others or themselves. (See chapter 3.) On the other end we will find interpretations that did not satisfy the two constraints. On encountering them, we ask: why were they proposed as serious interpretations? Between the two ends we will find interpretations that are defended indirectly by showing that the interpreters proposing and agreeing with them were qualified interpreters.

We must reconsider a further weakening of the admittedly weak Restrictive Principle: instead of claiming that *all* who agree with a given interpreter are reasonable and knowledgeable about what is at issue, we claim only that *some* who agree with that interpreter are reasonable and knowledgeable about that issue. As mentioned in chapter 3, the weaker formulation of one of the principles is useful in some contexts. A reconsideration of this topic serves a more important purpose here: it permits and facilitates a comparison between consensus-driven views of interpreting with the views presented here.

An appeal to the weakened form of one of the two principles has a very limited use in two cases. An interpreter appealing to the Restrictive Principle may be aware of a person who agrees with him although he is unreasonable or unfamiliar with the issues. This interpreter can no longer defend all who agree with him. He must withdraw to an even weaker claim: "Some persons who understand this as I do are reasonable and familiar with the issues."

A second case arises in the context of defending an eccentric interpretation. The interpreter may appeal to the claim contained in the weaker formulation of the Restrictive Principle. For example, an agent of ethnic cleansing or terror may specifically appeal to this claim in order to show that more than one interpreter shares his understanding of the issues. He could not reach this goal by appealing to the Restrictive Principle as originally formulated, for this principle defends all who happen to agree with him but does not require empirical evidence that there are persons sharing his views. The mere assumption that there are such persons is sufficient for appealing to this principle. But he wants to show more: he wants to show that there is empirical evidence that others share his views. He needs such evidence in trying to persuade others that neither he nor his views can be easily dismissed as irrational. And this evidence is available only through an appeal to a weakened form of one of the principles. To be sure, such evidence is seldom persuasive; nonetheless it may be sufficient for admitting serious consideration of eccentric interpretations.

It may be useful to point out that these two cases have a common feature. In the first case the interpreter is forced to withdraw to a weakened version of the Restrictive Principle, because he has evidence of an unqualified interpreter who shares his views. Hence, he can no longer defend all who share his views. In the second case, the interpreter defends his views by insisting on his qualifications. By saying that others share his eccentric views, the interpreter defends himself. The terrorist in the above example could just as well say: "Look here! I am not mad."

We are now in the position of comparing consensus-driven interpretive theories with the interpretive theory proposed here. Consensus-driven theories implicitly rely on a weakened form of one of the principles proposed. By saying that we adopt a given interpretation because this is the consensus of interpreters, we imply that we agree with the opinions of some interpreters considered to be reasonable and knowledgeable about the issues.

Interpretations relying on consensus-driven theories can be supported only by a statistical inquiry: how many interpreters support a given interpretation? By answering this question we can establish only a quantitative difference between standard and eccentric interpretive choices of one and the same object of interpretation. If we wish to establish a qualitative difference, we must appeal to what is beyond the limits of consensus-driven theories. An appeal to either of our two principles will be useful.

Let us assume the sincerity of a given interpreter. Suppose he suggests what by his own lights is an eccentric interpretation. He can support such an interpretation only by appealing to the Restrictive Principle. He cannot acknowledge the eccentricity of his interpretation and at the same time appeal to Universalizability. Alternatively, if he suggests what by his own lights is a standard interpretation, he must support such an interpretation by appealing to Universalizability. He may even acknowledge disagreement with those who hold an eccentric interpretation of what is at issue. By saying that their interpretation is eccentric, he implies that their views must not be taken seriously, for they are either insufficiently reasonable or insufficiently knowledgeable about the issues. A qualitative difference between standard and eccentric interpretations is thereby established.

Two problems arise. Can we assume by any realistic calculation that an interpreter offering an eccentric interpretation is ever sincere? The answer is that—at least occasionally—sincerity is the best policy, when he wants to secure a hearing for his eccentric interpretation. (A case in point is the terrorist's interpretation mentioned previously.) Secondly, even a sincere interpreter offering an eccentric interpretation may believe erroneously that he has suggested a standard interpretation. Such errors are quite common, but if an eccentric interpretation is defended as if it were a standard interpretation, the interpreter's error can be easily discovered. It can be expected that eccentric interpretations appearing in the guise of standard interpretations will be buried beneath an avalanche of counterexamples. After all, even standard interpretations are vulnerable to counterexamples that must be dealt with.

7. Do Numbers Count in Appealing to a Principle?

Interpretations supported with an appeal to Universalizability are neither strengthened nor weakened by the agreement or disagreement of other interpreters. In recommending an unimpeachable interpretation, interpreters are entitled to demand the agreement of others. The fact that some agree or others disagree has no bearing on their recommendation.

The number of interpreters agreeing with their recommendation cannot establish that interpretation. After all, any appeal to Universalizability can be defeated by just one dissenting voice of an interpreter who satisfies all relevant conditions. Appeals to Universalizability are not problematical because the number of persons in agreement with an interpretation does not count. Such appeals become problematical if a given interpreter automatically excludes all persons who disagree with his interpretation. Of course, a disagreement with an interpretation may trigger a reexamination of the recommendation, but as long as the interpretation's unimpeachable character can be defended, the recommendation need not be withdrawn. Unimpeachable interpretations can be supported with a second appeal to the Universalizability Principle: interpreters can claim that others who disagree with their recommendation of a given interpretation are either not reasonable or not knowledgeable about what is at issue.

Can we avoid vacuous or idle appeals to Universalizability? We cannot, but we need not worry about this matter, for the appeal to Universalizability does not by itself support a given interpretation; it is merely an opening move in support of that interpretation. To establish that interpretation, the interpreter must show that he has satisfied the factual and normative constraints on interpreting, and this cannot be achieved by using a rhetorical device of appealing vacuously to Universalizability.

Matters are different concerning interpretations supported by an appeal to the Restrictive Principle. Interpretations supported by this principle acquire strength from the number of other interpreters in agreement with that interpretation. After all, this principle merely claims that interpreters who agree with a given interpretation are reasonable and knowledgeable about the issues. This strength in numbers provides support by moving the essentially contestable character of interpretations supported only by the Restrictive Principle slightly offstage. This is especially important in the context of eccentric interpretations. For the purposes of elaborating on an example that I have used previously, let us agree that an interpreter's judgment that a given interpretation is eccentric is self-confirming. The judgment of one interpreter concerning the eccentric character of an interpretation need not be shared by any other interpreters.

Suppose a terrorist of fundamentalist religious persuasion tries to convince those of us who do not share his views about an interpretation of a religious document that seems to support his acts of terror. He appeals to the Restrictive Principle: he claims that all who agree with him are reasonable. We reply: provided that he is reasonable, he is right, for he is the only one who holds the eccentric views that we consider nonsense. He responds by pointing to one or more persons (other than himself) who share his views—they are reasonable. In providing this information, he secures a hearing for his views. At this stage it would not make sense to tell him that he is mad. We may even take a further step and agree that no terrorist of fundamentalist religious persuasion is mad or ever was mad. But now we examine the eccentric interpretation that we previously called nonsense. Does it satisfy the factual and normative constraints on interpreting? It does not. So even if he is reasonable and knowledgeable about what is at issue, we cannot accept his views. What he believes is still nonsense. However, if he is reasonable and knowledgeable, why does he believe such nonsense? We could answer that he must be self-deceived. In providing such an answer, we are fully aware that we are offering a controversial interpretation. Such an interpretation cannot be defended from center stage and overtly by an appeal to Universalizability. After all, we have admitted that he is reasonable and knowledgeable, yet he does not agree with us. In defending those who share our views, we can overtly appeal only to the Restrictive Principle—while leaving the appeal to Universalizability to our backstage voice. No doubt, our speaking with two voices defeats the claim that we are sincere. So if we wish to regain our claim of sincerity, we must reject the overt appeal to the Restrictive Principle and appeal only to Universalizability. But in this case we must also reject our previous judgment that he is a qualified interpreter. What was previously a deep interpretation becomes a natural interpretation in the subjunctive mood.

Note that his interests dictate that he should appeal to the weakened form of the Restrictive Principle ("Some qualified interpreters agree with me"). Also, we can support our interpretation by arguing that it satisfies the factual and normative constraints on interpreting. We are entitled to appeal to Universalizability, even if we appeal (insincerely) only to the Restrictive Principle. But he cannot support his interpretation by arguing that it satisfies both of these constraints. If his interpretation did satisfy them, he could appeal to Universalizability rather than to the weakened form of the Restrictive Principle.

Numbers also count in legitimating interpretive goals. Since the demand of agreement with an interpretation is limited to persons sharing the interpreter's goals, ordinarily their number will contribute to the strengthening of a given interpretive tradition. This does not exclude the possibility that a new interpretive tradition could be started from the viewpoint of a single interpreter's goals. We may consider interpretive traditions that we do not share mistaken, but we can hardly consider them eccentric if they are shared by a large number of other interpreters.

8. Interpretive Traditions

The appeal to Universalizability can be iterated for interpretations. An important feature of repeated appeals to Universalizability emerges if we focus on interpretations that are unimpeachable for a given time. Suppose an interpreter argues that since he has satisfied the factual and normative constraints on interpreting, all reasonable and knowledgeable persons would agree with his interpretation of what was said in a given document (henceforth: p). Suppose also that the same interpreter or his successor argues that all reasonable and knowledgeable persons are in agreement on this topic. The second interpretive claim about the agreement among all reasonable and knowledgeable persons also satisfies the factual and normative constraints on interpreting; hence, it is an unimpeachable interpretation (p_1). If we admit a second interpretive claim about the agreement concerning the first unimpeachable interpretation about what was said in that document, we have no reasons to reject a third interpretive claim concerning the unimpeachable character of the second interpretive claim (p_2). At this point we cannot reject a successive interpretive claim (p_n) concerning the unimpeachable character of its predecessor (p_{n-1}). At each successive stage, an interpreter iterates his appeal to Universalizability. The question arises: can a successive interpretive claim, grounded on Universalizability, reinforce a preceding interpretive claim that is also supported by an appeal to Universalizability?

Such reinforcement is indeed plausible. Before discussing this matter, an obvious objection must be answered. The iterated appeal to Universalizability from p to p_n is possible only if we admit that there is a difference between the claim that all reasonable and knowledgeable persons would agree about a given interpretation (p) and the claim that all reasonable and knowledgeable persons agree that they agree with one another about that interpretation (p_1). Why do we differentiate between the two cases? Among the many answers to this question, three must be mentioned here.

(1) There are absurd beliefs that were widely held at one time. For example: "We live in a geocentric Universe" or "Some men are slaves by nature." (For a more detailed discussion of these examples, see chapter 9.) Although reasonable and knowledgeable persons shared these beliefs, each interpreter could appeal to Universalizability about these beliefs. As soon as the absurdity of these beliefs became evident for a later generation of interpreters, they could suggest that notwithstanding the absurdity of their ancestors' beliefs, they were entitled to appeal to Universalizability. Alternatively, they could suggest that they were not entitled to such an appeal. Either way, each interpreter could appeal to Universalizability in

support of his own interpretation of his ancestors' appeal to Universalizability. We can argue for either of the two suggestions only if we admit the distinction between p and p_1.

(2) In many interpretive contexts, the interpreter is expected to offer his own interpretation, regardless of other interpreters' contribution to what is at issue. For example, professional critics in art, literature, or music are expected to provide their own interpretations. They may demand that others agree with their interpretations, but the fact that some or all other professional or amateur critics agree or disagree with their interpretations must remain irrelevant for them while they are engaged in interpreting a work of art. (For a more detailed discussion of interpreting in the arts, see chapter 5.) If each professional critic provides his own interpretation of a given artwork, yet there is a consensus among professional critics about that artwork, then there is a distinction between p and p_1.

(3) Finally, the distinction between p and p_1 and between the successive appeals to Universalizability from p to p_n permits us to become clearer about the notion of an interpretive tradition. The absurd beliefs mentioned previously exemplify this point. Interpreters who no longer shared their remote ancestors' belief that they lived in a geocentric universe (p) were nonetheless willing to concede that these ancestors were entitled to appeal to Universalizability in support of their mistaken belief (p_1). The claim that their ancestors were entitled to appeal to Universalizability (p_1) was also grounded on Universalizability. Successive generations of interpreters appealed to Universalizability in arguing that the previous generations of interpreters were right to appeal to Universalizability in supporting the claim that their remote ancestors grounded their absurd belief on Universalizability (p_2 to p_n). Interpretive traditions emerge through such successive appeals to Universalizability. Relying on such interpretive traditions, historians often suggest that their remote ancestors could not help but to hold some widely shared absurd beliefs.

But the spell of interpretive traditions can be broken at any time. For example, it has been argued that contemporaries of Plato and Aristotle could not help but accept the absurd belief that some men are slaves by nature. According to a well-established interpretive tradition, they should not be blamed for having defended the institution of slavery, for without it they could not have imagined the organization of their society. However, this tradition would be discredited if historians found more evidence for doubt about this belief—at a time when it was widely shared—than what is presently available.

Interpretive traditions have a conservative bias. In order to fight that bias, the reader may object against the hypothesis that a successive interpretive claim on a given topic (p_n), grounded on Universalizability, can reinforce a preceding interpretive claim on the same topic (p_{n-1}) that is also supported by an appeal to Universalizability. The objection is useful for urging us to focus on the high price of accepting an interpretive tradition. The answer to the objection is that in accepting an interpretive tradition, we accept its conservative bias. If we wish to reject this bias, we must discredit that interpretive tradition. But in discrediting an interpretive tradition, we are just taking the first step in establishing a new interpretive tradition. Subsequent charges about the conservative bias of the newly established tradition can be expected.

Dissatisfied with this answer, a reader may wish to reject the very notion of an interpretive tradition. The price for doing so is even higher than accepting the conservative bias of interpretive traditions. If it is argued that a following interpretive claim on a given topic (p_n) cannot reinforce a preceding claim on the same topic (p_{n-1}), then—by parity of reasoning—it must be argued that a following interpretive claim cannot weaken a preceding claim. Let us assume, for example, a difference of opinion between two groups of historians. According to some, the contemporaries of early Stoic philosophers were just as entitled to believe that some men are slaves by nature as the contemporaries of Plato and Aristotle (p). According to others, contemporaries of the early Stoic philosophers were no longer entitled to this absurd belief (not-p). Both groups of historians support their own interpretive claims with an appeal to Universalizability. As long as the slaveholders accepted this absurd belief about natural slavery, they were entitled to appeal to Universalizability (p_{n-1}). If we argue that one group of historians weakens this appeal, then we must admit that the other group strengthens it. In either case, we admit an interpretive tradition. Alternatively, if we argue that the historians cannot strengthen or weaken the (p_{n-1}) appeal to Universalizability, then we not only reject the notion of an interpretive tradition, but also of an assessment of the widely shared absurd beliefs of our remote ancestors. And this price is too high for rejecting the notion of an interpretive tradition, for historians are expected to tell us not only what has happened, but also how they understand what has happened. In foreclosing on an assessment of widely shared absurd beliefs, we undermine their ability to tell us about their understanding of what has happened.

9. Universalizability within the Limits of Interpretive Goals

An orderly redescription of the interpreting activity that is compatible with a wide variety of theories of interpretation must provide an account of controversies about interpretations. Some theories insist that interpretations must be judged as true or false; others argue that they are neither true nor false but more or less plausible. Both views can be defended against criticism at the cost of accepting views that run counter to our intuitions. If interpretations are truth-valued, how can two contradictory interpretations survive and prosper side by side? If interpretations are not truth-valued and are only more or less plausible, how do we explain the convergence to the best interpretation? These problems can be avoided if we understand interpretations as recommendations that must satisfy both factual and normative constraints.

We have further limited the appeal to Universalizability to interpreters sharing the same interpretive goals. It did not seem necessary to suggest a further limitation of the appeal to persons sharing the same interpretive tradition. Differences between interpretive traditions of two interpreters can be accounted for as differences between the goals of these interpreters. Granted, each interpreter recommends his interpretation within the framework of his tradition. His recommendation is either addressed only to others who share his interpretive tradition or to all whom he wishes to convert to his tradition. Regardless, the scope of his appeal to Universalizability will depend on his goal. A further limitation of the appeal to a given interpretive tradition seems superfluous.

We are now in the position of judging the scope and limits of the appeal to either of the two principles. The next two chapters discuss the appeal to these principles in the context of interpretations in the arts and in the context of essentially contestable interpretations. What has been said so far prepares the ground for two further claims: (1) In the context of interpretations in the arts there is no difference between natural and deep interpretation, and we can only appeal to Universalizability. (2) In the context of essentially contestable interpretations we can appeal only to the Restrictive Principle, and only deep interpretations are essentially contestable interpretations.

CHAPTER FIVE

Contestable Interpretations: Interpretations of Artworks

Marx directed attention to what became the central problem of contemporary aesthetics. In the introduction to *A Contribution to the Critique of Political Economy* (1857, first published in *Neue Zeit,* 1903) Marx wrote:

> . . . is Achilles possible when powder and shot have been invented? And is the *Iliad* possible at all when the printing press and even printing machines exist? Is it not inevitable that with the emergence of the press bar the singing and the telling and the muse cease, that is the conditions necessary for epic poetry disappear?

> The difficulty we are confronted with is not, however, that of understanding how Greek art and epic poetry are associated with certain forms of social development. The difficulty is that they still give us aesthetic pleasure and are in certain respects regarded as a standard and unattainable ideal.

Marx raises a fundamental philosophical question; his answer to the question, rooted in speculative psychology, need not be taken seriously. In trying to answer his question we must confront a central topic in the understanding of artworks. Ordinarily we understand others as they understand themselves. But it would be futile to try to understand Greek art as if we still believed Greek mythology. Our only option is to accept a radical break between what is available to us and what was available to the poets and artists who produced Greek art. The same break appears when we speak about the art of the present. Just as we must disregard Greek mythology in our approach to Greek art, we must disregard the artists' private mythology in our approach to the artworks of our contemporaries. In the context of artworks the umbilical cord connecting a creation and its creator is broken. Once this cord is broken, the difference between natural and deep interpretation can no longer be maintained. A critic's interpretation of an artwork may be the same as or different from its creator's interpretation. But it is not a decisive argument in favor of an artwork's interpretation that it has been endorsed by the artwork's creator. To be sure, disagreement with such an interpretation must be accounted for, but agreement with the artist's interpretation of his own work need not be the aim of interpreting artworks.

1. The Fragility of the Intentional Tie

We steer by facts when interpreting others. What facts can orient us when we interpret the artworks of others or our own? It won't do to say that we must find out what the creators wanted to say in their artworks. In an obvious sense what they wanted to say is in front of us, and we can derive what their intentions were from what is presented. Their beliefs could guide us to illuminate how they wanted their audiences to understand the words they used or the artworks they created. Again in an obvious sense, we can derive their beliefs from what is in front of us. But it won't be useful to insist that we must be always guided by their intentions and beliefs.

At issue is not merely that these intentions and beliefs are not always available. More important, even if they are available, they could fail to illuminate the artworks we are interpreting. What motivated Iago's desire to destroy Othello? The text is quite clear on this matter:

> I hate the Moor,
> And it is thought abroad that 'twixt my sheets
> He has done my office; I know not if't be true,
> But I, for mere suspicion in that kind,
> Will do as if for surety.
> (*Othello*, 1.3.392–96)

The literal-minded reader wants to know: was Iago's suspicion justified? In the reader's world such questions have answers, and these answers are available at least in principle, if not in fact. Concerning Iago's world only those questions have answers that are provided in *Othello*. These answers together with their logical consequences leave many of the literal-minded reader's questions unanswered. If Shakespeare did answer such a reader's questions, his answers would be constitutive of the world of Othello only if it is provided in *Othello*. Shakespeare's answer about *Othello* is admitted as a regulative principle for interpreting *Othello* only if such an interpretation is considered to be better than other available interpretations. The reader may wish to question the sharp distinction between what is within an artwork and what is said about that artwork. Ordinarily we accept a poet's revision of his poems for a second edition of his poems, just as we accept a painter's and a composer's changes in their creations, even after they have entered the public domain. Nevertheless, an artwork's creator is not necessarily its best interpreter. The interpreter providing the best available interpretation is its privileged interpreter, regardless of whether she is or is not its creator. Before providing reasons for what opponents would recognize as an endorsement of the anti-intentionalist dogma (to be discussed in the next section), it should be mentioned that reasons and arguments only partially support either intentionalism or anti-intentionalism. Both views are supported by decisions that are deeply rooted in the critics' understanding of artworks. The charge of dogmatism against the opponents has a point—but it should be mentioned that defenders of either side in this debate are in very good company. In discussing the problem of intentionality, I shall at first restrict my remarks to literary artworks.

In our world, middle-sized objects are fully determined: a given object either does or does not have a certain property; an event either did or did not take place. In a literary artwork, objects and events have only those characteristics that have been assigned to them or are consequences of what have been assigned to them within that artwork. To be sure, interpreters of such artworks are encouraged to fill in the gaps and to suggest characteristics of objects and events. The filling in of gaps is regulated by the text. The only characteristics admitted are those that are consistent with the text, and among them only those are admitted that enhance the value of the text as a literary artwork. Although other answers to the literal-minded reader's questions may be consistent with the text, it could be suggested that *Othello* is a better literary artwork if we do not fill in the gaps mentioned previously. Evaluative considerations guide us when we decide whether we should fill in a particular gap and how we should fill in that gap.

A comparison with texts that are not artworks is useful. The genre of a given text regulates not only whether we can fill in a given gap, but also the standards of evidence that must be satisfied in filling such gaps. In historical narratives, neither the historian nor the reader is at liberty to fill in the gaps between events, unless these additions can be documented. The agents' desires, beliefs, and their understanding of their own actions can be made explicit in a historical narrative or can be suggested by the reader of such narratives, provided that the available evidence supports the historian's or reader's claims. Although it may be acceptable to attribute to literary characters whatever a critic or reader suggests, as long as this is consistent with the text of a given literary artwork, evaluative considerations may counsel against the attribution. Racial prejudices, anti-Semitic sentiments, sexist views, offensive moral or political motivations that are consistent with but not explicitly stated within a literary artwork must not be attributed to literary characters. With such attributions the focus of the interpretation shifts from the text to the interpreter. If a critic's and her reader's views about a given moral or political view do not happen to coincide, the reader will reject the critic's attributions as sheer propaganda for her ideological commitments. If their moral or political views happen to coincide, the attribution may not be rejected, and it may even go unnoticed. Yet even in these cases the question can be raised: does the attribution shed light on the artwork? Or, is its goal to illuminate the critic's moral or political values reflected in the artwork?

2. Intentionalism and Anti-Intentionalism

It is tempting to submit what can or cannot be attributed to a given artwork to the virtual approval of its creator: would he agree with or approve of the critic's attribution of a given characteristic that is consistent with, but not stated within, his artwork? Intentionalist critics require such virtual approval, but they fail to note that only in a few cases can the artwork's creator transform a virtual approval into a real approval. In all other cases, it is the critic who claims that the artwork's creator would approve, if he were in the position to do so. Secondly, even dyed-in-the-wool intentionalist critics—E. D. Hirsch, Jr., is one example—agree with their anti-intentionalist colleagues that the actual—or virtual—disapproval of the artwork's creator must be disregarded whenever characteristics attributed to the work are considered to be causally dependent on its creator's unconscious intentions.

Anti-intentionalist critics are in no better position than their intentionalist colleagues. In attributing to the artwork characteristics that are consistent with that work, they must distinguish between what is internal and what is external to that work. If they succeed in attributing internal characteristics, they illuminate that work. If they fail and attribute external characteristics, they manage to obscure it. Even consummate anti-intentionalist critics—Monroe C. Beardsley, for example—agree with their intentionalist colleagues that if they attribute an external characteristic to the work, they superimpose their own views on that work, and instead of illuminating it they obscure it. The question arises: what are our criteria for distinguishing between what is internal and what is external to a given artwork? Intentionalist critics urge reliance on a virtual approval of the artwork's creator. Such temptation must be resisted, for it will not solve the problems intentionalists and anti-intentionalists intend to solve.

An agreement of intentionalists and anti-intentionalists in their critical practice is compatible with disagreement about the justification offered in support of such practice. An intentionalist critic could attribute a characteristic to a given artwork and support her judgment by claiming that if the artwork's creator were in the position to do so, he would agree with her judgment. Her anti-intentionalist colleague could attribute the same characteristic to that artwork and support her judgment by claiming that she attributed a characteristic that is internal to the artwork. For the anti-intentionalist the characteristic is internal to that work; for the intentionalist the characteristic at issue is causally dependent on the creator's unconscious intentions. Finally, characteristics that anti-intentionalists consider external to the artwork can be easily rejected by intentionalists by claiming that this was not intended by the artwork's creator.

Arguments supporting the views of each side can be easily answered by the opposite side. So far, neither a counterexample discrediting the views of one side nor a knockdown argument in support of one side is available. The debate between intentionalists and anti-intentionalists has been going on for a very long time. Its antecedents can be traced to the Hebrew Bible and to Plato. Interest in the topic has been central in American aesthetics since Wimsatt and Beardsley's discussion of the intentional fallacy. There are reasons to believe that the debate is an endless philosophical one. This does not mean that it is a futile debate. Its pursuit is useful not because we can expect to discredit one of the two sides. Basic issues in the philosophy of criticism are illuminated by the debate. While recognizing the merits of the other side, I shall defend the anti-intentionalist side in the debate.

3. The Interpreter's Perspective

The interpreter asks: how must I understand what has been said or what has been done? The question is raised in the first-person singular, regardless of whether account is taken of the speaker's or agent's intentions. Moreover, the interpretation provided will be informed by how others understood what was said, and by the interpretive tradition—if there is one. In testing her interpretation against others, she tries to find grounds for believing that her interpretation is the best for a given purpose. No matter in what direction, her effort at understanding continues: interpretations always start from the interpreter's perspective.

In contexts outside of art and literature, the interpreter is guided by what she knows about the facts and what she would say or do if she were in the speaker's or agent's place. Suppose now that in the case of the arts she included among these facts the intentions of the artwork's creator. Intentionalist and anti-intentionalist critics agree that such intentions must be accounted for as long as they can be traced within a given artwork. Intentions that are internal to a given artwork are not subjects of disagreement. At issue are only intentions that are unrealized within a given artwork or that cannot be traced within that artwork. Such intentions are among the characteristics of the artwork's world that are external to that artwork.

Artworks do not contain secrets. Whatever they contain is, in principle if not in fact, available to all interpreters of a given artwork. No doubt, artists can hide in their creations secret messages that are decipherable only by their friends and acquaintances. If their creations contain such secrets, they are external to their artworks. If what is internal to a given artwork is in principle available to all interpreters, then its professional, amateur, or ignorant critics have the same perceptual experiences of that artwork. The differences among interpreters emerge when we focus on what they bring to their perceptual experiences. For example, the professional, the amateur, and the ignorant critic see the same painting; what they notice and find important to talk about in the context of that painting depends on their different contributions to what they see. If what is internal to an artwork is in principle open to examination, then there cannot be a difference between surface and deep interpretations of an artwork. On this topic both intentionalist and anti-intentionalist critics agree. To be sure, both can shift their focus from the artwork to its creator and provide a natural or a deep interpretation about the artist.

Some critics endorse the intentionalist view motivated by conservatism, others by what they misunderstand to be a moral issue. They seem to believe that by relying on the intentions of an artwork's creator they are serving the artwork by preserving its spirit and by excluding unwarranted interpretations. Their aims are laudable; the means used to achieve them are questionable. Insistence on intentions that are unrealized within a given artwork shifts the focus of criticism from the artwork to its creator. Artworks are better served by focusing on the artwork rather than its creator; unwarranted interpretations can be excluded by concentrating on the distinction between internal and external characteristics of a given artwork. There are no criteria that could be used for making that distinction for all artworks. We must rely on our critical judgment in making that distinction for each. We must be prepared to defend our critical judgment just as we must be prepared to defend our interpretation and evaluation of each work of art. Interpretive practice can only offer guidance, and we must decide what guidance we consider to be relevant. No doubt, interpretations of any one artwork are contestable and they are often contested. It is the convergence of interpretations about individual artworks that requires explanation. How is such convergence possible?

4. Levels of Understanding Artworks

Notwithstanding their different philosophical views, intentionalist and anti-intentionalist critics agree not only on some interpretations about individual artworks, but also on some standards of correctness about such interpretations. What is contestable and contested must be understood against the background of considerable agreement. None of this should be surprising. After all, different philosophical views in the philosophy of mathematics or physics are compatible with agreement in the practice of mathematics or physics. Disagreements among critics holding different philosophical views must be also understood against the background of agreement in critical practice. Three levels of understanding artworks can be distinguished from the interpreter's viewpoint.

In our remote past, when we still played make-believe games, we were introduced to the foundation of understanding artworks. In the context of these games we took the first steps in learning to differentiate between fact and fiction. We used our imagination, and we practiced skills which we could not even name at that time: differentiating between a story and history, between an image and its counterpart in reality, between seeing a given object and seeing something as a certain object, between seeing a picture and seeing something in a picture. Additional support of this basic understanding was provided when we learned about the conventions of language use and the practices associated with such use. In the process of assimilating these conventions and practices, we reached the second level of understanding artworks that can be expected of educated laypersons. The third level of understanding is reached by experts, connoisseurs, or critics within a given field of art, literature, and music.

There are no sharp lines separating the novice from the educated layperson or the latter from the expert. The novice believes that the artwork's creator provides the best guidance to the understanding of a given artwork. This naive belief is shared by some of the more sophisticated experts. To be sure, the novice does not rely on a theory when he asks the artist for help in understanding his artwork. The novice reasons about artworks as he would reason in contexts outside of the arts: we rely on speakers and agents to tell us about their words and deeds, so why couldn't we rely on an artwork's creator to tell us about his creation? The sophisticated expert relies on a false belief when he calls on the artwork's creator to provide understanding of his creation. The false belief is that only the artist understands completely the work of art he has produced. It becomes an ideology when it is allied to a second false belief: because an artwork's creator is an expert in his field, he is also an expert in talking or writing about his own artwork. Philosophers from Socrates to Ryle seem to have argued in vain against the second mistaken belief, that agents know how to talk about a certain skill because they have that skill or have achieved mastery in exercising that skill.

"Criticism can talk, and all the arts are dumb," Northrop Frye once wrote. Even if some artists are good critics of their own artworks, the information they offer about them must be tested against the work itself. If the information is contained in the work—or is a logical consequence of what is in the work—then the information is at least in principle available to all interpreters and critics of that work. Such information is not privileged, and whether it is provided by the artwork's creator in his capacity as its interpreter or by any other critic of that artwork is irrelevant. If the information is not contained in the work, then the information provided by the artist can contribute only to our information about his biography, but not to our understanding of his artwork. This much must be conceded to anti-intentionalist critics. Yet intentionalist critics have an intuition that deserves to be preserved. If we fail to maintain some connection between the artist and his artwork, then the liberty we gained in interpreting his work easily becomes a license to project the interpreter's own beliefs, desires, and understanding onto that work. In such cases the interpreter literally superimposes his own views and values onto the artwork. The superimposition obscures rather than illuminates the artwork. The connection to the artwork's creator can be reestablished by distinguishing between internal and external characteristics of the artwork.

5. The Internal versus External Distinction

At first, we must focus on artworks that admit nontrivial answers to the questions about their subject matter. Within literary works of art we can ordinarily answer questions about the events that occur in the world represented in a given artwork. We can talk about the fictional characters within that world, about their actions and their motives. Within some visual works of art—figurative paintings, for example—we might have questions about what is represented within a given artwork, and how it is represented. It is trivially true, but not unimportant, that when we cannot otherwise understand a given artwork, we can always say that it is about itself.

First example: the Biblical story about David and Bathsheba in 2 Samuel 11. The reader may object to my choice of a religious document as an example for literary artworks. One answer is that there are no good reasons to believe that a religious document cannot be a literary artwork. Also, the methods available to literary criticism have been very fruitfully employed in interpreting this story. Another reason for choosing a Biblical story is that these stories do not admit questions about unrealized authorial intentions. Believers and nonbelievers have different reasons for not admitting such questions: for the believer, all authorial intentions are realized within the text; for the nonbeliever, authorial intentions unrealized within the text happen to be unavailable.

The David and Bathsheba story is told in the Hebrew Bible in 538 words; it has been discussed and interpreted for at least two thousand years. Meir Sternberg, an Israeli literary critic, provided an interpretation of the story that focuses on the text rather than its interpretive tradition.* His essay is a paradigm of literary criticism. This does not mean that the interpretations offered in this essay are uncontestable. They are not only contestable, but also controversial.

No synopsis can substitute for quoting the whole story—instead of a full-length-quotation, a rereading of the story is recommended—for any synopsis must be guided by an understanding of what the story is about, and this is already a result of an interpretive decision. What is the story about? The obvious answer is that it is about King David. What about King David? The narrator leaves it up to the reader to decide what the story is about and what moral lessons must be drawn from it. Some readers claim that it is about an embarrassing situation that King David tries to cover up by committing a crime. Its moral: the cover-up of an embarrassing situation is always more harmful than the original embarrassment. Other readers claim that the story is about the abuse of power. Its moral: even the pious author of the Psalms is not immune to the corruptions of power. There are many excellent alternative interpretations of this story: what in one reading is considered an internal element of the story will be considered in another reading an external element.

* Meir Sternberg, *The Poetics of Biblical Narrative* (Bloomington: Indiana University Press, 1985), 186–229.

If we focus on the facts that are related, the following must be mentioned. While his army is fighting a war, King David—usually at the head of his army—stays at home in Jerusalem. One evening, while on the roof of his palace, he notices a good-looking woman bathing. She is Bathsheba, the wife of Uriah. David sends for her and has sexual relations with her. Bathsheba conceives and informs David of this fact. So far, we are told only about an embarrassing situation. King David resorts to intrigue and murder only after receiving the message from Bathsheba that she is pregnant. What up to that time was merely a peccadillo is now a case of adultery warranting extreme measures. Under a pretext, Bathsheba's husband is recalled from the front and is repeatedly urged by David to stay with his wife. Uriah refuses, whereupon David sends with him an order to his commander, Joab, to bring about his death by the enemy. Joab arranges for Uriah's execution, which leads to the death of other soldiers.

If we opt for reading this story as telling us that in trying to cover up his tracks King David committed murder, then we want to know more about Uriah. Did he know that David had sexual relations with his wife? Did he know that in the letter he carried to Joab was an order for his execution? The story can be interpreted on the hypothesis that he knew about his wife's unfaithfulness, and also on the hypothesis that he did not know about this matter. It can be read on the hypothesis that he did know about the contents of David's letter, and also that he did not know about that matter. Moreover, did David think that Uriah did (or did not) know about his wife's unfaithfulness? Must we understand Uriah's refusal to return to his house as a rebuke to David, who stayed out of the war by remaining in his palace in Jerusalem? Did Joab know that the point of David's order of execution was to cover up an embarrassing situation? Did Joab decide that the execution of Uriah required that he cover up the tracks of the execution by letting a number of other soldiers be killed at the same time?

The answers to these questions are of importance only if we claim that this story is about the cover-up of an embarrassing situation; if it is about the abuse of power, then the character and motivation of Uriah and Joab are without interest. In that case we need not even know about David's emotions: was he motivated only by passion or by love for Bathsheba? Did he commit a crime of passion or was he motivated only by political considerations in ordering Uriah's execution?

The story offers multiple interpretations; each interpretation raises questions about different gaps in the narrative. Depending on a given reader's level of understanding literary artworks—the novice's, the educated layperson's, or the professional critic's—some gaps in the story are recognized, while others are not even noticed. Guided by her critical judgment, the reader will fill in the gaps that she recognizes. She may claim that she has subordinated her critical judgment to a theory, an interpretive tradition, or an authority within a given field in the arts. But no matter how she tries to support—or conceal—her judgment, even the choice of that support is embedded in her critical judgment. If the interpreting activity always starts from her own viewpoint, then her claim that a given theory imposes a certain interpretation is at best circular: after all, she herself chose that theory. Her critical judgment is at work at every step: in recognizing a gap within a literary artwork, in filling that gap, and in deciding what is an internal and what is an external element in a given artwork. Just as speculation about Iago's motivation can be judged to bring an external element into Othello's story, speculation about Uriah's or Joab's motives can be also judged to introduce an external element into King David's story.

6. On- and Off-the-Wall Interpretations

Another example: Heidegger's remarks on one of Van Gogh's paintings of shoes and its subsequent criticism. What is this painting about? According to Heidegger, it is about a pair of peasant shoes—specifically, female peasant shoes. In Der Ursprung des Kunstwerkes, (Holzwege, 1950), he describes what he saw in the painting:*

> . . . There is nothing surrounding this pair of peasant shoes in or to which they might belong, only an undefined space. There are not even clods of soil from the field or the path through it sticking to them, which might at least hint at their employment. A pair of peasant shoes and nothing more. And yet.
>
> From the dark opening of the worn insides of the shoes the toilsome tread of the worker stands forth. In the stiffly solid heaviness of the shoes there is the accumulated tenacity of her slow trudge through the far-spreading and ever uniform furrows of the field, swept by a raw wind. On the leather lies the dampness and saturation of the soil. Under the soles there slides the loneliness of the field-path as evening declines. In the shoes vibrates the silent call of the earth, its quiet gift of the ripening corn and its enigmatic self-refusal in the fallow desolation of the wintry field. This equipment is pervaded by uncomplaining anxiety about the certainty of bread, the wordless joy of having once more withstood want, the trembling before the advent birth and shivering at the surrounding menace of death. This equipment belongs to the *earth,* and it is protected in the *world* of the peasant woman. From out of this protected belonging the equipment itself rises to its resting-in-itself.

---

* Martin Heidegger, "The Origin of the Work of Art", trans. A. Hofstadter, in A. Hofstadter and R. Kuhns, *Philosophies of Art and Beauty* (New York: Random House, 1964), 662.

Guided by his critical judgment, Heidegger claimed that he saw in the painting what he described. He insisted that what he saw in the painting was not a superimposition of external elements unto the painting: "The art work let us know what shoes are in truth. It would be the worst self-deception to think that our description, as a subjective action, had first depicted everything thus and then projected it into the painting." Readers who become persuaded by his description and agree that the world of the peasant woman is internal to one of Van Gogh's paintings of shoes must be prepared to claim that they see in that painting what he described.

Readers who cannot see what Heidegger described in any of Van Gogh's paintings of shoes must claim that the world of the peasant woman is external to these paintings. In a now-classic note, Meyer Schapiro demonstrated that Heidegger was mistaken: Van Gogh's paintings of shoes were not peasant shoes, but the painter's own shoes.[*] All art critics and art historians admit this much: Heidegger produced a wide-of-the-mark interpretation. They are even ready to explain it away: after all, the metaphysical speculation that came in tow of the misinterpretation is interesting in its own right. But Schapiro's readers did not notice that Heidegger stands corrected not for a wide-of-the-mark interpretation, but for an off-the-wall interpretation. Whatever Heidegger said about the painting of a pair of shoes could be said about a pair of shoes but not about the painting. The philosopher, looking at a painting, superimposed his fantasies, free associations, and metaphysical speculations on the painting. There is no better judgment of the currently fashionable interpretive practice than Schapiro's remarks on Heidegger:

> Alas for him, the philosopher has indeed deceived himself. He has retained from his encounter with Van Gogh's canvas a moving set of associations with peasants and the soil, which are not sustained by the picture itself. They are grounded rather in his own social outlook with its heavy pathos of the primordial and earthy. He has indeed "imagined everything and projected it into the painting." He has experienced both too little and too much in his contact with the work.

> The error lies not only in his projection, which replaces a close attention to the work of art. For even if he had seen a picture of a peasant woman's shoes, as he describes them, it would be a mistake to suppose that the truth he uncovered in the painting—the being of the shoes—is something given here once and for all and is unavailable to our perception of shoes outside the

* Meyer Schapiro, "The Still Life as a Personal Object—A Note on Heidegger and Van Gogh," in *The Reach of Mind: Essays in Memory of Kurt Goldstein*, ed. M. L. Simmel (New York: Springer Publishing, 1968), 203–9. For a reference to the reprint, see below.

painting. I find nothing in Heidegger's fanciful description of the shoes pictured by Van Gogh that could not have been imagined in looking at a real pair of peasants' shoes. Though he credits to art the power of giving to a represented pair of shoes that explicit appearance in which their being is disclosed—indeed "the universal essence of things," "world and earth in their counterplay"—this concept of the metaphysical power of art remains here a theoretical idea. The example on which he elaborates with strong conviction does not support that idea.

Schapiro's six-and-a-half-page note demonstrates the failure of all interpretive practices modeled on Heidegger's essay. Jacques Derrida noticed the note's importance. He must have understood that it threatened his own interpretive practice, for he tried to bury it underneath a tumble of words. Derrida's essay *La vérité en peinture* contains more than twenty times as many words as Schapiro's note.* The more recently published volume 4 of Schapiro's *Selected Papers* contains an addition: "Further Notes on Heidegger and Van Gogh."† Derrida is not mentioned in this additional note. On one reading of the controversy—and this is my preferred reading—his essay does not deserve an answer. On another reading, anything that could be said in answer to Derrida's interpretation of Van Gogh's painting would be irrelevant.

In discussing Schapiro's critique of Heidegger's interpretation, Derrida changed the subject of the controversy. Schapiro talked about an artwork, Van Gogh's representation of his own shoes; in Derrida's reading of Heidegger and Schapiro the painting is not only a still life, an artwork or a representation of reality. It is transformed into that kind of a self-contained object that not only admits Heidegger's interpretation but also creates agreement between Heidegger's and Schapiro's interpretations. This much will be granted: just as some icons or relics were not only artworks, but served also within a religious practice, Van Gogh's paintings of shoes are not only artworks but are also endowed with religious significance. Schapiro himself drew attention to the religious significance of those shoes in Van Gogh's life, but when speaking about the painting, he spoke as an art historian about the representation of an object in a work of art—the painter's life and art are separated in both of his notes. Derrida blurs the distinction between Van Gogh's life and art; as a philosopher he not only meditates about the significance of the shoes in the painter's life, but also

---

* Jacques Derrida, *La vérité en peinture* (Paris: Flammarion, 1978), 291–436.

† Meyer Schapiro, *Theory and Philosophy of Art: Style, Artist, and Society*, Volume 4 of *Selected Papers* (New York: George Braziller, 1994). "The Still Life as a Personal Object—A Note on Heidegger and van Gogh" 135–42, "Further Notes on Heidegger and van Gogh" 143–51.

claims—allegedly on Schapiro's authority—that the painting is a self-portrait of "Van Gogh (alias J.C.)."[*] On this reading of the controversy, anything that could be said in answer to Derrida's transubstantiation of Van Gogh's painting would be irrelevant.

Is Derrida's interpretation (1) the best available interpretation, is it (2) wide-of-the-mark, or is it (3) off-the-wall? If we accept it as the best available interpretation, we blur the distinction between the painter's art and life. If we cannot accept it, we must decide whether we wish to differentiate between off-the-wall and wide-of-the-mark interpretations. Completely mistaken or wholly insincere interpretations, those that do not at all offer an interpretation of the purported objects, are off-the-wall interpretations; they are merely stories about what the interpreters claim to have interpreted. Partially mistaken or halfway sincere interpretations are at least on-the-wall, they are competing against other available interpretations; they can be considered misinterpretations as soon as a better interpretation for a given purpose becomes available. Even a misinterpretation must contain some connection to the artwork that is its object.

Some—but not all—critics agree that there is a difference between wide-of-the-mark and off-the-wall interpretations. If they claim at the same time that Derrida offered the best available interpretation, then those who argue against their view can at best suggest that it is mistaken. On the other hand, if they claim that Derrida did not offer the best available interpretation, they must show either that he offered a wide-of-the-mark interpretation or that he superimposed another object on the purported object of interpretation—that is, he suggested an off-the-wall interpretation. The very notions of a wide-of-the-mark and an off-the-wall interpretation are interdependent. After all, a wide-of-the-mark interpretation is just a partially, but not totally, mistaken or insincere interpretation; an off-the-wall interpretation is nothing but a wholly mistaken or insincere interpretation.

If we erase the lines separating the three different cases—the best available, the wide-of-the-mark, the off-the-wall interpretations—we obliterate the lines separating (1) good works of art, (2) bad works of art, and (3) what are not artworks at all. What Derrida said about Van Gogh's painting could be said about a devotional picture painted by a Sunday painter. The difference between bad artworks and what are not artworks at all is just as fundamental as the difference between wide-of-the-mark and off-the-wall interpretations. In some cases it is a mistake to admit as an artwork what is presented as a work of art. For example, pornography is often presented as art; critics must judge whether it is art, bad art, or not art at

---

[*] Derrida, *La vérité en peinture*, 434

all. The judgment deserves to be accepted if it is based on the best available interpretation; it need not be taken seriously if it is based on an off-
the-wall interpretation.

7. Application

If the goal of interpreting is the understanding of what was said or done,
then the notion of understanding at issue covers a very wide field. I have
argued that interpretations are application-driven. Ordinarily religious or
legal documents are interpreted to provide guidance for religious or legal
practice. If guidance for such practice is not included in the notion of
understanding in these fields, then such a narrow notion cannot serve the
goal of interpreting. Interpreting serves other purposes in other contexts.
Most artworks were created to provide aesthetic delight, entertainment, or
amusement. Accordingly, a wide notion of understanding in the context
of art interpretation includes appreciation. In exceptional cases, a narrow
notion of understanding is also at issue in the interpretation of literary artworks. An interpretive commentary to *Finnegans Wake* is a case in point. But
in the large majority of cases a wider notion of understanding—inclusive
of appreciation—is the goal of interpreting literary artworks. The reader
will object that there are no limits to such a wide notion of understanding:
it includes at one time appreciation and at another time guidance for religious or legal practice. Moreover, this wide concept of understanding is
dependent on an equally wide concept of interpretation. Such unlimited
concepts are ordinarily useless. The answer is that these concepts appear
to be unlimited only as long as we talk about them within a theory of interpretation. Within our interpretive practice they are contained within manageable boundaries. The interpretation of an artwork that does not
contribute to its appreciation will be faulted for failing to satisfy the factual
and normative constraints on interpreting. Also, the interpretation of a
religious document that does not advert to guidance in religious or moral
practice will be criticized. Often there are good answers to such criticism.
(See for example my reporting on the Biblical story about David and
Bathsheba as if it were a literary work of art.) The oceanic concepts of interpretive theory become limited and manageable in interpretive practice.

Since interpretations are application-driven, it is understandable that
amateur and professional critics within the audience of an artwork aim
at different interpretations. Amateurs need not search for the best available interpretation. An amateur critic may adopt an interpretation of a
given artwork and at the same time admit that there is at least one better

interpretation, but for want of sufficient knowledge or an adequate education that interpretation is unavailable to him. Professional critics could not admit that they are satisfied with the second-best interpretation within their field of expertise. Also, within that field they must provide their own interpretation and speak about it with a universal voice. Amateurs need not satisfy these conditions. As mentioned before, in the interpretation of artworks there is no difference between surface and deep interpretation. Even if an amateur critic appeals only to the Restrictive Principle, this does not imply that his interpretation is an essentially contestable or deep interpretation. It is merely an acknowledgement that it is a contestable interpretation. Since within the limits of his knowledge the amateur critic has offered the best available interpretation for his purposes, he could have appealed to Universalizability. He is in a similar situation as our remote ancestor who believed that he was living in a geocentric universe: both could appeal to Universalizability in support of their views. (See chapter 9.)

8. Blurring Distinctions

It could be argued that in speaking about artworks, the internal versus external distinction is artificial. Moreover, if we disregard this distinction, then the sharp demarcation line between art and life also appears to be mistaken. Finally, if we erase the line separating art and life, then the difference between wide-of-the-mark and off-the-wall interpretations is useless. Why should we maintain these three distinctions? Why shouldn't the biographical information that is at our disposal about a given artist influence our understanding of what he has created? After all, the historical setting in which an artwork was created leaves an indelible mark on what has been created. In fact, much of what educated laypersons know about ancient Greece or medieval England, they have learned from reading Homer, Shakespeare, other poets, and other artists. What they know about our history was mediated by their knowledge of art and literature. So why do we insist on maintaining these distinctions?

Critics who consider these distinctions mistaken have a point that deserves to be preserved: the insights gained from art and literature are certainly relevant to our lives. They believe that by erasing distinctions, we can make the insights more directly relevant, for the rigid separation of art and life undermines the value of art and literature for our lives. In extreme cases, the complete separation of art and life makes art and literature irrelevant. They are thereby degraded to the level of entertainment. On such a level, we escape from rather than turn to issues of concern in our lives.

Our attempt at understanding what concerns us recedes into the background. Our effort at caring for what is dear to us is suspended. The mirror offered to us by art and literature, wherein to catch our conscience, no longer does its duty.

Both extreme positions—the erasing of the three distinctions and the complete separation of art and life—deserve to be rejected. If we reject them, the insights motivating them can be preserved. The internal versus external distinction permits the understanding and appreciation of artworks in their historical context. The ways of seeing the world at a certain time, an artist's unique way of seeing the world—the style of a period and the artist's individual style—leave internal marks on artworks, regardless of the artist's intentions. Just as our own ways of seeing are transparent to us, the style of a period and an artist's individual style are transparent to those who share that style. Nonetheless, stylistic features are internal elements of artworks that can be discerned at a later time or by viewers who no longer share the style that left its mark on the artwork. Moreover—as we have seen before—this distinction also admits accounting for the artist's intentions, insofar as they are realized in the artwork.

The distinction between art and life permits the splitting of fictional sentences in literature from our beliefs about the world, and facilitates the anchoring of art and literature in our make-believe activities. Depending on the reader's views about these matters, the statement "Desdemona is a woman" is either false or does not have a truth-value. The statement " 'Desdemona' is used as a name for a fictional character, about whom we make-believe that she is a woman" is cumbersome but true. It is part of our make-believe that she suffered the fate related in Shakespeare's *Othello* and that we pity her for her undeserved suffering. What we know about our own world permits the understanding of artworks. Occasionally this relation is reversed, and what we know about literary artworks facilitates the understanding of our own experiences. We presuppose the distinction between art and life in both cases: when we bring to bear what we experience in life to the understanding of art, and when the imaginative engagement with art facilitates the understanding of our own experiences.

The distinction between wide-of-the-mark and off-the-wall interpretations is primarily useful in the context of interpreting art and literature. As mentioned earlier, interpretations have a normative character: they are presented as the best available for a given purpose. In ordinary contexts, when evaluating an interpretation of what another person has said or done, we can easily dismiss interpretations that fail to satisfy the factual and normative constraints on interpreting. Even if a given interpretation is so wide-of-the-mark that it no longer counts as a misinterpretation, we need not insist that it is either an off-the-wall interpretation or no interpretation at all of what has been said or done. To be sure, honesty suggests such insistence, but politeness urges silence on the matter. After all, the interpretation will be dismissed, regardless of whether it is evaluated as a misinterpretation or an off-the-wall interpretation.

The prompting of politeness must be resisted when we are confronted with a fundamental confusion between art and life. Interpretations rooted in such confusion need not be taken seriously as interpretations of artworks, even if offered by the sophisticated rather than the ignorant. The ignorant may believe that the purpose of one of Michelangelo's frescoes is to serve as a resting place for flying insects, or he may wish to jump on the stage and rescue Desdemona from the hands of Othello. The sophisticated may tell a story about what he claims to have interpreted, but in telling that story he confuses what he saw in a painting with what he brought to the painting and superimposed on what is represented. The sophisticated and the ignorant share the same confusion between art and life. Their beliefs, wishes, and grasp of what is at issue are based on interpretations that do not compete with misinterpretations or wide-of-the-mark interpretations; they are based on off-the-wall interpretations.

9. Art and Life

Sophisticated off-the-wall interpretations of artworks, rooted in the confusion between art and life, may serve other purposes than the interpretation of artworks. Philosophical speculation is often attracted to great works of art and literature. The content of such speculation need not be rejected just because it is dependent on an off-the-wall interpretation of an artwork. Even if the interpretation is rejected as bad art criticism or bad art history, it can contribute to the understanding of what concerns us and to supporting the care for what is dear to us in our lives. Since the historical setting in which an artwork was created leaves a mark on that artwork, the artwork can also guide us to the understanding of our history. Art and literary critics of both conservative and radical persuasions always insist that great art and great literature provide us not only with aesthetic delight, but also with a better understanding of our own lives: what is presented in great art and literature is not true of life, but it aspires to being at least true *to* life. Accordingly, art and literary criticism discusses not only the interpretation and evaluation of art and literary works, but also the relevance of art to life, and of literature as a guide to a good life. The modern reader's skepticism about exaggerated claims submitted on behalf of the relevance and value of art and literature is warranted. At the same time, these claims cannot be dismissed.

If any of these claims are admitted, Marx's problem deserves to be reexamined. For Marx, it seemed paradoxical that the art of the past provides aesthetic pleasure long after the disappearance of the social conditions that brought it about. What is seen to be a paradox at one time can easily become a defining characteristic at a later time. For example, prior to the late nineteenth century, philosophers of mathematics questioned the existence of an actual infinite; at the same time they knew, and found it paradoxical, that there were as many natural numbers as there were even numbers. The paradox disappeared as soon as they accepted as a defining characteristic of infinite sets that they have proper subsets that are also infinite. Similarly, Marx's paradox disappears if we accept as a defining characteristic of great art and literature that it gives us aesthetic pleasure after the disappearance of the social conditions that brought it about. Marx's question contains implicitly a better philosophical answer than the explicit psychological answer that he suggested.

CHAPTER SIX

Essentially Contestable Interpretations

All deep interpretations are essentially contestable interpretations. But are all essentially contestable interpretations deep interpretations? So far, I have argued that deep interpretations are appropriate only if (natural) interpretations in either the indicative or subjunctive mood are insufficient for understanding the speaker's or agent's words or deeds. A deep interpretation is required if, in the interpreter's judgment, the speaker is a victim of self-deception. If I now wish to claim that all essentially contestable interpretations are deep interpretations—in other words: only deep interpretations are essentially contestable interpretations—I must establish the connection between essentially contestable interpretations and self-deception.

1. On the Contents of Belief Box #1

I have suggested a distinction between two kinds of beliefs. Belief box #1 contains all my deeply entrenched and compelling beliefs; as long as I am the same person as I am now, I am prepared to hold on to these beliefs no matter what happens. I can defend the contents of my belief box #1 only with the Restrictive Principle. Belief box #2 contains all my other beliefs; they must be defended with the Universalizability Principle. As mentioned before, the contents of these boxes will differ from one person to the next. Some keep their views about religious or philosophical matters in box #1, while others keep them in box #2. Essentially contestable interpretations are often beliefs concerning religious or philosophical topics; they are the best examples for such interpretations.

You don't know about all your beliefs that are in your box #1. But you think that some beliefs are in that box. They have a common characteristic: you don't know how you could be wrong about them. When asked, you may not wish to offer reasons for holding these beliefs, or for holding them in your belief box #1. To be sure, these reasons are based on other beliefs that are also in either your belief box #1 or #2. But you may not wish to be embarrassed into admitting that the so-called privileged facts—that is, the contents of your belief box #1—are supported by less certain beliefs. Accordingly, you may argue that anything said in their support is less certain than what is in that box. Now, if you tell us what is in that box, we can at least start our inquiry.

We must first dispose of a preliminary objection. Suppose you tell us that your belief box #1 is empty. Is this possible? This is not possible. Either your belief box #1 contains at least one belief or you have found ways for being wrong about any one of your beliefs. At least since Descartes, philosophers have been trained to find ways for being wrong about any given belief. Suppose you succeed in showing how you can be wrong about any given belief. Would not at least one belief remain in your belief box #1—namely, that your belief box #1 is empty? A similar objection can be raised against your claim that although your belief box #1 is not empty, as soon as you find a belief in that box, you will show that it must be either abandoned or placed in your belief box #2 and supported by an appeal to Universalizability. If you are right about this matter, your belief box #1 contains at least one belief—namely, that your belief box #1 can be emptied in this fashion. If you are wrong, your belief box #1 contains at least one belief that could be neither discarded nor relegated to your box #2. So, your belief box #1 contains at least one belief.

Your interpreter has three choices concerning any belief, including the contents of your belief box #1. (1) She understands you as you understand yourself, and she agrees with you. She interprets your words in the indicative mood, and the question of an appeal to a principle does not arise. If others happen to disagree with her understanding of what you were saying, the interpreter who agrees with you will appeal to Universalizability. (2) Your interpreter disagrees with you. According to your judgment, your belief box #1 contains a given belief. She either holds that belief to be false or claims that the belief in question is in your belief box #2. She interprets what you said in the subjunctive mood, and she supports her interpretation with an appeal to Universalizability. (3) In the same situation as choice 2, your interpreter defends her views by appealing to the Restrictive Principle.

If your interpreter disagrees with you about a belief that in your judgment is in your belief box #1, she must appeal to one of the two principles. What decisive consideration will influence her choice? If she appeals to Universalizability, she will have to claim that your judgment need not be counted. In her judgment, all reasonable and knowledgeable persons agree with her understanding of what is at issue, and persons who disagree with her simply do not count among the reasonable and knowledgeable persons. Note that if she appeals to Universalizability, she cannot at the same time claim that her interpretation of your words or deeds is an essentially contestable interpretation. On the other hand, if she appeals to the Restrictive Principle, she is free to admit that you are reasonable and knowledgeable about the issues, and that her interpretation is an essentially contestable interpretation. The incompatibility of essentially contestable interpretations with the appeal to Universalizability is not surprising. After all, an interpreter cannot speak with a universal voice and at the same time claim that her interpretation is essentially contestable. But if essentially contestable interpretations are considered to be sufficiently important to generate interminable controversies, then charges of self-deception will always be heard or implied in such controversies.

2. Interminable Controversies

When asked about the contents of your belief box #1, you tell your interpreter that your beliefs about your ethnic origins are in that box: you are a Serb, a Croat, a Jew, or a Gypsy—and you don't know how you could be wrong about this matter. Your childhood memories about your caregivers are supported by documents, witnesses will testify to your claims, and the inscriptions on the gravestones of your relatives provide additional evidence for what you consider not just a belief but a privileged fact. Your interpreter disagrees, but the topic is of little interest to her, and she may not even voice her objections to your claim.

Another interpreter will be more interested in this matter. An example: an employee of a relief agency is charged with dividing the agency's meager funds among this week's and this region's underprivileged. If she disagrees with your claim, and simply overrides it, she is rejecting your request for assistance. In her judgment your request is either fraudulent, or based on a mistaken belief, or on self-deception. She will support her judgment by appealing to Universalizability, and she will provide an interpretation of your words in the subjunctive mood.

The controversy about your roots in a given community can be terminated. Your interpreter decides on the matter; if you appeal the decision to the relevant authorities, they will adjudicate what is at issue. Some beliefs in belief box #1 cannot be decided in this manner. Among them are philosophical and religious beliefs. You hold fundamentalist religious beliefs, while your interpreter is a freethinker—or the other way around. You believe that we see sense-data and that physical objects are logical constructs out of these data, while your interpreter holds that we see physical objects and that sense-data are philosophers' daymares—or the other way around. It is irrelevant how you acquired these beliefs that are presently in your belief box #1. In some cases childhood training is the origin; in others reasons and arguments provided by a charismatic teacher are the basis of what you consider not only beliefs but also privileged facts. Your interpreter's contrary beliefs are ingrained in her belief box #1, and she considers them privileged facts. Neither you nor your interpreter knows how to be wrong about a given topic of fundamental importance for both of you. When professing your beliefs you have learned to avoid a futile discussion by a show of tolerance. Your opponent is entitled to her opinion, as you are to yours—at least, this is what you say. But tolerance has its limits. At some time both you and your interpreter must ask: am I really serious about this topic? I cannot hold it in my belief box #1, consider it a foundation for many other beliefs in my belief box #2, and at the same time say that it is just a matter of opinion. To be sure, I can and do say this, but do I believe what I say? Of course, I believe it—otherwise I wouldn't support all beliefs in my box #1 with an appeal to the Restrictive Principle.

By appealing to the Restrictive Principle, I merely claim that all persons who agree with my interpretation are reasonable and knowledgeable about what is at issue. For all I know, persons who disagree are also reasonable and knowledgeable about the same issue. This is my concession to tolerance. But if I don't know how to be wrong about this issue, isn't such a concession just an empty formula that permits me to avoid the debate with those who disagree with me? How can they believe the contrary of what I consider a privileged fact? I don't know how I can be wrong about this issue. They not only claim to know how to be wrong about it, but in fact think that I am mistaken about it. They claim to know something I can neither know nor learn from them. Are they mistaken? Are their claims fraudulent? Are they benighted? Are they suffering from self-deception?

We arrived from essentially contestable interpretations to an overt or covert claim that states dissenters with such an interpretation are victims of self-deception. I suspect them of self-deception, for they claim to know what I cannot know and what they cannot teach me. But if these are all my reasons for suspecting them of self-deception, they have even better reasons for suspecting me of self-deception. After all, it was I who argued that I don't know how to be wrong about this issue, and that I cannot learn from them how to be wrong about it. From their viewpoint such claims show that I am mistaken, or that my claims are fraudulent, or that I am benighted or self-deceived. As opponents in the context of an essentially contestable interpretation, we will try to negotiate our differences, but as long as one side does not succeed in convincing the other, we will be divided on the very issue that made each of us suspect of self-deception in the eyes of the other. They know and I do not know how to be wrong about the very same issue, and we cannot teach one another about this matter.

3. Tolerance

Your ethnic origins, your sexual preferences, your views about matters of religion or philosophy are different from your interpreter's. You think of beliefs about these topics as privileged facts. They are in your belief box #1, and your interpreter agrees that they are in that belief box. In some cases, your opinions, beliefs, or convictions about them are of no importance to your interpreter. She does not share your beliefs, but she considers you at least her equal and in some respects her better. She would not say that she is tolerant of your diversity or of your alternative persuasions, because she never thought that tolerance is called for in this case. For all that she knows, your beliefs and convictions are just as well-founded as hers. And even if they are not well-founded, they are irrelevant to her concerns. Another situation arises if the content of your belief box #1 is important for her. What is a false belief in her judgment is true according to you—or the other way around. While she holds on to her own convictions, she can learn to become tolerant of your different beliefs. Even if she considers your beliefs somewhat second-rate, she would not regard this a reason for denying you the opportunities that you seek. Moreover, she would urge others not to deny you the opportunities that may arise. In her judgment, your beliefs about these matters are just irrelevant to the tasks you will have to perform when you are provided with these opportunities. A third situation arises when her wanting to become tolerant of your divergent views is at loggerheads with the contents of her belief box #1.

Interminable controversies about matters of philosophy or religion provide examples for the tension between tolerance and the contents of belief box #1. Religious fundamentalism and political fanaticism are ordinarily considered beneath notice in serious discussions. Advocates of such views are marginalized in a culture deeply rooted in the traditions of liberalism and skepticism. But the extremists' insights deserve to be taken seriously. A firm conviction about the truth of a belief and its importance as a guide to life cannot be easily reconciled with tolerance of alternative beliefs. Of course, we can learn to become tolerant. Yet if the scuttlebutt about philosophers can be believed, even they find it difficult to reconcile their wanting to be tolerant with a firmly held belief they consider to be important. It is easy to see why philosophers become intolerant of alternative views.

Ordinarily we acquire our religious beliefs or agnostic convictions at a relatively early age. They can become so deeply rooted in us that they are considered privileged facts and are placed in our belief box #1. Once they are placed in that box, we are seldom called to defend them. If occasionally we must defend them, an appeal to the Restrictive Principle seems to be sufficient. Compared with religious beliefs, philosophical views are adopted at a much later age. Although they are accepted on the grounds of reasons and arguments that leave the door open for being mistaken, philosophers are ordinarily quite confident in the view they have accepted and certain they have examined all available alternatives. Having rejected the alternatives and adopted a view as their own, they are willing to claim that their beliefs concerning that view are in their belief box #1. If required to defend their own view, prudence suggests an appeal to the Restrictive rather than the Universalizability Principle. After all, if you want to convince others of your views, you may not wish to tell them that as long as they disagree, they are either not reasonable or not knowledgeable about what is at issue. But the arguments at their disposal are presented with a universal voice. (It would be absurd to restrict the scope of philosophical, logical, or mathematical arguments to a given segment of the population. It is not at all absurd to restrict the scope of arguments supporting a religious conviction to members of a given religious community. In fact, some religious communities even prohibit proselytism.)

Prudential considerations suggest that philosophical arguments appeal to the Restrictive Principle; yet the universal voice of these arguments requires an appeal to Universalizability. These two claims are at loggerheads. The tension between them can be resolved if a given argument succeeds in convincing the audience to whom it was presented. Let us say, for example, that your interpreter is a phenomenalist; she believes physical objects are logical constructs out of sense-data, whereas you believe that you see physical objects. While she only claims that all persons who share her views are reasonable and knowledgeable about the issues, she must argue with a universal voice—even if she is tolerant of all available alternative views. If you become convinced of her views, you will not object to her tolerance of alternative views or to her claim that those who hold such views are also reasonable and knowledgeable about the issues. Converts of recent vintage are ordinarily more zealous than the long-standing faithful: according to your judgment, she merely shows tolerance and appeals vacuously to the Restrictive Principle. Be that as it may, the tension between her universal voice and her appeal to the Restrictive Principle is, in your judgment, of no consequence.

Should you—contrary to her denial—persist in believing that you see physical objects, then the tension between her universal voice in presenting her reasons and arguments and her protestation of appealing only to the Restrictive Principle turns out to be of fundamental importance. You persist in maintaining your views and place your beliefs about this matter in your belief box #1. Your interpreter also persists in holding on to her views and places her beliefs about the matter in her belief box #1. Both of you appeal to the Restrictive Principle, yet each of you—having rejected all available alternative views—must present his or her own arguments with a universal voice. If each of you considers the content of the other person's belief box #1 of sufficient importance, then you will claim one of three things: the other is either mistaken, lying, or deceiving himself.

These are harsh words. However, there are two alternatives that are less offensive than any of the previous three choices: disregarding the content of another philosopher's belief box #1 or avoiding arguments on behalf of the content of one's own belief box #1. We might try to disregard the contents of another philosopher's belief box #1 by claiming that "he pursues other interpretive goals," or that "he is a different kind of a philosopher," or by making similar remarks. Short of these two alternatives, each of the three choices has offensive connotations. In the context of long-standing philosophical controversies, the claim that another contemporary philosopher is mistaken is just as offensive as the charge that he is lying or a victim of self-deception. Why is this so?

Ordinarily, when we claim that another person's beliefs are mistaken, we override his views and in interpreting his words and deeds, we support our (natural) interpretation with an appeal to Universalizability. Our interpretation is in the subjunctive mood, and we suggest that he would agree with us if he were both reasonable and knowledgeable about what is at issue. Some historians of philosophy would even argue that philosophers of a bygone age are honored—*Ehrenrettung* is the German word used in such circumstances—by a natural interpretation in the subjunctive mood.

To be sure, if they were mistaken about a given topic, then they were not as knowledgeable about that topic as their successors. They were the giants of their time, and their successors were the dwarfs standing on their shoulders; yet had they seen and known what their successors saw and knew, they would have agreed with them, and they would have avoided being mistaken. Such considerations are inapplicable to contemporary philosophers. If the content of a contemporary philosopher's belief box #1 is at issue and this is contradicted by the content of his interpreter's belief box #1, then the claim that the philosopher is mistaken amounts to the charge that he has failed to examine the available alternatives prior to placing a given view in his belief box #1. The charge that he is mistaken casts on him a shadow of suspicion. The focus of attention shifts thereby from the topic that is discussed to the philosopher: he is at fault for taking a wrong turn. In saying to him that he is mistaken in contradicting well-known reasons and arguments, we imply that something is wrong with him if he does not mend his ways. Remember that philosophical arguments are always presented with a universal voice, even if we claim to appeal only to the Restrictive Principle in support of the arguments and appear to be tolerant of alternative views.

Contemporary philosophers are discredited by our setting aside their views and claiming that they are mistaken. Forced to speak with a universal voice, we can at best argue that they failed to examine all available alternatives before adopting their own views. Even this charge is offensive, however: it suggests that they failed to answer the call of duty. If we take another step and interpret their words in the subjunctive mood, we further imply that they literally don't know what they are talking about. We tell them not only that they are either not reasonable or not knowledgeable about a given topic, but also that if they were both reasonable and knowledgeable, they would adopt our views about that topic. In interpreting the words of contemporary philosophers in the subjunctive mood, we do what the physician does when she interprets her illiterate patient's complaint about a pain in an organ he has located incorrectly. Our interpreting a contemporary philosopher's words in the subjunctive mood is at least as offensive as telling him that he is either lying or deceiving himself.

We attack either his professional competence or his personal integrity. Our choices are quite limited if we become convinced that he is either mistaken, lying, or a victim of self-deception. After rejecting his views, we must either ignore them as viable alternatives to our view or interpret his words in the subjunctive mood and appeal to Universalizability. Prudential considerations require that we appeal to the Restrictive Principle if we want to convince him. Since philosophical arguments must be presented with a universal voice, the appeal to the Restrictive Principle could be just a rhetorical device used in the debate. Once we become convinced that he is mistaken or lying, the appeal to the Restrictive Principle is no longer needed. It continues to be needed if we are convinced that he is a victim of self-deception and we wish to continue the debate. It could not be continued unless we acknowledge that all who share his views are just as reasonable and knowledgeable about the issues as all who share our views.

In appealing to the Restrictive Principle, we defend the views of interpreters who agree with our own views. At the same time, we speak with a universal voice in presenting our arguments on behalf of our views. Accordingly, in arguing for our views we appeal to Universalizability. From center stage we appeal to one principle, while in our backstage whisper we appeal to the other. We encounter this pattern whenever it seems prudential (or convenient) to hide our claim that we have satisfied the factual and normative constraints on interpreting, and accordingly we are entitled to appeal to Universalizability. Speaking with two voices provides evidence of hypocrisy or self-deception: we become insincere in the process of professing to be tolerant of alternative opinions.

There is another insincere strategy that we can pursue if we wish to appear tolerant. Convinced that we have satisfied both constraints on interpreting, we appeal to Universalizability. When asked whether we really believe that all qualified interpreters agree with our interpretation, we can avoid answering the question and respond that they *ought* to agree. After all, we cannot be faulted for recommending an interpretation we propose. At the same time, the statement that all qualified interpreters agree with a given interpretation is moved to the backstage area, while the recommendation that they ought to agree is moved to the center stage. Here, dodging the question is a way to appear tolerant, but is further evidence of insincerity.

4. Interminable Controversies and Deep Interpretation

You believe that we see sense-data and that physical objects are logical constructs out of these data. You do not know how to be wrong about this matter—accordingly, you place this belief in your belief box #1. Your interpreter believes that we see physical objects and that sense-data are philosophers' constructs. She does not know how to be wrong about her belief—accordingly, she places this belief in her belief box #1. Since both of you appeal to the Restrictive Principle in support of your own view, both of you claim that reasonable and knowledgeable persons agree with either view. You could teach each other how each of you could be wrong about a belief each holds in his or her belief box #1. But the lesson each of you is willing to give to the other turns out to be unacceptable. You may say that the other is both reasonable and knowledgeable, and you even try to convince the other. Both of you make every effort, but after a while each of you considers the discussion with the other an exercise in futility. It turns out that the other is not an *interlocuteur valable* about what is at issue. Since you consider each other's view profoundly mistaken, your choices are limited: ignore the other's view, refuse to discuss your own view with the other, question the other's professional competence or personal integrity.

These choices are not unique to professional philosophers. Impressionist painters thought of their contemporaries' academic art as *l'art pompier*— fireman's art—while the academic painters considered the great impressionists incompetent. Nonspecialist visitors of the Musée d'Orsay, where impressionist and academic paintings could be seen in the same exhibition hall, discovered that there was considerable talent on both sides. Just as two philosophers who have incompatible beliefs about a given topic that is of central importance to both, most painters on both sides of that divide—Edgar Degas was a notable exception—did their best either to ignore those on the other side or to question their professional competence or personal integrity.

Historians of philosophy try to show the merits of both sides of a controversy in presenting their predecessors' incompatible beliefs. Although museums enable us to see art on both sides of a given divide—as long as a controversy is still open—historians of philosophy cannot reach the goal of permitting us to discover the philosophical merits of both sides of the controversy. What divides painters is the way they see and represent the world, in short: they have their own *style*. In some cases, ways of understanding philosophical problems—style differences—account for two philosophers adopting incompatible views concerning a given topic. More often and more importantly, philosophers sharing the same style have incompatible views concerning a given topic. Historians of philosophy have a choice as long as a given controversy is open. They can act as curators and guardians of our philosophical museum and limit their purview to the presentation of all sides of a controversy and the preservation of the insights gained from each side. Or they can intervene in the controversy and become actively engaged in philosophical debate—thereby losing their positions as mere curators and guardians.

The debate about phenomenalism in epistemology serves here only as an example of a philosophical controversy. It was chosen because it is not now in the foreground of the discussion among philosophers. The issues raised in that controversy have not been resolved. Philosophical controversies find a satisfactory resolution if one and only one side of the debate has been discredited. If a debate has been going on for a long time without a satisfactory resolution, then three alternatives must be considered. Either both sides are mistaken and their views must be rejected; both are right, but focus on different issues; or the two sides have different conceptions of the same issue, and the judgment about which side is considered to be right depends on the conception endorsed. The first two alternatives are taken from Kant's discussion of the antinomy of pure reason. The third alternative raises a problem that even a historical perspective finds intractable.

Philosophical controversies are not subject to the judgment of history. They are interminable; we are not nearer to their resolution than our predecessors were. There are, of course, controversies among philosophers that have been terminated because of a discovery in the sciences. Once terminated, they are understood as controversies among philosophers and not as philosophical controversies. Participation in an interminable philosophical controversy often seems to be futile, even for those who have strong convictions on a given topic. Both sides appeal to the same facts, and the arguments on either side are continually recycled. Such controversies yield clarity and better understanding of arguments in this field, but they do not thereby find satisfactory resolutions.

The strongest motivation for participating in an interminable philosophical controversy is a philosopher's conviction that—after many false starts and detours—he has found the decisive reasons and the conclusive arguments supporting either one side or the undecidability of the controversy. (He need not enter the controversy if he has found the difference between the two sides from a philosophical viewpoint irrelevant; a historical account of the controversy would be sufficient.) If he is right, then the facts of the matter have been discovered, truth has been reached, and the search for a successful resolution has been achieved. His belief that he is right permits and facilitates his participation in the controversy. Let us assume that his conviction about what he calls the facts of the matter is in his belief box #1, and his belief that he is right is either in the same box or in belief box #2. In supporting his conviction, he appeals to the Restrictive Principle. The seemingly modest claim that all who agree with him about the facts of the matter are both reasonable and knowledgeable about what is at issue hides his self-deception: he claims to have resolved a philosophical controversy, in the teeth of his knowledge that such controversies are interminable.

Even if he does not believe that he is right, and he believes only that his view is more plausible than his opponents' view, he cannot escape placing his conviction about what he calls the facts of the matter in his belief box #1. If he would place it in his belief box #2, he would have to support his conviction by appealing to either the Restrictive or the Universalizability Principle. He cannot appeal to Universalizability and at the same time admit that he is participating in an interminable philosophical controversy. Just as neither side of an essentially contestable interpretation can be supported by Universalizability, neither side of an interminable controversy can be so supported. Since only the appeal to the Restrictive Principle is available, he must at least affirm his conviction by placing it in his belief box #1. Remember, he not only has an opinion, a persuasion, or a conviction about the matter; he also claims to know the facts of the matter. Does he know how to be wrong about these so-called facts of the matter? If he did, he would not enter the debate, and he would only report about it as a historian of philosophy. He can enter the debate only if he succeeds in convincing himself—without leaving room for being mistaken—that he has discovered either the decisive reasons and the conclusive arguments in support of one and only one side of the controversy, or its undecidability. His belief about what he calls the facts of the matter must be at least as privileged a belief as all other beliefs that are placed in his belief box #1. If he is right, then what was a philosophical controversy turns out to be a controversy among philosophers. If he is mistaken, his view will be just one link in the long chain of philosophers' views in the controversy. Either way, much is gained and little is lost by convincing himself—even at the cost of self-deception—that his belief about what he calls the facts of the matter is properly placed in his belief box #1.

Placing a belief in one's belief box #1 at the cost of self-deception may be considered too onerous. So, let us suppose that the road to self-deception outlined previously is mistaken. Notwithstanding the reasoning that led one philosopher to place his belief about what he calls the facts of the matter in a philosophical controversy in his belief box #1, another philosopher places her belief in a similar situation in her belief box #2. She can choose to support that belief by appealing to either the Universalizability or the Restrictive Principle. If she appeals to Universalizability, she must succeed in convincing herself that such an appeal can be reconciled with her knowledge that she is supporting either one and only one side of an interminable philosophical controversy or its undecidability. Self-deception has elastic limits, and it must be granted that she can convince herself that all reasonable and knowledgeable persons agree with her claim about what she calls the facts of the matter. If she appeals to the Restrictive Principle, she is required to believe that (1) all those who agree with her are both reasonable and knowledgeable about the issue. Philosophical argumentation requires that (2) arguments of both sides of an issue appeal not only to some but to all philosophers. Her placing her belief in box #2 requires that (3) she knows how to be wrong about her belief. Having satisfied all three requirements, she must convince herself that her reasons and arguments in support of her beliefs are better than what can be marshaled on behalf of contrary beliefs—otherwise, she would have no good reasons for entering the debate. She knows how to be wrong, yet she must insist that she is not wrong. If she convinces her opponents, then what was a philosophical controversy turns out to be a controversy among philosophers. If she fails to convince her opponents, she must reconcile her appeal to the Restrictive Principle with her philosophical argumentation. She must resolve the tension among three claims: (1) Her opponents are reasonable and knowledgeable, in accordance with the Restrictive Principle; (2) yet they did not yield to reasons and arguments that were addressed to all, in accordance with the requirement for argumentation in philosophy, (3) despite the fact that—at least in her judgment—her reasons and arguments were better than what was available elsewhere, for otherwise she would not have entered the debate.

The least interesting alternative for resolving the tension among the three claims is her withdrawal from the philosophical controversy. Another alternative is the replacement of her appeal to the Restrictive Principle with an appeal to Universalizability: she no longer needs to maintain that her opponents are both reasonable and knowledgeable about what is at issue. Although her conviction about what she calls the facts of the matter is in her belief box #2, she must maintain that all reasonable and knowledgeable persons agree with her. Self-deception would surely help in maintaining such a view in the context of an interminable philosophical controversy. The third alternative is that she holds on to all three claims simultaneously. The cost exacted for placing the belief about what one calls the facts of the matter in an interminable philosophical controversy in one's belief box #2 is the same as the price paid for placing it in one's belief box #1. Either way, the price is self-deception!

5. Deep or Subjunctive Mood Interpretation

In the light of the onerous price exacted for entering the debate on either side of an interminable controversy, the subsequent choices become clearer. We must now examine what is an available alternative to a given view. The reader will remember that this notion surfaces repeatedly in different contexts. We are expected to be tolerant of them, we are expected to examine them as professionals, and we are expected to reject them before adopting our own views. Who decides what is an available alternative view? Is phenomenalism an available alternative to philosophers who are convinced that they see physical objects—or the other way around? Is religious fundamentalism an available alternative for agnostics, or is agnosticism such an alternative to religious fundamentalists? No religious fundamentalist would agree that agnosticism is an available alternative view; nor would a convinced phenomenalist accept as an available alternative the view that we see physical objects directly and without the help of any intermediary. The interpreter of a given view must decide in any given case what is considered to be an available alternative. She must also decide— this is merely a repetition of what was said earlier—in any given case whether a natural interpretation in the subjunctive mood or a deep interpretation is appropriate. Although the interpreter must decide on these matters, this does not imply that she is free of any constraint. (For example, institutional constraints would prevent untenured teachers of philosophy from accepting the teachings of their favorite guru or public philosopher as an available alternative to the views of canonical figures in the history of philosophy or of academic philosophers.)

Suppose the interpreter—having entered the debate on one side of an interminable philosophical controversy—decides that her opponents' view is an available alternative to her view. In defending her own view she appeals to the Restrictive Principle. As mentioned previously, prudential considerations prompt such an appeal. After all, her primary goal is to convince her opponents. As a secondary benefit of her entering the debate, she is also preaching to the converted. As long as she expects to convince her opponents, she must either believe or make-believe that her opponents are just as reasonable and knowledgeable about what is at issue as all who agree with her view. She would not enter the debate unless she was convinced that the preponderance of the evidence is on her side of the issue. Since her reasons and arguments are addressed to all—in accordance with argumentation in philosophy—and if she does not convince her opponents, her choices are limited as long as she continues to participate in the debate. (Of course, she can withdraw from the debate at any time.) Either she no longer counts her opponents' views among the available alternatives to her own view (at the same time, her opponents cease to be valid conversation partners in a philosophical conversation concerning the case in point); or she questions their professional competence or personal integrity. In either case she must decide whether in interpreting her opponents' views she appeals to Universalizability and interprets their words in the subjunctive mood or she continues to appeal to the Restrictive Principle and provides a deep interpretation of their words. Either way, she will not understand her opponents' views as they understand their own views.

Her interpretation of her opponents' words and deeds in the context of this debate is initially an essentially contestable interpretation: what in their understanding is true is, according to her, false—or the other way around. But what starts as an essentially contestable interpretation need not continue to be such an interpretation. In some cases the disagreement will prompt her to end the engagement with her opponents' views. In her judgment, these views no longer count among the available alternatives to her own view, nor can their proponents be counted among those who are reasonable and knowledgeable about what is at issue. At this stage she no longer considers her understanding of their words and deeds as an essentially contestable interpretation. Henceforth, she supports her own view by appealing to Universalizability. Since her opponents' views are no longer among the available alternatives, they can be ignored. When searching for a reason why her opponents do not agree with her, she is free to question their professional competence or personal integrity.

In all other cases, she will continue the debate. Her understanding of her opponents' words and deeds continues to be an essentially contestable interpretation. She still hopes to convince her opponents, but at the same time she wishes to find reasons for their mistakes without attacking their professional competence or personal integrity. It would be a covert attack if she charged that they are just mistaken, or lying, or that they happen to hold a false belief. (Have they examined all available alternatives before adopting their own view?) Prudence suggests that she support her own view by appealing to the Restrictive Principle, thereby providing room for the claim that both she and her opponents are qualified interpreters. Although the appeal to the Restrictive Principle is merely a ruse in her own case—it permits her to continue the conversation with her opponents—it is a necessity when arguing with her opponents. After all, she cannot say to her opponents that they do not count among those who are reasonable and knowledgeable about what is at issue. As we saw previously, she can appeal to Universalizability in support of her own view and interpret her opponents' words in the subjunctive mood, if she questions their professional competence or personal integrity. Charging her opponents with self-deception is less offensive than questioning their professional competence or personal integrity. Having eliminated the more offensive charges, she can claim only that they are self-deceived.

I have argued that all deep interpretations are essentially contestable interpretations, and that deep interpretations are appropriate for interpreting others only if (natural) interpretations in the indicative or subjunctive mood are insufficient for the understanding of their words and deeds. Deep interpretations are required if, in the interpreter's judgment, the speaker is a victim of self-deception. Here I argue that as long as we continue the debate with our opponents in the context of an essentially contestable interpretation, and it is necessary to appeal to the Restrictive Principle in support of our understanding of their words and deeds, then our interpretation is a deep interpretation, and we, at least covertly, claim that they are victims of self-deception. There are good reasons for believing that all deep interpretations and only deep interpretations are essentially contestable interpretations.

6. Should We Appeal to Principles or to a Consensus?

An interpretation satisfying the normative and factual constraints on interpreting may be the best available for our purposes, but this does not imply that it is a good interpretation or that it will be the preferred interpretation at a later time. Even our successors who share our goals may prefer alternatives to the interpretations we defend. The theory of interpretation presented here is in this respect neither better nor worse than other theories. In other respects a comparison with alternative theories, such as consensus-driven theories, will be useful.

The unattractive features of the appeal to either of the principles are in evidence. We have seen that the appeal to Universalizability can easily yield intolerance. The appeal to the Restrictive Principle brings us close to charging others—or being charged by them—with self-deception. Also, the appeal to the Restrictive Principle often hides the interpreter's backstage appeal to Universalizability—a concession to tolerance at the cost of sincerity. Finally, it can be shown that our desire to steer by the Restrictive Principle can be easily defeated. For example, an interpreter suggests that all who agree with him must be counted among the qualified interpreters, but unbeknownst to him some unqualified interpreters also agree with him about the issues. This will prompt a retreat to a weakened form of the Restrictive Principle (see chapter 4). Instead of defending *all* interpreters who agree with him, he must retreat to the claim that *some* who agree with him are reasonable and knowledgeable about the issues. Can we consider the Restrictive Principle a good principle if it is so easily falsified? It may be a deficient principle, a principle only in scare quotes, yet—as our only candidate for an alternative to the appeal to Universalizability—it is an indispensable principle. For how long? As long as deep-level interpretations, supported by theories of deep interpretation, fail.

Consensus-driven interpretive theories are clearly alternatives to the principle-driven theory of interpretation presented here. To be sure, when searching for what is considered a standard interpretation about a topic in a given field, we often ask what is the consensus of professionals or experts in that field. Outside of our own field of expertise, we would not presume to rely on our own judgment in interpreting. Guided by those we consider experts in a given field, we accept the best available interpretation for our purposes. When we ask how consensus-driven interpretations fit with a view that recognizes only an appeal to Universalizability or to the Restrictive Principle, the answer is that such interpretations fit only with the weakened form of either of our principles. This answer is surprising, and if it is the right answer, it provides grounds for either dismissing or accepting a principle-driven theory of interpretation.

Consensus-driven theories derive the strength for standard interpretations from statistical or empirical data about the number of qualified interpreters who agree on a given interpretation. Since we cannot examine the views of all qualified interpreters, at best we can reach the conclusion that some qualified interpreters agree with a given interpretation. In other words, at the end of the statistical inquiry we arrive at the same result that has been reached by a defender of an eccentric interpretation. Earlier I have suggested: when a solitary interpreter defending an eccentric interpretation points to others in his surroundings and argues that they are qualified interpreters, he could just as well say: "Look here! I am not mad." Such a remark would be a gross misunderstanding when an interpreter appeals to the weakened form of one of the principles in the context of his search for a standard interpretation. An example will be useful here.

Suppose two interpreters reach incompatible interpretations on the same issue. A third interpreter could either dismiss both interpretations as irrelevant for his purposes or accept one of the two interpretations. He could support the accepted interpretation either by appealing to one of the two principles or by claiming that he is following a consensus of qualified interpreters. Assuming that in search of a standard interpretation he follows a consensus, he must satisfy a precondition: prior to counting the judgments of interpreters, he must decide if their judgments count. If he appeals to one of the two principles as originally stated, then he need not satisfy this precondition. He must satisfy it only if he appeals to the weakened form of one of the principles or to the consensus of interpreters. In either case, he will not choose to accept what *he* considers an eccentric interpretation: this would be incompatible with his search for a standard interpretation. Hence, we can always distinguish between two contexts of the appeal to a weakened form of either principle: the search for a standard interpretation and the defense of an eccentric interpretation.

It is possible that—contrary to my overconfident prediction in the previous paragraph—an interpreter does choose to accept what he considers an eccentric interpretation. Since this was *his* choice, we are entitled to understand his appeal to the weakened form of either principle as saying in other words what defenders of eccentric interpretations are saying by such an appeal: "Look here! I am not mad—others share my views." The case for a clear distinction between the two contexts of an appeal to the weakened form of either principle is thereby strengthened.

A first comparison between consensus-driven theories of interpretation with the principle-driven view presented here must point to the following:

1. Consensus-driven interpretations rely on a preliminary decision of counting only those qualified interpreters whose judgment counts. Interpretations incompatible with what is accepted by a consensus of interpreters must be considered only if this leads to a reexamination of the interpretive consensus.

2. Principle-driven interpretations are vulnerable to counterexamples. Interpreters appealing to Universalizability in support of an interpretation must be prepared to respond to the interpretation of every qualified interpreter who disagrees with the interpretation presented. Interpretations appealing to the Restrictive Principle in support of an interpretation must be prepared to withdraw to the weakened form of this principle if an unqualified interpreter happens to agree with the interpretation presented.

7. Conciliatory Remarks

It cannot be too strongly emphasized that ordinarily we understand each other as we wish to be understood. When asked to interpret another person's words or deeds, most often we are able to provide an interpretation that is consistent with that person's self-understanding. Our first suspicion that all is not well with our understanding of what was said arises when the content of what was said cannot be reconciled with facts that are known to us. It bears repeating that most often there are innocent explanations for what seems to be or is a discrepancy between what we know about the facts and our understanding of another person's words. For example: we were mistaken about what we claimed to be facts, we misunderstood what was said, they were mistaken about the facts, they were engaged in a make-believe game, or they were lying. The claim that they were victims of self-deception indicates that the more innocent explanations are insufficient. Theories of interpretation do not deserve a hearing if they suggest that we maintain a charge of self-deception in cases in which innocent explanations are available and preferable.

Popular wisdom recommends stock phrases to be used when we encounter opinions, beliefs, persuasions, and convictions that we do not share. Most often we do not engage others in discussing our disagreements. If we do engage them in a debate, we try to convince them that they are mistaken. We overtly charge them with insincerity only in exceptional cases, even when all innocent explanations have failed. Theories of interpretation must discuss such topics, for the covert charge of insincerity is important in trying to understand another person's words and deeds.

Depending on the circumstances, interpreters must choose and remain free to choose between a natural interpretation in the subjunctive mood and a deep interpretation. Occasionally the interpreters' choices will be contrary to what has been claimed here. Legislating every choice of every interpreter would be an exercise in futility. Yet what has been said here finds support in the explanations offered for a divergence from the view defended here. For example, one interpreter appeals to the Restrictive Principle in the context of a deep interpretation, although she is entitled to appeal to Universalizability in the context of an interpretation in the subjunctive mood. Explaining her choice, she argues that she was motivated by prudential considerations or by a desire to convince the speaker whose words she has interpreted. A second interpreter, entitled only to appeal to the Restrictive Principle, nonetheless appeals to Universalizability in the context of a deep interpretation, while claiming that the speaker whose words she interpreted is guilty of self-deception. Explaining her choice, she informs us that she was motivated by rhetorical considerations: in her judgment appealing to the Restrictive Principle is less persuasive and is less likely to bring about a change in the speaker's life than an appeal to Universalizability.

But let us set aside these explanations, and ask: can we reconcile two of my claims that seem to clash? I urge admitting the interpreters' freedom of choice between natural interpretation in the subjunctive mood and deep interpretation. I also argue that when interpreting others, an appeal to the Restrictive Principle is appropriate only in the context of deep interpretations. No doubt, prompted by prudence, or the desire to be persuasive, or by some other hidden—or not so hidden—agenda, interpreters occasionally appeal to one principle when an appeal to the other is more appropriate. In some cases the appeal to the less appropriate principle is insincere; these cases do not require detailed discussion. In all other cases, we must remember that the appeal to either of the two principles must be supported by good reasons—otherwise, the recommended interpretation falls short of the normative constraints on interpreting. Suppose one interpreter tried to support a natural interpretation in the subjunctive mood with the Restrictive Principle; this interpretation could be discredited—in accordance with the normative constraint on interpreting—by another interpreter providing the same interpretation supported by the stronger Universalizability Principle. Or suppose an interpreter tried to support a deep interpretation by appealing to Universalizability; this interpretation could be discredited as insincere by another interpreter providing the same interpretation supported by the weaker—but in this case more effective—Restrictive Principle, also in accordance with the normative constraint on interpreting. Even if interpreters occasionally appeal to the less appropriate of the two principles when interpreting others, the claim that the appeal to the Restrictive Principle is appropriate only in the context of deep interpretations is not an arbitrary stipulation.

Another matter requires explanation. I have argued that it is sufficient to support the content of our own belief box #1 by appealing to the Restrictive Principle. The reader may suggest supporting at least part of the content of our belief box #1 by appealing to Universalizability. Nothing is gained by adopting this suggestion. Essentially contestable beliefs and interpretations cannot be supported by Universalizability, and whatever can be so supported can be moved to our belief box #2. What we lose by adopting the reader's suggestion is our free choice between the two belief boxes. We would have no choice but placing only essentially contestable beliefs in our belief box #1 and placing all other beliefs in our belief box #2.

Yet if we maintain our free choice over the content of our own belief box #1 and support the contents of that belief box with the Restrictive Principle, then we must add a condition to our claim concerning the appropriateness of the appeal to that principle: the appeal to the Restrictive Principle is appropriate only in the context of deep interpretations, *when interpreting others*. Without that additional clause, we would be defending three jointly incompatible claims: (1) The appeal to the Restrictive Principle is appropriate only in the context of deep interpretations. (2) Deep interpretations imply overt or covert charges of self-deception. (3) We can entertain charges of self-deception about ourselves, but we cannot admit to such charges. With a condition added to the first claim—when interpreting others, the appeal to the Restrictive Principle is appropriate only in the context of deep interpretations—the three claims are no longer jointly incompatible. A secondary benefit of maintaining our free choice over the content of our belief box #1 is a constant reminder: when interpreting others, we appeal to the Restrictive Principle while implying charges of self-deception. Could it not be that the possibility of self-deception is ever present whenever we place a given belief in our belief box #1 and thereby claim it to be a privileged fact? Could it not be that the appeal to the Restrictive Principle about the contents of our own belief box #1 shares guilt by association with such an appeal when interpreting others? Appealing to the Restrictive Principle when interpreting others implies an overt or covert charge of self-deception; appealing to the same principle when trying to understand ourselves serves as a welcome reminder that even in our own case we should at least entertain the possibility of being self-deceived. The intellectual advantage of such a reminder of philosophical skepticism cannot be overestimated.

CHAPTER SEVEN

Grasping, Understanding, and Interpreting

1. Understanding and Translating

When interpreting and translating for another person, we provide understanding of what was said or written. The two activities are in some respects similar, yet their differences are sufficiently large to argue that each activity has its own unique characteristics. However, most people assume interpreting and translating are one and the same. A pretheoretical and false claim about translating is often extended to interpreting. We are told that the French sentence "Elle travaille avec son père" can be translated into the English sentence "She works with her father," because they have the same meaning. But how do we compare the meaning of the French sentence with the meaning of the English sentence? A French speaker may say, " 'Elle travaille avec son père' veut dire qu'elle travaille avec son père." An English speaker may say, " 'She works with her father' means that she works with her father." But how can we infer from what the French and the English speakers said that " 'Elle travaille avec son père' means that she works with her father"? We cannot, for the sentence between the quotation marks could be false or meaningless. If you admit that an English sentence may contain a clause in French, then the sentence could be false, for the French sentence could also mean that she works with *his* father. If you don't admit that an English sentence can contain a clause in French, then the sentence is meaningless.

Translating relies on a guiding principle: what can be said in one natural language can be said in any other natural language. Since we do not know how to argue for this principle, we must stipulate it and be prepared to withdraw it in the unlikely event that we are provided with a counterexample. This principle does not imply that we can always translate what was said in another language. At issue is not the trivial claim that in distant times or places there were no words for "Holy Ghost" or "neutrino"—missionaries or physicists could be trusted to introduce these words into the natives' language, while providing instruction in religion or physics. A more important claim is under consideration: not everything that relates what has been said in another natural language counts as a translation of what has been said in that language. A case in point is the problem of translating self-referential sentences.* As we shall see, a translation problem arises even in the context of referential sentences.

Suppose we find a sample sentence, "Apjával dolgozik," in a Hungarian textbook, and our task is to translate that sentence into German, French, and English. We will notice that such translations are not transitive.

(1) Apjával dolgozik.

(2) German	*(3) French*	*(4) English*
(a) Er arbeitet mit seinem Vater.	(a) Il travaille avec son père.	(a) He works with his father.
(b) Er arbeitet mit ihrem Vater.	(b) Il travaille avec son père.	(b) He works with her father.
(c) Sie arbeitet mit seinem Vater.	(c) Elle travaille avec son père.	(c) She works with his father.
(d) Sie arbeitet mit ihrem Vater.	(d) Elle travaille avec son père.	(d) She works with her father.

Every sentence labeled "(a)" is a translation of two other sentences labeled "(a)"; the same is true of sentences labeled "(b)," "(c)," and "(d)." These tables would be larger if we tried to remove all ambiguities, or if we tried to emphasize the progressive aspect of the activity. (For example, 4(d) is ambiguous as to whether the subject works with her own father or with another woman's father; "He is working with his father" and analogous sentences in German and French emphasize the progressive aspect of the collaboration.) Also, since 3(a) is identical with 3(b), and 3(c) is identical with

---

* See W. D. Hart, "On Self-Reference," *Philosophical Review* vol. 79 (1970): 523–28 and Tyler Burge, "Self-Reference and Translation," in *Meaning and Translation*, ed. F. Guenther and M. Guenther-Reutter (New York: New York University Press, 1978), 137–53.

3(d), four German, two French, and four English sentences are correct translations of the Hungarian sentence (1). No doubt, some information provided by these ten sentences is lost when they are translated into Hungarian, yet the Hungarian sentence is a correct translation of each of these sentences. Hence, translations on this model are symmetrical. But while 3(a) is a correct translation of 2(b), and 4(a) is a correct translation for 3(a), 4(a) is unacceptable as a translation of 2(b). Hence, translations on this model are not transitive. This model will be called the first model of translation.

Translations on the first model are symmetrical as I have said, yet some information is lost when the German, French, or English sentences are translated into Hungarian. Isn't there a tension between these two claims? Or, to put it less politely: isn't there a contradiction between these two claims? There is indeed, and for this reason I will introduce a second model of translation. On this model, translations are neither symmetrical nor transitive. Even before providing details about this model, I hasten to add that professional translators would not admit it as a translation model. (I am grateful to Professor Ágnes Erdélyi for demonstrating the scope and limits of this model.) Now for the details. The rules of grammar constrain the information provided by the four sentences in these four languages. Except when indicating special significance, the personal pronoun is not used in Hungarian; the possessive pronoun appears as an inflection of the noun designating the subject of the sentence; finally, all pronouns are gender neutral. Personal pronouns in German and French follow the same gender rules as in English. In German, possessive pronouns satisfy the same gender rules as in English, but in French, the gender of the possessive pronouns must agree with the gender of the noun designating the object possessed. The information derived from the gender of the possessive pronoun in 2(d) and 4(d) can be provided by the sentences surrounding the French sentence 3(d). Similarly, the information available from the gender of the personal and possessive pronouns in 2(c) and 4(c) can be provided by the sentences surrounding the Hungarian sentence (1).

Suppose a translator insists on providing the same information in one Hungarian sentence that is embedded in 2(c) or 4(c). Let us call that sentence (1'). (For Hungarian readers it would be superfluous to write out this sentence; for non-Hungarian readers it would be senseless.) An English translation of (1') is sufficient for showing its problematic character as a translation of 2(c) or 4(c): "That girl (or woman) works with the father of a boy (or a man)." Professional translators would admit that (1') provides the same information as 2(c) or 4(c), yet they would reject it as a relevant translation of the German or English sentences because such a translation is not even symmetrical; and except for poetry, symmetry is a necessary condition for the acceptability of translations. If (1') were offered as a translation of 2(c) or 4(c), we could not derive from (1') a German or English translation that would be sufficiently close to 2(c) or 4(c). Professional translators would suggest that (1') *says* what is said in 2(c) or 4(c), but it is not a translation of the German or English sentence indicated. (It will be shown later that (1') is not an interpretation of the indicated sentences either.) They would agree that the second model is useful in preparing for a translation, for it says in the target language what has been said in the source language. But the preparatory work for a translation is unacceptable for it to be a translation.

However, the same Hungarian sentence (1) can be used to make a statement in a real-life situation about individuals known to both the speaker and his audience. The third model of translation emerges in this context. Suppose that the Hungarian sentence refers to a woman who works with her half brother's father, and the translated sentences are expected to preserve references to the same persons; then only the following sentences are acceptable as translations of the Hungarian sentence:

(1) Apjával dolgozik.

(2) German	*(3) French*	*(4) English*
(c) Sie arbeitet mit seinem Vater.	(c) Elle travaille avec son père.	(c) She works with his father.

Sentences 2(c), 3(c), and 4(c) are correct translations of (1), for they pick out the same individual and say about her what is said in (1). Such translations are transitive. It would not make much sense to wonder or to ask whether the statement "She works with his father" means or says the same as that she works with his father. But it certainly makes sense to ask whether (1) means or says the same as 2(c) or 3(c) or 4(c) in the specific circumstances we have supposed. If we correctly answer that the four sentences make the same statement, we must explain: what is the difference among these four sentences? Frege answered similar questions by referring to *die Art des Gegebenseins*, the mode of presentation of the same fact or the same state of affairs. In the specific circumstances we have assumed, each of these four sentences replicates in a given language what the other three sentences mean or say in each of the other three languages; moreover, none of the other seven sentences—2(a), 2(b), 2(d), 3(a), 4(a), 4(b), and 4(d)—can be used to say or mean what is said in (1).

Accordingly, if we agree with the professional translators and set aside the second model of translation, two ways of understanding translations are at our disposal. One is appropriate when translating sample sentences in books about learning a second language. The referring expressions in these sample sentences do not pick out individuals known to the speaker and his audience, and they do not state what is true (or false) about these individuals. Target-language sentences become candidates for translating source-language sentences if it is at least possible for the target-language sentence to pick out the same individuals and to say about them what the source-language sentence says. If we focus exclusively on such translations, we will find it difficult to resist the claim that a given target-language sentence is a correct translation of a source-language sentence if and only if the two sentences have the same sense or the same meaning. As soon as we speak about sentences that in one language have the same or different sense or meaning as sentences in another language, we find that we are committed to the existence of whatever is designated by such words as "sense" or "meaning." But even if we admit the existence of such objects, it is not quite clear how we establish that (1) has the same sense or meaning as the ten other sentences listed in three languages. Are multilinguists expected to inspect these senses or meanings while they are detached from their linguistic expressions, and establish whether they do or do not find them identical? Multilinguists cannot satisfy such expectations. At best, they can claim that whenever (1) is used in Hungarian, 2(a)-2(d) would be used in German, 3(a) or 3(c) in French, and 4(a)-4(d) in English. Even if they add that all these sentences have the same sense or meaning, the reference to a sense or meaning does not do any work—it is idle.

Real-life situations are paradigmatic for the second way of understanding translations. Statements about objects or concepts are translated most often for the benefit of someone unfamiliar with the source language. Suppose (1) "Apjával dolgozik" refers to Pillangó Mária, who happens to work with her half brother's father, Rikkantó János. The multilinguist provides information about this fact to a listener who does not know Hungarian but is familiar with German, French, or English. The translations provided by 2(c), 3(c), or 4(c) preserve the references to Pillangó Mária and Rikkantó János and say about them exactly what is said in (1). Accordingly, all four sentences make the same statements and have the same truth-value. Only the mode of presentation of the same fact is different in the four languages. Unless we are burdened by a philosophical view—independently of the issue discussed here—requiring intermediary objects, such as a sense or a meaning to mediate between statements and what they are about, we have no reason to believe that such a detour is needed when we translate from a source language to a target language. The multilinguist grasps directly what is said in any of these four languages, just as the monoglot understands directly what is said in his native language. Only the mode of presentation of the same fact is different in all four languages.

Provided that the four sentences refer to the same individuals, and state the same fact about them, each of the four sentences is an exact translation of each of the other three. Translations so understood are symmetrical, transitive, and partially reflexive. (Partial reflexivity is a logical consequence of symmetry and transitivity.) A translation that has these three properties establishes an identity between the statements made by the source and the target-language sentences. The multilinguist's task is to find a sentence in the target language that provides for the monoglot in that language the same information that is provided by the source-language sentence, while respecting the rules of grammar of the target language.

The multilinguist uses any of the four sentences to record her grasping of the fact that Pillangó Mária works with her half brother's father, Rikkantó János. After grasping that fact, she is in a different state from before; she understands now what she did not understand before. If the multilinguist switches to one of the other three languages in order to provide information to a monoglot, she replaces the source-language sentence with one of the other three target-language sentences. Before being provided with the required information, the monoglot in one of these four languages is in the same situation as our remote Babylonian ancestor who either asked or wondered whether Hesperus is the same heavenly body as Phosphorus. The monoglot may also ask or wonder whether (1) makes the same statement as 2(c), 3(c), or 4(c).

The first and third models of translation are idealized versions that permit us to become clearer about grasping and understanding what has been said. But I must add: adopting real-life situations as models for translations—a multilinguist provides information about one and the same individual for monoglots in another language—does not make many problems connected with modes of presentation any easier to understand. For example, having read some articles in German by John Maynard Keynes on economics, and other articles in French by John Maynard Keynes on probability theory, I came to believe when I was a student that the economist Keynes was different from the probability theorist Keynes. English readers of Keynes's articles on two subjects can replicate such confusion. The fact that the articles on different subjects were in different languages probably had a marginal role in determining the relatively long time it took for my becoming aware of the confusion. Other examples show that switching from one language to another plays an essential role in problems about modes of presentation. Saul Kripke's example of luckless Pierre who does not know that "London" refers to the same city as "Londres" is at times replicated in the experience of multilinguists. For example, the title of the movie *Sunshine* is a partial translation of its Hungarian title, *A napfény íze.* (The full translation would be "The Taste of Sunshine.") Yet after reading approximately twelve articles in Hungarian about a movie referred to by its Hungarian title, and two articles in English about a movie referred to by its English title, I did not know—even after seeing that movie—that the articles in both languages referred to the same movie. Leibniz's law applies to the third model of translations: if Z is a translation of Y, and Y is a translation of X, and the translations are symmetrical and transitive, then if F is an intrinsic property of what is designated by the use of the referring expressions in X, it is also an intrinsic property of what is designated by the use of the referring expressions in Z and Y. ("Intrinsic" does the work of excluding irrelevant counterexamples; for instance, from "John is thinking *de dicto* about what is designated in X" we cannot conclude that "John is thinking *de dicto* about what is designated in Z or Y.") The fact that Leibniz's law applies to this model of translations does not entail that a monoglot is aware of the fact that Z or Y is a translation of X. It is more surprising—nonetheless true—that a bilingual speaker of the two languages can be unaware of the translation relation between Z or Y and X.

2. Modes of Presentation

In discussing a model of translations that is symmetrical, transitive, and partially reflexive, I have avoided talking about senses or meanings. We would lose all the advantages we have gained so far if we followed Frege in identifying modes of presentations with senses. We need not do so. For Frege, coreferential terms have different senses—a sense is an abstract, nonmental object. He argued that if it were a mental object, we could not understand how the members of a jury could agree or disagree on finding a defendant innocent or guilty. By stipulating that senses are publicly available abstract objects, he solved this problem at the cost of reifying the senses of expressions. No doubt, the reader may find it necessary to assume that senses have their permanent abode in some Platonic heaven. But the reader's reasons for this assumption are independent of the requirements of translating, for the reference to a sense is idle while we are engaged in translating.

What was said in the source language is literally gibberish for a monoglot in the target language until she is provided with a translation. We must focus on this triviality if we wish to understand what motivates the value placed on sense in talking about translations. From the monoglot's viewpoint, the foreigner, the barbarian, and the linguistic outsider speak gibberish. She wants to make sense of what they say, but this does not imply that she wants to know the sense or meaning of the sentences in the foreigner's language. As a matter of fact, given favorable circumstances she could even provide us with that sense or meaning without her understanding a single word of what she was saying. (Sopranos or tenors who sing entire stanzas in a language they do not understand nonetheless convey what they are singing to their audiences who understand that language.) She is not engaged in a translation exercise that falls under the first model of translation. What she wants to know falls under the second or third model of translation. A purely syntactic specification of what was said in the source language is sufficient in these two models. Such a specification enables a bilingual speaker in the source and target languages to provide the required information for a monoglot in the target language.

The need for talking about senses or meanings as abstract objects arises if we sever the connection between the sentences that are used to make statements and the objects or concepts that are talked about in these statements. It is misleading to claim that translations are grounded on the following three steps. (1) A monoglot of the source language says p. (2) A bilingual speaker asserts that p in the source language means the same as q in the target language. (3) Based on what she was told by the bilingual speaker, the monoglot of the target language accepts the claim that q is a translation of p. We are further misled if we add to the second step that an interpretation is the ground of the bilingual speaker's claim that p in one language means the same as q in the other. No doubt, in some cases these steps correctly describe the way information is conveyed from a monoglot in one language to a monoglot in another language. Such a description can be fitted to the first model, but it is insufficient for the second and third models of translation.

A better description of translations becomes available if we retain the connection between what is said and what is talked about. On this assumption, translating is grounded on the following three steps. (1) In saying that p, a monoglot makes a statement in the source language about what is being referred to in that statement. (2) A bilingual speaker grasps p and replaces it with q, a statement in the target language that refers to what is being referred to in p and says about it what is said in p. (3) Informed of q, a monoglot of the target language grasps what is referred to and said in q. In these three steps, the two monoglots and the bilingual speaker grasp one and the same fact. How do they grasp a fact? We may not be able to provide a satisfactory answer to this question, but what the monoglots and the bilingual speaker say provides sufficient evidence that they have grasped one and the same fact. If we examined the reactions of the three speakers, we could demonstrate that they have grasped the same fact and as a result now understand what was at issue.

The second and third models of translation rely on the bilingual speaker for conveying to the monoglot in the target language all the relevant information that has been provided to her by the monoglot in the source language. As mentioned before, professional translators accept the second model only for the purpose of guiding the preparatory work for a translation. The third model requires that the translator provide a grammatically correct target-language sentence that can be used for saying what was said by using the source-language sentence. As another part of the preparatory work for such a translation, we may assume a dialogue between the translator and the monoglot in the source language. In this dialogue the translator is provided with all the relevant information for her translation. She could even take a further step and test her proposed translation in a second dialogue with the monoglot in the target language. Does it convey the same information that the monoglot of the source language provided? Unless it contains the same relevant information, the translation is not suitable for replicating what was said in the source language. The point of the translation is the replacement of the source-language text by the target-language text, and only translations that are both symmetrical and transitive can be substituted for what was said in the source language. What is relevant information in one context may not be relevant in another. The translator must rely on her own judgment for deciding what information is relevant in order to provide a sentence in the target language that is suitable for replacing what is said in the source language.

I have suggested that in specific circumstances 2(c), 3(c), and 4(c) are correct translations of (1). Since in the same circumstances these translations are symmetrical and transitive, each of these four sentences is a translation of the other three. A slight change in the circumstances surrounding the example can render one of these translations inadequate, however. For instance, if in our example the Hungarian, German, or English speaker has been informed by the sentences surrounding the translation that Pillangó Mária works with the father of a man, but the monoglot French speaker has not been provided with this information that is considered relevant, then 3(c), "Elle travaille avec son père," must be rejected as an inadequate translation of the other three sentences; the gender of the possessive pronoun in 3(c) does not contain information about the gender of the person designated by that pronoun.

When translators accept the guiding principle of translations—what can be said in one natural language can be said in any other natural language—

they must make every effort to provide translations that are symmetrical and transitive. They may not succeed in their task, but unless they reject the guiding principle, they are committed to the claim that such a translation is available—it is always available in principle, but not always in fact. The preparatory work necessary for a translation cannot be always completed. Concerning documents, translators are seldom able to consult with the documents' authors about the relevant information for the translation. Unable to ascertain the facts of the matter, they are forced to interpret. It is for lack of relevant information that interpreting gains a foothold in the translating activity. Before discussing this topic, two objections must be answered.

I spoke about syntactically specified modes of presentation that permit a monoglot in the target language to grasp what has been said in the source language and thereby to grasp the same fact as the monoglot in the source language and the bilingual translator. The point of his grasping that fact is understanding what is at issue. As a result of understanding the issue, he is in a different state than before. Some readers may say that "grasping" is a metaphorical expression and that its repeated use does not explain how we came to understand what we did not previously understand. The answer is that it is at least uncertain whether "grasping" is a metaphor. If it is a metaphor, it stands for many other metaphors that describe our getting hold of some facts, hooking onto what is the case, and their cognates. If there are literal expressions that do the same work, I would be glad to replace "grasping" with that expression.

The second objection concerns the transitivity requirement in translation. From the viewpoint of the monoglot in the target or the source language, whether a given translation is transitive is irrelevant. The monoglot in the target language may be concerned with the symmetry of the translation, for he wants to be sure that the monoglot in the source language understands the same facts that he understood; but why should either monoglot be concerned with the transitivity of the translation?

The answer is that they need not be concerned with transitivity. This is only the translator's or the multilinguist's concern. As mentioned earlier, translations that have the properties of symmetry and transitivity establish an identity between the statements made by the source and target language sentences. Professional translators ordinarily avoid translating into a third language a text that is itself a translation from another language. If the translator had evidence that her translation from the source to the target language satisfied the third model of translation, then not only would she have proof of its adequacy, but she would also have an additional warrant for her translation. Such evidence could serve as a satisfactory basis for a translation into a third language.

3. Interpreting

Both translating and interpreting lead to the understanding of what has been said. Except for this goal they do not have much in common. Facts are at the center of adequate translations. The content and the truth-value of what has been said in one language must be preserved by the translation in another language. By contrast, facts appear only beyond the limits of adequate interpretations. To be sure, interpretations must be consistent with the facts that are known to the interpreter, and interpretations are guided by the facts but do not describe facts. The proponents and defenders of interpretations may hold their recommended interpretations to be true. Yet if they were true, they would be descriptions of facts rather than interpretations. Translating and interpreting are not different aspects of the same activity. No doubt, interpretations are often embedded in translations, and the examination of a difficult text's translations is always useful for an interpreter. How did the translators of Kant or Joyce understand the difficult passages in the writings of these authors? The translators' understanding of these passages provides a clue to their interpretations, and these become useful even for interpreters who do not need the translations.

Interpreting does not enter the translating activity as long as facts are available to the translator. She is not engaged in interpreting if she follows the second model of translating and is able to relate in the target language what has been said in the source language. If she has grasped the relevant factual content of all that has been said in the source language, and only that content is talked about in her translation, then there is no need for an additional interpretation. The need for an interpretation arises if she did not understand part of the relevant factual content of what has been said in the source language. How could she translate it if she did not understand it? Her lack of understanding shows up as a gap in the seemingly seamless web of what has been said in the source language. The gap may be due to an obscurity in the text: readers of difficult passages in philosophical or literary texts at times have the impression that not only they do not know what the author wanted to say, but that the author himself did not know what he wanted to say. Intralanguage interpreters can easily hide their lack of understanding: instead of reporting about a given passage in indirect speech, they can reproduce it between quotation marks. Translators cannot hide so easily either the shortcomings of the source-language text or their own failure in understanding that text.

Interpretations in the context of translations are prompted by a gap in the translator's knowledge. If she is aware of the gap, the interpretation is arrived at deliberately and is grounded on the available information. If she is unaware of the gap, she may not even realize that her translation was grounded on an interpretation. For example, if a bilingual speaker who is ignorant of the earlier specified circumstances were asked to translate 3(c), "Elle travaille avec son père," into English, she would answer 4(c), "She works with his father," without realizing that her answer presupposes an interpretation. Another interpretation would have prompted her to answer 4(d), "She works with her father." As mentioned earlier, the preparatory work required for a translation in the context of documents cannot always be completed. The translator ordinarily learns about the facts described in a document from that document and from its historical or cultural context. If she had more evidence about those facts, she could provide a translation that falls under the third model of translation. For lack of relevant information, she must interpret. She could be a conscious or an unaware interpreter. After reflecting on the surrounding sentences, she could decide whether 3(c) should be translated into English as 4(c) or 4(d); or she could choose one of the two English sentences without any reflection. If she is a conscious interpreter, she will try to find plausible interpretations for filling the gaps in the relevant information that is provided by the document she is translating. As long as the Universalizability Principle can support her interpretations, her translation will be accepted as falling under the third model of translation. If they cannot be so supported, her translation will be accepted only as falling under the first model of translation. Under this model, she need not even grasp what has been said in the source language about the facts in order to produce a translation. She can approach her task as if she were translating sentences from a source-language exercise book. For such purposes, 4(d) and 3(c) are acceptable translations of each other, for it is at least possible that in a real-life situation these sentences could be used to state the same facts in English and French. The adequacy standards of such translations are quite low. They are produced by translators who are insufficiently informed about the subject matter of the writings they are translating.

We raise these standards if we insist that translations must satisfy the third model of translation. In accordance with this model, translations are expected to provide the monoglot in the target language the same relevant information of what has been said that is available to the monoglot in the source language. Especially concerning documents, this places an added burden on the translator. Her judgment is required for deciding what information is relevant for inclusion in her translation. Her understanding of the source-language text, her interpretation of the difficult passages in that text, and her knowledge of its subject matter ordinarily support her judgment. Her critics will judge her translation to be adequate if she convinces them that she has conveyed in the target language the same relevant information about the facts that were available in the source language, and that the interpretations recommended for filling the gaps in the document can be supported by the Universalizability Principle.

4. Paraphrases

It is a widely held and firmly entrenched belief that every translation presupposes interpretation. The reader who shares this belief will object to the views presented here by directing attention to the second model of translation. On that model, the translator says in the target language what has been said in the source language, without even attempting to provide a translation that is symmetrical. If she did not translate into the target language and only reported in indirect speech what had been said in the source language, we would claim that as long as she did not quote directly the words of others, she offered a paraphrase of what had been said. Such intralanguage paraphrases often serve for testing students about their understanding of the material that was presented to them, and paraphrases rely—at least partially, if not always—on interpretations. If intralanguage paraphrases rely on interpretations, then by parity of reasoning, interlanguage paraphrases must also rely on interpretations. Translations on the second model of translation are interlanguage paraphrases. So how can we argue that they do not rely on interpretations?

Attention to the presuppositions of paraphrases is required for discussing the role of interpretations in translations. No doubt, grasping what has been said or written—at least partially—is a necessary condition for producing its adequate paraphrase. If the objector believes that grasping and subsequent understanding of what has been said always presupposes its interpretation, then paraphrases indeed presuppose interpretations. If we accept this view, our notions of interpreting and interpretations would become oceanic to the point that they would be useless. By contrast, if the use of the notions of interpreting and interpretation is restricted to the cases in which they are needed, then it must be admitted that interpretation occasionally plays a role in paraphrasing, but it is not its presupposition. Paraphrases are expected to provide significant and important information of what has been said or written. For example, if a novice provided us with a paraphrase of every sentence in one section of Kant's or Joyce's text, we would not be sure that he understood what was said in these texts. We would fault him for not having a principle of selection that permitted him to single out what is significant and important. We would fault him for not bringing enough to these texts, for not interpreting them sufficiently, and for not making them sufficiently perspicuous prior to producing a paraphrase. But if an expert on Kant or Joyce offered a paraphrase of every sentence in a difficult passage in these texts and commented on every sentence of her paraphrase, we would evaluate the contributions of her interpretations to our understanding of these texts, and if successful, gratefully acknowledge such a contribution. In one case we deplore the lack of interpretation prior to a paraphrase; in the other case we applaud the role that interpretation plays in a paraphrase. But in both cases interpretation, or its lack, is judged in its own right and in response to a need to understand better rather than as a presupposition of a paraphrase.

If monoglots grasp what was said or written and paraphrase it, they are not always interpreting. Similarly, if in the home language a paraphrase is available to the bilingual speaker without interpreting, she can also provide a paraphrase in a second language without interpreting. The need for an interpretation arises when mutually exclusive alternative paraphrases are at least plausible. If the facts determine a paraphrase, then there is no need for an interpretation. Interpretations are needed if the facts merely guide but do not determine a paraphrase and if different interpretations supporting different paraphrases are plausible. What has been said or written must be grasped and at least partially understood for it to be a paraphrase or translation. We value paraphrases and translations only if they contain the significant and important information contained in the texts paraphrased or translated. How much detailed information must be included in a paraphrase? What information is sufficiently significant for inclusion in a translation? These questions are answered differently in each case. If in a given case the facts leave open more than one plausible answer to these questions, then that paraphrase or translation relies on an interpretation.

5. Deficient Understanding

Translations on the second and third model require understanding; translations on the first model can be produced even with a deficient understanding of what is at issue. Translators have learned from their patron saint, St. Hieronymus: he admitted that he did not understand the Book of Ezekiel—so, he proceeded to translate it *verbum a verbo*. A word-for-word translation provided by a bilingual speaker who understands every word of a source-language text without understanding the content of that text is certainly possible. Such a translation can provide understanding of that text to others who are unfamiliar with the source language. After finishing the translation, the translator himself can come to understand it, even if he could not understand it while it was in preparation. Philosophers often suggest that their classicist colleagues translated the writings of Plato or Aristotle without understanding them. Readers of the classicists or St. Hieronymus's translations succeeded in making sense of what they read. As long as a translation satisfies the minimal standards of translations on the first model, it conveys sufficient information to readers ignorant of the source language for a rudimentary understanding of the source-language text's content. The translators' understanding of the source-language texts may have been deficient, and upon reading the translations, the readers' understanding of that text's content may have been rudimentary. Yet translators and readers learn to understand these texts as soon as they become more familiar with their topics.

It would be desirable if translators were experts not only in both the source and target languages, but also in the subject matter of their translations. Since the target language is ordinarily their native language, translators usually satisfy one of these three conditions. Often they learn about the other two conditions, the subject matter and the source language, while they are engaged in translating. Infrequently they may be deficient in the subject matter and in both languages. Nonetheless, they are capable of preparing an adequate translation. For example, curious schoolboys trying to translate Ovid's *Ars Amandi* into their native language must overcome deficiencies in all three contexts. They must learn Latin, learn the vocabulary in their native language that is relevant to the subject matter, and become acquainted with an unfamiliar subject matter. How do they succeed in overcoming their deficiencies? To the extent that they are unaware of the facts, they rely on interpreting for filling the gaps in their knowledge.

As we have seen, translations on the second model are not symmetrical. They rely on understanding of what has been said and provide its paraphrase. By contrast, translations on the first model are symmetrical, yet they are compatible with a deficient understanding of what has been said. In preparing such translations, the translator—he need not yet be a bilingual speaker—makes use of dictionaries, grammar books, and other sources of information that may be helpful in this task. He is not engaged in the same kind of real-life situation as a translator on the second or the third model of translation. His situation is comparable to that of a student who is engaged in learning a second language. He tries to replace words or sentences in one language with words or sentences in another language. In replacing, for example, 3(a), "Il travaille avec son père," with 4(a), "He

works with his father," he does not know who is designated by the personal
and the possessive pronouns in the source language. For all he knows, these
are just sample sentences and no one is designated by these pronouns. He
can only claim that if one or more persons are referred to by the pronouns
in the source language and something is said about them, then it is at least
possible that the same persons would be referred to by the pronouns in the
target language and the same thing would be said about them.

Bilingual speakers in the source and target languages can always improve
on translations on the first model. Relying on the translator's spadework,
the translator's critic can often reach a better understanding of the texts in
both languages than the translator. Unless the translator himself assumes
the role of a critic at a later time, the critic enjoys an advantage over the
translator, for the critic can always ask: was it a result of interpretation that
3(a), "Il travaille avec son père," was translated as 4(a), "He works with his
father"? Shouldn't we entertain the interpretive hypothesis that 4(b), "He
works with her father," is the correct translation? Perhaps other interpretive hypotheses must be accounted for, such as "He works with his own
father," or "He works with someone else's father," or "He is working with
his own father." Such variants are always available. As soon as a variant is
seriously entertained and the critic compares her interpretive hypothesis
with the translator's hypothesis, she tries to discover whether there are facts
of the matter that decide the issue. If there are such facts, then one variant
is accepted, while all others are rejected. What starts as a translation on the
first model becomes a translation on the third model. If there are no such
facts, then the most plausible interpretation will support one variant over
all others. But if a translation is supported by an interpretation rather than
a fact, then there is a gap in our knowledge of the facts, and that gap is the
same in the source and the target language. For example, if a monoglot
French speaker cannot inform us whether in a real-life situation the possessive pronoun in 3(c), "Elle travaille avec son père," refers to a man or a
woman, then his understanding of that situation is just as deficient as the
translator's who cannot determine whether 4(c), "She works with his
father," or 4(d), "She works with her father," would be appropriate.

Translations on the first model need not be as well anchored to the
objects, concepts, and states of affairs of the world in which we live as the
texts they are translations of. When it is said, "Something was lost in the translation," it is suggested that significant information that was available to the
monoglot in the source language has not been conveyed to the monoglot in
the target language. By transforming a first-model translation into a third-
model translation—a transformation that is available at least in principle, if
not in fact—the translator conveys to the monoglot in the target language

the same information that was available to the monoglot in the source language. The monoglot in the target language is now able to grasp the same facts and to achieve the same understanding as the monoglot in the source language and as the bilingual speaker in both languages.

6. Are Interpretations Intralanguage Translations?

It is misleading to think about interpretations as intralanguage translations if the notion of an intralanguage translation is formed by analogy to interlanguage translations, for the supposed analogy does not yield understanding of the scope and limits of interpretations. Interlanguage translations are governed by the grammatical rules of the source and target languages. Because of discordant grammatical rules, information available to the source-language speakers is unavailable to the target-language speakers. For this reason, I have argued that if we wish to respect the conventions of translating and provide the same information in the target language that is available in the source language, we must choose the third model of translation. Since all of this is irrelevant when we speak about intralanguage translations, the notion of intralanguage translation does not seem to be useful in illuminating interpretations.

The reader may object: the ordinarily accepted proximity of interpreting and translating suggests the contrary of my view. The short answer is that unless I am provided with instruction on how interpreting can be understood better in the reflected light of intralanguage translating, I cannot agree with the objector. Independently of any analogy between translating and interpreting, I would argue that we do not engage in either activity in order to discover the meaning of what another speaker has said. Just as the reference to a sense or a meaning is idle when we are translating, so it is when we are interpreting. This view does not rely on any alleged analogy between translating and interpreting. The need for an interpretation arises because from the listener's viewpoint there is a gap between what has been said and his understanding of what has been said. Guided by common sense the interpreter attributes reasons to the speaker's or agent's words and deeds. Interpreters make sense of what has been said, and if they are sincere, the point of their activity is to provide others with the same understanding of what has been said (or done) as they possess.

The longer answer to the reader's objection requires that we become clear about the claim that when interpreting or translating we do not discover the meaning or the sense of what another speaker has said—we make sense of what he has said. A comparison between two views will be helpful in explaining this point. Ulrich von Wilamowitz-Moellendorff, Nietzsche's conservative opponent and a leading classical philologist of his age, wrote the following on translating: "*Das Kleid muss neu werden, sein Inhalt bleiben. Jede rechte Übersetzung is Travestie. Noch schärfer gesprochen, es bleibt die Seele aber sie wechselt den Leib: die wahre Übersetzung ist Metempsychose.*" ("The clothing must become new, its content remain the same. Every correct translation is a change of costume. Speaking more pointedly, the soul remains but the body changes: the true translation is metempsychosis.")* In this view, the translator must "carry" the meaning of a sentence from the source to the target language. As an etymological ground for this view it is usually pointed out that in many languages the words for the translating activity ("translation," "*translatio,*" "*Übertragung,*" "*traduction,*" "*átvitel*") suggest the carrying of a load from one place to another. If meanings could be identified independently of words or sentences in a language, we could speak about carrying the meaning of a word or a sentence from one language to another. For those of us who cannot identify a soul independently of a body, the concept of metempsychosis is just as confusing as the concept of translation grounded on etymology.

Meaning realism, or the view that meanings are real independently of words or sentences in a given language, is rejected by most contemporary philosophers. On this point there is agreement among many philosophers of both the analytical and the Continental European philosophical traditions. Contemporary philosophers in the analytical tradition have learned from Wittgenstein, Quine, and Davidson that in translating or interpreting we do not discover the sense of what was said or done; we make sense of it; we attribute to it a sense. Davidson's remark against meaning realism contains one of the clearest statements on this topic:

> . . . when we learn or discover what words mean, the process of learning is *bestowing* on words whatever meaning they have for the learner. It's not as though words have some wonderful thing called a meaning to which those words have somehow become attached, and the learning process is just putting us in touch with that meaning. What the teacher may well think of as a matter of bringing the learner into step with society is, from the learner's point of view, giving the word what meaning it has. The appreciation of this point, and of its consequences, constitutes the biggest forward step in our understanding of language since the onset of the "linguistic turn."†

---

* Ulrich von Wilamowitz-Moellendorff, *Reden und Vorträge* (Berlin: Weidmann, 1901), 7.
† Donald Davidson, "Intellectual Autobiography," in *The Philosophy of Donald Davidson*, ed. L. E. Hahn, Library of Living Philosophers, vol. 27 (Chicago: Open Court, 1999), 41.

It does not diminish the great achievements of Wittgenstein, Quine, or Davidson if we acknowledge other predecessors in our thinking about meaning, interpreting, and translating. Philosophers of the Continental European tradition can trace their skepticism about words' or sentences' independent meanings to Nietzsche, and ultimately to Pascal. According to Pascal, "*Les sens reçoivent des paroles leur dignité, au lieu de la leur donner.*" ("Meanings receive their dignity from words, instead of giving it to them.")* Pascal's understanding of meaning, translation, and synonymy is certainly closer to contemporary philosophical views than to Wilamowitz-Moellendorff's views.

7. Criteria of Adequacy

If meanings are rejected as grounds for the adequacy of translations and interpretations, we must provide viable alternatives to the rejected views. One such alternative first distinguishes between what a speaker wanted to say by using certain words and what is said by using these words. Since in the large majority of cases we understand directly what has been said without any need for interpretation, most of the time we need not pay attention to this distinction. There is often an innocent explanation for the speaker's seemingly deviant use of words. We misheard or misread what he said, he was joking, irony or ignorance played a role in his choice of words, and so on. In these and many similar cases, the speaker's aim is decisive. How would he understand his own words if he were in the interpreter's place? In answering this question, the interpreter understands not only what the speaker said, but also why he chose the words that he did. In such cases the differences between the speaker and his interpreter can be negotiated in principle. When they cannot be negotiated in fact, the interpreter can always appeal to Universalizability either in the indicative or the subjunctive mood. He will appeal to the Restrictive Principle only if a deep interpretation is appropriate.

Ignorance is at the root of the interpreter's misunderstanding of what has been said or written. For example, what seemed to him a deviant use of a word is in fact its standard use. What he construed as an expression of irony or as a joke turns out to be a report of past events. What he took to be just a story happens to be history. What the speaker said in these and similar cases will not be understood by the interpreter until he receives further instruction from the speaker, from other interpreters, or from his learning about the facts of the matter without the help of others. As long

* Blaise Pascal, *Pensées*, fragment 50 in the Brunschvicg edition, 789 in the Lafuma edition.

as the reader agrees that in translating or interpreting we bestow meaning of what has been said, he will find the appeal to the two principles useful. If, contrary to Pascal, he claims that words receive their dignity from meanings, then the appeal to the two principles becomes idle. Such reified meanings are objects that wait to be discovered in a successful interpretation, or "transported" from one language to another in a useful translation. For want of adequate identity criteria for reified meanings, we would not know whether they have been discovered or transported.

The appeal to the two principles presented in this work is expected to be consistent with all other theories of interpretation. Occasionally a theorist argues for the reification of meanings—a case in point is Wilamowitz-Moellendorff's view—but even he could support his interpretations by showing that they satisfy the two constraints on interpreting; hence, he could appeal to Universalizability or defend those who agree with him with an appeal to the Restrictive Principle. Theorists who reject the reification of meaning will find their interpretations strengthened by such appeals. Concerning every verbal or written communication we can ask: what did its author want to communicate by saying what he said? How must we make sense of what he said? If what is to be interpreted is not considered a communication between its creator and his audience—for example, it is a literary artwork—then we ask: how must we understand what is presented to us, regardless of the author's understanding of what he has created? In appealing to principles in support of an interpretation or in defense of interpreters, we must ask: how does the interpreter avoid projecting his own beliefs, desires, and understanding onto what is being interpreted? How does he avoid this major pitfall of interpreting? This problem is at the center of the next three chapters.

CHAPTER EIGHT

Universalizability and Self-Deception

When we are not required to provide our own interpretation, we often ask: what is the consensus of qualified interpreters about a given topic? Even when we are guided by interpretations we accept from others, we must still account for our interpreting their interpretations. Each of us is a solitary interpreter at a given stage of the interpreting activity. Moreover, even if we were at all times conscious of the rules regulating the interpreting activity, we would be left to our own devices in deciding whether we should apply one rule rather than another. Ordinarily we steer by facts that we claim to know in framing an interpretive hypothesis, but if we automatically reject every interpretive hypothesis contradicting what we claim to know, we do not leave room for an examination of our own knowledge claims. At times we must be willing to disregard what we claim to know; we must be prepared to suspend a rule guiding us in most cases in order to entertain an interpretive hypothesis that is incompatible with our belief or knowledge claims. Each of us is alone in deciding when to apply and when to suspend a rule governing the interpreting activity.

Earlier I suggested that unless we understand interpreting from the viewpoint of a solitary interpreter, we cannot make sense of professions that require creativity and originality and at the same time rely primarily on interpreting. Other professionals—such as judges and physicians—must

follow guidelines for their judgments, but the application of the guidelines
is still dependent on their own judgment. Such examples require that we
focus on interpreting from the viewpoint of a solitary interpreter. Two problems arise. The interpreter starts with a claim about how *he* sees what is at
issue, and continues with a stronger claim about how *we* see it or a different
claim about how *we* ought to see that issue. To be sure, when challenged,
he can always answer that he has satisfied both constraints on interpreting.
Hence, he is entitled to appeal to Universalizability. Still, on what grounds
are his interpretive choices universalizable? Moreover, how does he know
that he relies on his own judgment in claiming how *he* sees that issue? Maybe
he is only following a consensus on the matter. The possibility of self-deception arises in this context.

Before discussing these two problems, I must answer an objection. It is
often suggested that the widespread agreement among professional
interpreters within a given field is incompatible with the view that the
interpretive choices were reached as a result of a solitary inquiry. The
answer is that the solitary inquiry of many interpreters need not yield disagreement. An important paradigm of a solitary inquiry in the context of
interpreting is the philosopher's confrontation with the problem of skepticism. While confronting this problem and trying to find an adequate
answer, it would be ludicrous and self-defeating if he were to ask for help
from a fellow philosopher. As a result of a solitary inquiry, each philosopher understands skepticism and finds an answer to its most radical formulation. Yet there is remarkable agreement among these answers. Could
it be that there is an invisible hand directing their attention to the same
solution? If there were such a hand, and they did not know anything
about it—for example, an evil genius directing every one of their
actions—then they would have to start their solitary inquiry about skepticism all over again. So they must find ways to convince themselves that
there is no such invisible hand. Could it be that a common philosophical
culture determined their answer? If this were the case, then the solitary
inquiry would be a sham, and each of them would have to be prompted
to learn philosophy all over again. Could it be that the widespread agreement among philosophers on the answer to the most radical formulation
of skepticism is based on each philosopher's success in finding temporarily—until the next skeptical challenge—a right answer to the problem?
This could indeed be the case. As we will see, it will be useful to remind
ourselves of this paradigm of a solitary inquiry. For ease of exposition, I
will speak in the first-person singular about the solitary segment in the
interpreting activity.

1. Universalizability

When I understand another person's words as a joke, an expression of irony, or a malapropism, I do not claim that my understanding is dependent on my unique characteristics. I came to my understanding not as a result of an extraordinary intelligence, insight, or cleverness, but as a consequence of my knowing some facts about the world in which we live. I listened to what was said and how it was said. I took into account what the speaker or writer could be expected to know, what I attributed to him concerning his beliefs, desires, and understanding of the situation about which he spoke. I did not rely on any special talent that I have when I framed the hypothesis that a nonliteral understanding of his words was warranted. Of course, I could ask my friends whether they agreed with me. But asking my friends has limits. To be quite sure about the matter, I would have to ask other friends whether they agreed with my first set of friends, and yet another set of friends whether they agreed with my second set of friends, and so on. The consultation with friends is limited only by practical considerations; from a theoretical viewpoint it is unlimited. But it seems to be fairly easy to avoid even the first consultation. I imagine what they would say if they were consulted on this matter. They could agree with me, and then I would take this to be a reinforcement of my claim; or they could disagree with me, and then I would either revise my judgment or claim that they are mistaken.

Still, isn't my imagination dependent on my unique characteristics? If it is, then my interpretation will be idiosyncratic. Ordinarily, my goal is to find a natural interpretation of what was said. Of course, idiosyncratic interpretations have their uses. Storytellers often rely on a pretended misunderstanding for the sake of a joke; attempts at deep interpretation often start with an eccentric understanding of what was said. However, now I wish to find a natural interpretation. Accordingly, I would not want to stray far from the beaten path, and if I do, I must be prepared to provide an explanation for my unconventional choice. Yet no matter how careful I am about this matter, as long as I try to steer by the viewpoint of others and adopt what I believe to be a conformist choice, I could be mistaken. Maybe I do not understand their viewpoint well, or the choice that I make is not as conformist as I imagine. So I take a radical step that excludes the possibility of this kind of mistake. Up to now I wanted to conform to the viewpoint of others and to provide a conventional interpretation. Now I simply declare: my unique characteristics are independent of my interpretive choice in this particular instance; this is how I see what was said, and I am reporting only on what has become evident to me. Since I am not relying on my unique characteristics in my judgment about this matter, I am entitled to add: if others were in my situation, they would agree with me. I am not trying to conform to the judgment of others. It is up to them to conform to my judgment concerning my interpretive choice.

The reader will object: what I offer is not much of a bargain. I have eliminated the possibility of one kind of mistake at the price of opening a door that will invite another kind of mistake, and that mistake is not only possible, but also probable. Instead of relying on a consensus of interpreters for validation, I demand that other interpreters agree with my interpretation. Many may argue that even if they were in my situation, they would not agree with my interpretive choice. Or they may ignore my demand and offer an alternative interpretation. Either way, it can be expected that others will not comply with my demand. Moreover, when I tried to conform to the viewpoint of others, my interpretation was validated or undermined by consensus or dissent. As soon as I demand that others conform to my interpretation, and that demand is based on what is evident to me independently of how anyone else understands what is at issue, I cannot count either compliance or opposition as confirming or undermining my interpretation. After all, my interpretation relies solely on what is evident to me—and it is merely a matter of coincidence if others comply with my demand or dismiss it without further discussion. Whenever I am confronted with the rejection of my demand, I have only one of three choices. I can withdraw my demand and claim that I have been mistaken; I can revise my interpretive choice and agree with the consensus about the matter at issue; or I can maintain my interpretive choice, regardless of the disagreement of others. The first two choices are uninteresting; the third deserves detailed discussion. Before engaging in that discussion, however, a reminder is in order.

2. Kant

There is at least one strand in the philosophical tradition that is hospitable to the understanding of the interpretive choice that is at issue here. What Kant said about pure judgments of taste—such as "this is beautiful"—provides a good starting point for the kind of consideration that may lead to the demand that one person's interpretive choice be accepted by all. According to Kant in the *Critique of the Power of Judgment*:

> For one cannot judge that about which he is aware that the satisfaction in it
> is without any interest in his own case in any way except that it must contain

a ground of satisfaction for everyone. For since it is not grounded in any inclination of the subject (nor in any other underlying interest), but rather the person making the judgment feels himself completely **free** with regard to the satisfaction that he devotes to the object, he cannot discover as grounds of the satisfaction any private conditions, pertaining to his subject alone, and must therefore regard it as grounded in those that he can also presuppose in everyone else; consequently he must believe himself to have grounds for expecting a similar pleasure of everyone.[*]

In saying that a given object is beautiful, the interpreter speaks about that object with a universal voice. He does not ask whether others agree with him; "he *demands* that they agree."[†] The force of a pure judgment of taste is closer to a perceptual judgment ("This thing is round") than to a statement of individual taste preference ("I like it"). If challenged, he must be able to provide good reasons for his pure judgment of taste. After all, his judgment claims that an object can be seen *as if* it had the properties he assigned to it. But he is not required to defend his individual taste preferences, although in extreme cases he may be thought of as having bad taste.

Even in matters of individual taste preferences, however, the "everything goes" approach is unacceptable for Kant. He does not spell out the details, but it can be assumed that bad taste is at the origin of eccentric or idiosyncratic taste preferences. Constraints on an interpreter's preferences within the limits of good taste provide ways of separating the acceptable from the unacceptable interpretations. Do these constraints counsel conformism? They certainly counsel caution, but not conformism. If my interpretation is adjusted so that it agrees with the understanding of others, then I am no longer speaking with my own voice when I demand agreement with my interpretation; I am speaking only for a consensus. In speaking for a consensus, I merely repeat the chatter overheard in public places. As Heidegger's readers will agree, the chatter of "what people say" is not the same as a universal voice, for I must be able to speak in my own voice in order to demand that others agree with my interpretive choice. The content of "what people say" cannot be traced to the judgment of a single individual; hence, the call for agreement with the overheard chatter is at best an appeal to public opinion. Constraints on interpreters' preferences suggested by philosophers can be expected to appeal to reason and critical judgment, but not to public opinion.

[*] Immanuel Kant, *Critique of the Power of Judgment*, ed. and trans. Paul Guyer (Cambridge: Cambridge University Press, 2000), sec. 6, pp. 96–97.
[†] Ibid., sec. 7.

3. Interpretive Choices and Aesthetic Judgments

The analogy between Kant's view about pure judgments of taste and our understanding of interpretive choices is not accidental. A pure judgment of taste is not a perceptual judgment. "This object is beautiful" does not have the same force as "This object is round." A pure judgment of taste merely asserts about a given object that it can be seen *as if* it had a certain property; it can be seen *as if* "beautiful" predicated the same sort of thing as "round." It is not a fact that it is beautiful, but it is—as I will argue—asymptotically close to being a fact. By contrast, the *as if* locution would be misleading in the context of perceptual judgments. In saying that an object can be seen *as if* it were round implies that it may not be round. (For example, it is a very small object that is sometimes seen as if it were round.) True perceptual judgments establish facts about the world in which we live, whereas pure judgments of taste merely establish that a given object can be seen by an interpreter *as if* it had a certain property. What is the force of the *as if* locution in the context of pure judgments of taste? My concern here is neither an exegesis of what Kant has said nor an eisegesis of what he should have said. Accordingly, I will speak about the *as if* locution in the context of aesthetic judgments rather than in the context of pure judgments of taste. What will be said here about aesthetic judgments may or may not be relevant to Kant's views; judgment on this matter must be left to Kant scholars.

Singular aesthetic judgments are based on interpretations attributed to a given artwork. An interpretation attributed to it must be anchored to that artwork. Outside of the arts, statements of facts or descriptions of objects are ordinarily attached to what they are about by our claim that the statements are true. But if an interpretation is hooked to an artwork by a truth claim, then either the truth claim or the claim that it is an interpretation must be rejected. Facts or descriptions are not interpretations. So if we wish to reach beyond facts and descriptions, we must find a way of anchoring the interpretation to the artwork without claiming that it is true of that artwork. For example, we speak about balance, intensity, and other formal properties that we attribute to a given painting, but we speak about these properties *as if* we found them in that painting. If it were a fact that they could be found in that painting, they would be available for anyone capable of seeing and noticing properties of objects outside of the arts. Yet in speaking about these properties *as if* we found them in that painting, it is clear that we did not find them there. In attributing relevant formal properties to that painting, we do not talk about what we see in that painting. We speak about what our understanding and imagination have shaped out of what we see. We talk about what we "see." The scare quotes around the perceptual verb indicate that the verb is used in an unusual sense. Perceptual objects are the proper objects of perceptual verbs; interpreted perceptual objects are the proper objects of perceptual verbs in scare quotes.

We are all critics when offering an aesthetic judgment about an artwork. Some of us are professionals in a specialized field; others are amateurs. Even a person incompetent about a given field of the arts is a critic as soon as he provides an aesthetic judgment in that field. The difference between professional and amateur critics is not only that we expect the professionals to do better than the amateurs, but also that the professional critics make their own aesthetic judgments. When speaking in their fields of interest, professional critics would be discredited if in making their judgments they relied on what they have learned from their teachers or colleagues, or if they merely accepted the views prevalent in their social circles. They are expected to speak with their own voice, but as soon as they say what they have "seen" in a painting, what they have "heard" in a symphony, or what they have "read" in a poem, they speak with a universal voice.

Yogi Berra reportedly said, "You can observe a lot by watching." In the context of aesthetic judgments, professional critics turn this play on words into "If you watch, you will observe (or 'see') a lot." It would not serve the critic's purposes to say this, for the point of the *as if* locution is to convince herself and everyone else that she found the interpretation she is presenting in the artwork. Of course, she did not find it in the artwork; if she did find it there, her services would not be needed. If the properties she assigned to that artwork were found in it, they would be perceptual properties and anyone able to see, hear, or read could in principle if not in fact find them there. If they were perceptual properties, then statements affirming these properties of a given object would be truth-valued, and if they were truth-valued, they would not be interpretations. So if the statements affirming these properties are accepted or rejected as interpretations, they must be understood as a professional critic's recommendations to see that artwork as she "saw" it. The sleight of hand in the previous sentence must not escape the reader's attention. Everyone—including the critic whose understanding and imagination shaped an interpreted object out of the perceptual object she saw—ought to see the object as the critic "saw" it; everyone ought to believe that he sees a perceptual object, when in fact he "sees" an interpreted object. In demanding that everyone see it as she "saw" it, the professional critic speaks with a universal voice. Are we witnessing a sleight of hand when the critic first wants to report with her own individual voice what she "saw" in a given artwork, and then speaks with a universal voice in demanding that everyone see it as she "saw" it? One answer is that we must admit that this is indeed a sleight of hand. In accepting this answer, we admit that the formal properties attributed to a painting are understood *as if* they were found in that painting, *as if* they were perceptual properties—while in fact they are not found in it and they are not its perceptual properties. A second answer is that the assertion that this is a sleight of hand must be rejected, and that the formal properties attributed to a painting are its perceptual properties. This answer is unacceptable, for it collapses aesthetic judgments into perceptual judgments. The facts of the matter prohibit such a collapse. Good vision does not guarantee the ability of "seeing" balance or tension in a painting, just as good hearing does not secure the ability of "hearing" dissonance resolving into consonance in a symphony.

4. Two Kinds of Conflicts

We are now in the position to understand better the kinds of conflicts that may arise when I demand the agreement of all other reasonable persons with my interpretations. Suppose I am confronted with the rejection of my demand. No conflicts arise if I subsequently withdraw my demand and admit that I have been mistaken, or if I revise my interpretive choice and agree with the consensus about the issue. But if these two solutions are unavailable, and I maintain my interpretive choice—regardless of the disagreement of others—I must be prepared to defend it against all available alternatives. Two cases must be distinguished. In the first case, I demand agreement with my choice, but this choice happens to coincide with the consensus about the topic. This case is of limited interest. My choice was reached either because of or in spite of the consensus, but now I am certainly not alone in demanding the agreement of all reasonable persons with my interpretive choice. In demanding agreement, I may be merely acting on behalf of many interpreters who accept that choice. In the second case, I demand agreement with my interpretive choice that happens to be incompatible with the consensus about the issue. A conflict with others arises when my demand for agreement is questioned. Is my interpretive choice based on reason and argument or on sheer authoritarianism?

While I believe that good reasons and arguments are the only grounds for my authority in this matter, others suspect that in demanding agreement, I merely speak with the voice of authority. Their suspicion is based on my indignant reaction after they either ignored or rejected my reasons and arguments. They may be right, but it is also conceivable that I may be right in this matter. Moreover, the conflict with others may be replicated as an internal conflict: am I really right about this matter?

The two kinds of conflicts, the external and the internal, need not always arise. But they may arise whenever a solitary interpreter demands the agreement of all reasonable persons with his or her interpretive choice. Professional critics in art, music, or literature are often in the position of maintaining an aesthetic judgment about an artwork that is not shared or is shared only by a few within the public they aim to reach. As long as they do not have the power to enforce their judgments, we admire their courage for maintaining them even if it means facing opposition from the large majority of their contemporaries. We would consider them petty tyrants if they had the power and used it to enforce their views.

5. Internal Conflicts

The conflicts that may arise within the solitary interpreter who claims to rely only on his own judgment while demanding agreement with that judgment from all reasonable persons deserves detailed discussion. Suppose a professional critic "sees" or "hears" an aesthetic property in a given artwork. As a professional critic, she can demand of everyone that they see what she "saw" only if she is quite certain that she herself "saw" what she claims to have "seen." If her claims about that artwork were based on hearsay evidence or public opinion, then she would be acting as an amateur and not as a professional critic in her own field. She would be merely urging all reasonable persons to conform to a received or a sectarian opinion. Her situation is analogous to that of the philosophy student who has watched professional philosophers raise skeptical problems and provide answers to these problems. The student or the amateur can imitate the professional's voice about skeptical inquiries or aesthetic judgments, but the imitation cannot take the place of that voice. Reporting about skepticism or aesthetic judgments is not the same as confronting the problem of skepticism or making aesthetic judgments. A student or an amateur, while on his way to becoming a professional in his field of interest, must first convince himself that he is not merely replicating what he has heard from others. Doubt about this matter must be resolved entirely within the solitary interpreter. For brevity's sake, I will speak again in the first-person singular about the solitary interpreter.

As an interpreter of an artwork, I must be quite certain that I am not spreading over that artwork what is merely in my imagination. What I am saying must be anchored to that artwork. Similarly, as an interpreter in philosophy, I must confront the problem of skepticism and not just iterate the received wisdom about skepticism. From a psychological viewpoint, I may appreciate confirmation by others that I am relying on my own experiences. But such reinforcement does not provide evidence in this matter. If others were arguing that I merely relied on received wisdom, this would not necessarily defeat my contrary claim. As a solitary interpreter, I must first satisfy my own doubt whether my judgments are supported by my own experiences. Others may agree or disagree with me about this matter, but this does not decide the issue.

Do I speak about my own experiences, or am I deceiving myself on this matter? My demand that every reasonable person see what I have "seen" or accept the solution to the problem of skepticism that I have provided deserves to be rejected if I did not succeed in having my own experiences. However, I say I have had these experiences and I am able to speak about them; this amounts to the claim that I have an *individual* voice. I have such a voice not only in the trivial sense that everyone is endowed with an individual or unique voice, but also in the sense that I have shaped my voice on the basis of my own experiences. As soon as I use this voice, it becomes a *universal* voice. The solitary interpreter's individual voice is a precondition for his speaking with a universal voice. If others reject what I am saying in speaking with a universal voice, they have a powerful weapon at their disposal: they can cast doubt on the legitimacy of my speaking with such a voice. (For example: "He speaks as if he were a professional critic or a philosopher, but in fact he is merely reporting what he has heard from others.") Before they can use that weapon, I must decide whether I am entitled to demand the agreement of every reasonable person with my aesthetic judgments or with my solution to a problem of skepticism. If on reconsideration I decide that I did not speak about what I have "seen" in an artwork or confront a radical form of skepticism, then I must withdraw my aesthetic judgments or the solution to the problem of skepticism that I proposed. But if my internal conflict about this matter is resolved, and I am willing to maintain that I have an individual voice, then I am entitled to speak with a universal voice and demand the agreement of all reasonable persons.

The solitary interpreter's world may ignore, agree with, or disagree with such a demand. The first two possibilities—failure to notice or agreement—are for the solitary interpreter of considerable psychological, but of no theoretical, importance. Admittedly, the professional critic's or the philosopher's universal voice is most often ignored, and agreement with such a voice is quite infrequent. It is the disagreement with his demand that is of importance, for the disagreement is expressed by shifting the focus of the debate. The critic or the philosopher spoke about an artwork or a philosophical problem. When others reject his demand that they see in that artwork what he has "seen," or see the philosophical problem and accept the solution that he has proposed, their focus is on the critic or the philosopher. In rejecting his demand they claim that he is mistaken, insincere, or self-deceived. We must not insist that these are three different claims. All three rely on the conviction that he does not have an individual voice, and accordingly that he is not entitled to speak with a universal voice. (For example: "He believes he has had, or pretends to have had, certain experiences, or he succeeded in convincing himself that he has had certain experiences that he did not have.") He seems to have an individual voice, but in fact he relies either on an eccentric judgment, sectarian opinion, or a majority view. (And isn't a majority view often just a sectarian opinion that is held by many?) If he had an individual voice, he would be entitled to speak with a universal voice. His universal voice is impervious to criticism if we admit that he has an individual voice. Admittedly, this is a strong claim that requires proof.

At this stage, only preliminary support is provided from unexpected quarters. When art and literary critics concerned with issues of gender, class, or race argue against a traditional critic, or criticize a work of art or literature, they fault the critic or the work of art or literature for superimposing a gender-, class-, or race-determined viewpoint on an individual viewpoint. The traditional critic, poet, or painter is faulted for not having an individual voice. Critics of traditional persuasion find the insistence on such issues unwarranted. They fail to notice that their opponents defend deeply entrenched and quite traditional concerns for having an individual voice in creating works of art and literature or in speaking about them. Similarly, critics concerned with gender, class, and/or race issues fail to see that their more traditional colleagues cannot discover the individual viewpoint behind the veil of criticism from a social viewpoint.

Must we conclude that if a critic or a philosopher has an individual voice and uses his voice to speak with a universal voice, we are bound to accept what he says about his experiences? This conclusion requires detailed defense. Here we must ask: what are the solitary interpreter's grounds for believing that he has an individual voice? Since he excluded confirmation or disconfirmation by others, his only reason for believing that he has such a voice is through his own assertion. He may be mistaken, and in considering this possibility, he may ask whether he really did "see" the formal properties of a given artwork or whether he really did confront and answer a problem in the field of philosophical skepticism. For the solitary interpreter the claim that he has an individual voice is confirmed as soon as he has rejected the possibility of being mistaken about this matter. Agreement or disagreement with this claim is at issue only if he subsequently *uses* his individual voice.

6. Negotiating Conflicting Judgments

A solitary interpreter may "see" the formal properties of a given artwork, but he may be unwilling to speak about his experiences. The frequently heard disclaimer "I don't know what is art, but I know what I like" must not be understood too literally. The speaker may not be able to speak—or to speak well—about art, yet at the same time he may have an individual voice. (For example, artists and poets are notoriously bad critics; they have an individual voice, yet they are found wanting only when they try to use that voice.) Similarly, the novice in philosophy may confront a skeptical problem and find its solution, and at the same time be unable to speak clearly about what is at issue. So far, the solitary interpreter has established only that he has an individual voice. Only if he uses that voice can it become a universal voice. Only at this stage can questions arise about agreement or disagreement with what he says. Others could easily reject his claim that every reasonable person who is knowledgeable about what is at issue would agree with his judgment about the formal properties of a given artwork or his solution to a skeptical problem. The rejection can take three different forms.

First, his claim may be considered and rejected without being taken seriously. According to his critics, his idiosyncratic judgments would provide sufficient evidence that he himself was not among the qualified interpreters whose judgments must be considered. Secondly, his claim may be taken seriously, but his critics would suggest an apparently innocuous explanation for rejecting it—for instance, he does not share his critics' interpretive goals. Such an explanation would only seem to be innocuous, for his critics could just as well support their understanding of his words with a natural interpretation in the subjunctive mood: he would agree with them if he shared their interpretive goals and their knowledge of what was at issue. What seemed to be an innocuous explanation could be merely a covert way of dismissing his claim. Thirdly, his critics may accept him among the reasonable and knowledgeable persons but argue that his judgments are eccentric or sectarian. Only the rather weak Restrictive Principle can support such judgments. In other words, they may admit that all persons who agree with his judgments are qualified interpreters but contend that there are no good reasons to believe that all persons who are reasonable and knowledgeable about that issue agree with his judgments. What he says deserves to be rejected as an essentially contestable interpretation.

Let us take stock. The solitary interpreter convinces his audience when speaking with a universal voice, or he fails to convince them on either of the previously mentioned grounds. As long as no other interpretations satisfying the two constraints on interpreting are available, his audience will accept even an essentially contestable interpretation. But in this case the focus of the debate shifts from an interpretation to the defense of all who agree with that interpretation. Can the solitary interpreter improve the odds for the acceptance of what he says?

7. Facts and Interpretations

When the solitary interpreter convinces his audience, he is understood *as if* he discovered certain properties in an artwork. Had he in fact discovered such properties, he would not need to support the statement of his discovery with the Universalizability Principle. He would be entitled to claim that he has spoken accurately about facts or true descriptions concerning an artwork. At the other end of the spectrum, when his views are not simply ignored but rejected, the suspicion arises that he is not entitled to be speaking with a universal voice. According to his critics, he is at best a victim of self-deception if he believes that his idiosyncratic, sectarian, or essentially contestable interpretations can be defended by speaking with such a voice. From his own viewpoint, when he established to his own satisfaction that he had an individual voice, he excluded the possibility of self-deception. He would agree with his critics: if he were a victim of self-deception, he would not be entitled to speak with a universal voice. Interpretations supported by the Universalizability Principle occupy the space between idiosyncratic, sectarian, or essentially contestable interpretations on one side and facts or true descriptions on the other. It would be disingenuous for the solitary interpreter to suggest that the aesthetic properties he has ascribed to an artwork are facts about that artwork, or to claim support by the Restrictive Principle for what he has said about that artwork. If he claimed such support, he could just as well admit that his interpretation is idiosyncratic, sectarian, or essentially contestable. As long as he stands by his interpretation, he must dig in his heels, and support it with the Universalizability Principle.

We agree with or defend interpretations we happen to believe. This does not imply that what we happen to believe is true, but it does imply that we believe that it is at least possible for some interpretations to be true. We must distinguish two senses of the claim that a given interpretation is true. In one of its senses, this claim is harmless: interpretations are considered to be true by contrast to misinterpretations. In saying that we hold a given interpretation to be true, we are saying only that it is consistent with the facts as they are known to us, and it is the best available for a given purpose. We believe it has satisfied the factual and the normative constraints on interpreting. In the second sense, this claim is not at all innocuous. True interpretations are ordinarily called statements of facts and not interpretations. Statements of facts are true, and they are true not because they can be supported by the Universalizability Principle, but in virtue of their stating what happens to be the case in the world in which we live. Unscrupulous interpreters—aware of the falsity of their claims— use the transformation of successful interpretations into factual descriptions for their own purposes. They save themselves the effort of providing reasons and arguments for their interpretations: they gain all the advantages of theft over honest toil by presenting their interpretations as if they were factual descriptions. Mistaken interpreters claim falsely that they have discovered facts about what they have interpreted. Partially insincere interpreters, interpreters whose beliefs or understanding is deficient, or self-deceived interpreters succeed in convincing themselves that instead of interpretations they are arguing for descriptions. An entirely different kind of insincerity among interpreters has its roots in their appealing simultaneously to both principles: overtly to the Restrictive Principle in defense of interpreters who agree with a given interpretation and covertly to the Universalizability Principle in support of their interpretations. Sincere interpreters will rest their case on the Universalizability Principle, while holding their interpretations to be true without making premature claims that they are true. For how long? As long as their interpretations are either transformed into factual claims or discredited by better interpretations.

Two patterns emerge: the instability of interpretations and the transformation of successful interpretations. Interpretations are unstable, for they thrive as interpretations only as long as they are not considered to be factual descriptions. If they gain in stability, they are transformed from deep-level to surface-level interpretations, and from surface-level interpretations to what are considered factual descriptions. As we have seen, deep-level interpretations are contestable and the theories supporting them are controversial. Successful deep-level interpretations become natural or surface-level interpretations supported by the Universalizability Principle. Successful deep interpretation theories are upgraded and become either commonsense generalizations or theories about human nature. Successful natural or surface-level interpretations become factual descriptions. The very notion of a definitive interpretation implies success. But if interpretations are successful, accepted, and considered to be incontestable, they are transformed into true descriptions.

8. Objections

Four objections may be raised. Some critics may object that the transformation of what has been considered an interpretation into what is now a factual description provides evidence that it was always a factual description and not an interpretation. This is indeed the case. Prior to the work of Dedekind and Cantor, when philosophers and mathematicians claimed that there was an actual infinite, they were offering an interpretation. Since Cantor's work we have a definition of infinite sets—infinite sets have proper subsets that are also infinite—and what has been regarded as an interpretation concerning mathematical objects is now known to be a factual description of these objects. But if it is now a factual description, then it always was a factual description—at best, we could claim that prior to Cantor we were ignorant of the facts in this matter. A similar answer can be given in the context of philosophical problems. If a hitherto unknown fact would be decisive in solving a philosophical problem, we would argue that it was never a philosophical problem. We were merely ignorant of the facts of the matter. In this context it should be also mentioned that if good vision and hearing could guarantee the ability of "seeing" balance or tension in a painting and "hearing" dissonance resolving into consonance in a symphony, we would not need to distinguish between perceptual and aesthetic judgments of artworks. What we now consider a matter of interpretation would be a factual description.

A second objection suggests an escape from our conception of interpretations supported by the Universalizability Principle as occupying the space between interpretations supported by the Restrictive Principle and factual descriptions. One objector may stipulate that there are only interpretations, and whatever is not a misinterpretation is a more or less successful interpretation. Accordingly, there are no factual descriptions. Among the more successful interpretations there may be a convergence to the best interpretation and even to a definitive interpretation. The answer to this objection is that this view changes only the terms of the debate, but not the underlying conception of interpretations. If we stipulate that there are no factual descriptions, we will find the field of successful interpretations quite crowded. In that crowded field we must find order by distin-

guishing between the more and the less successful interpretations. Once
we introduce this ordering principle, we will find that we call factual
descriptions what the objector calls the more successful interpretations.
What the objector wanted to discard returns under a different name.

A third objection suggests that we erase the demarcation line between
misinterpretations and successful interpretations. According to this view
there are only interpretations—containing both misinterpretations and
what we would call successful interpretations—and factual descriptions.
The interpretations can be more or less fitting, to the point, relevant,
appropriate, and so forth. Interpreters of a relativist persuasion may welcome this suggestion. But if we accept this suggestion, we must still argue
for our interpretive choices. In a crowded field, when arguing for our
choices or agreeing with the choices of others, we must show why some
choices deserve to be discredited. Again, the erased demarcation line
between misinterpretations and successful interpretations that the objector wanted to discard will be reestablished.

Finally, a fourth objection adverts to the fundamental difference
between facts and interpretations. To be sure, interpretive claims may
approach factual statements asymptotically, but they cannot become factual statements. Even if interpreters believe, while recommending their
interpretations, that they are true, it does not follow that they are indeed
true. If we believe that interpretations are more or less plausible—and not
either true or false—we must hold that interpretive claims cannot become
factual statements. The answer is that even if we admit the fundamental
difference between facts and interpretations, we must decide between
accepting a given claim as interpretive or as factual. Yesterday's fact is today
seen as an interpretation, just as what was at one time an interpretation is
now understood as a fact. The distinction between what is a fact and what
is merely *seen* as a fact, or between what is an interpretation and what is
merely understood as an interpretation, depends on what appear to us as
other facts and other interpretations. Ultimately, it depends on the content of our two belief boxes. If we were endowed with intellectual vision
enabling us to distinguish between facts and what merely appear to be
facts, we could do without beliefs and interpretations. When confronting
problems of skepticism, we would welcome such a dispensation. In other
contexts we would deplore it as an unhappy arrangement, for it would
harm our powers of imagination and impoverish our lives.

9. The Self-Deceiver's Mistake

Having an individual voice is a necessary condition for speaking with a universal voice. Since some solitary interpreters who have an individual voice and are entitled to speak with a universal voice are unwilling or unable to do so, we cannot claim that having an individual voice is also a sufficient condition for speaking with such a voice. If all who are entitled to speak with a universal voice would in fact do so, we could argue that having an individual voice is both necessary and sufficient for speaking with a universal voice. As things stand, some are entitled to speak with such a voice, while others merely pretend to do so, for they have not satisfied its necessary condition. The question arises: what are we saying, implying or suggesting when we claim that a solitary interpreter has not satisfied the necessary condition for speaking with a universal voice? What Kant described as the solitary interpreter's ground for a pure judgment of taste has been adopted here as a basis for an aesthetic judgment. In a larger context, it has also been adopted as support for an interpretive choice satisfying the factual and normative constraints on interpreting. In answering my question, a reconsideration of Kant's point from the perspective of the solitary interpreter's critic will be helpful. (For ease of exposition, feminine pronouns will be used for the critic, and masculine pronouns for the interpreter.) A partial repetition of what has been said earlier is unavoidable, for in discussing the point that can be traced to Kant's views, we followed interpretive choices from their formation to their dissemination. Now we have to retrace our steps from their reception to their formation, which will lead us to a clear understanding of the self-deceiver's fundamental mistake.

The solitary interpreter could not discover "as grounds of the satisfaction any private conditions, pertaining to his subject alone (*keine Privatbedingungen als Gründe des Wohlgefallens auffinden, an die sich sein Subjekt allein hängte*), and must therefore regard it as grounded in those that he can also presuppose in everyone else. . . ." We have reached the end of the matter if a critic ignores an interpretive choice presented with a universal voice. But if she pays attention to what was said and chooses to reject it, then she can do so only by claiming—notwithstanding all contrary presuppositions—that there was a private condition grounding the other's interpretive choice. The private condition determined that his interpretive choice became idiosyncratic. In extreme cases of idiosyncrasy, she would claim that the interpreter must not be counted among the reasonable persons who are knowledgeable about the issue. In a less extreme case, she would argue that the interpreter provided us with an eccentric, sectarian, or an essentially contestable interpretation that can be defended only by the Restrictive Principle. A charge of self-deception is implied or suggested by the claim that a private condition determined the solitary interpreter's choice. What exactly was the self-deceiver's mistake?

We must recall that from the solitary interpreter's own viewpoint his claim that he has an individual voice is confirmed as soon as he has rejected the possibility of being mistaken about this matter. His claim that he has an individual voice rests merely on his belief that this is the case. If he is mistaken on this matter, he is mistaken about himself. In being mistaken about himself, he did not rely on the judgment of others. He himself is the only person who can be blamed for the mistake about him. He is a self-deceiver. He is deceived about his having an individual voice; hence, he is deceived about himself. To the extent that he is deceived about himself, he lacks self-knowledge. To be more precise, his lack of self-knowledge shields from him the fact that he does not have an individual voice. Caution is required here: not all lack of self-knowledge has untoward consequences in interpreting. At issue here is merely lack of self-knowledge about his failing to have an individual voice. (The Delphic oracle's admonition about self-knowledge deserves to be contrasted with Goethe's words to Eckermann: "I do not know myself, and God forbid that I should.")

In objecting to the interpretive choice of a self-deceived solitary interpreter who pretends to be speaking with a universal voice, we are saying that he does not have an individual voice. What he presented as an interpretation is not on that segment of the line that can be supported by the Universalizability Principle. He offered either a factual description or an interpretation. If it is the latter, then it is an idiosyncratic, sectarian, or essentially contestable interpretation. Support from the Universalizability Principle is available to him if and only if he has satisfied both constraints on interpreting. If he demands agreement with his interpretive choice while he claims to be speaking with a universal voice, we argue that such a voice is available to him only if he has an individual voice. In rejecting his interpretive choice, the shift of focus from what is at issue to the interpreter becomes understandable. While entertaining or judging his interpretive choice, we were prepared to admit that the interpreter spoke with a universal voice. When we concluded that he did not satisfy the necessary condition of speaking with a universal voice, and we did not choose to ignore him or suggest classifying him among the previously mentioned extreme cases, our only choice was to claim that if he believes he has an individual voice, he is self-deceived. The idiosyncratic, sectarian, or essentially contestable interpretation he presented with what seemed to be a universal voice is sufficient evidence that he does not have an individual voice.

The critic's only valid reason for rejecting an interpretive choice is the discovery of a private condition (to be discussed further in the next section) underlying that choice. If it is untainted by a private condition, then she is mistaken and the solitary interpreter is entitled to speak with a universal voice. Confronted with opposition, the solitary interpreter must either admit that he was self-deceived and withdraw his interpretation or maintain it while dismissing or criticizing the opposition. But we must notice that the positions of the solitary interpreter and his critic are reversible. It is now the solitary interpreter who either ignores the other or finds her interpretive choice tainted by a private condition. Each argues that the other does not have an individual voice—hence, he or she is not entitled to be speaking with a universal voice. If both dig in their heels, we are in the presence of an interminable controversy. Meanwhile, if we admit that one of them is entitled to be speaking with a universal voice, we thereby admit that he or she has an individual voice, and we are bound to accept the interpretive choice spoken with a universal voice. Can we accept both interpretive choices? The short answer is that we cannot accept both at the same time, but we can accept them at different times—but this topic remains to be argued in another context.

10. Tainted Interpretations

A solitary interpreter's private conditions provide the foundation for idiosyncratic, sectarian or eccentric interpretations. Some interpreters within a given society often share such private conditions. Shared private conditions provide support for sectarian interpretations, identified by opponents as biased or ideologically tainted.* In some cases, all interpreters within a given

---

*What Max Weber wrote in comparing a sect and a church is relevant for the understanding of sectarian interpretations:

> A sect in the sociological sense of the word is not a *small* group: the Baptists, one of the most typical sects, are one of the largest Protestant denominations in the world. Moreover, the sect is not a group that is split off from another that does not recognize it or persecutes it and condemns it as heretical. Rather, the sect is a group whose very nature and purpose precludes universality and requires the free consensus of its members, since it aims at being an aristocratic group, an association of persons with full religious qualification. The sect does not want to be an institution dispensing grace, like a church, which includes the righteous and the unrighteous and is especially concerned with subjecting the sinner to Divine law. The sect adheres to the ideal of the *ecclesia pura* (hence the name "Puritans"), the *visible* community of saints, from whose midst the black sheep are removed so that they will not offend God's eyes.

Max Weber, *Economy and Society: An Outline of Interpretive Sociology*, edited by Guenther Roth and Claus Wittich (Berkeley: University of California Press, 1978), 2: 1204.

society accept ideologically tainted interpretations. They no longer appeal to all reasonable persons who are knowledgeable about what is at issue, but to members of the sect who share the private conditions grounding the ideologically tainted interpretations. A question arises: if eccentric and ideologically tainted interpretations are considered essentially contestable and can be supported only by the Restrictive Principle, then how wide or narrow is the segment on the line between essentially contestable interpretations and factual descriptions? Earlier I argued: when interpreting the words of another person, an appeal to the Restrictive Principle is appropriate only in the context of deep interpretation, when we overtly or covertly charge that person with self-deception. Moreover, all deep interpretations and only deep interpretations are essentially contestable interpretations. Can we maintain that ideologically tainted interpretations are essentially contestable interpretations, and accordingly imply overt or covert charges of self-deception?

Every interpreter will draw differently the demarcation line between essentially contestable interpretations supported by the Restrictive Principle and interpretations supported by the Universalizability Principle. Interpreters will also differ about the demarcation line between interpretations and factual descriptions. What one interpreter claims to be a fact, another will identify as an interpretation supported by Universalizability, or the other way around. Similarly, what one interpreter insists is an interpretation supported by Universalizability, another will designate as an essentially contestable interpretation, or the other way around. Accordingly, the span between the two extremes will be different for each interpreter: it will be wide or narrow depending on the content of each interpreter's two belief boxes. Since the content of their two belief boxes is at issue, it is understandable that opponents will accuse each other of self-deception. According to his critic, if the interpreter were fully aware of the content of his belief boxes, he would agree with her that private conditions determined his interpretation—hence, it is an essentially contestable interpretation that can be supported only by the Restrictive Principle. In contrast to such cases, if a critic believes that the interpreter was mistaken in presenting a universalizable interpretation as an essentially contestable interpretation, or a factual description as a universalizable interpretation, she will not charge the interpreter with self-deception, for in both cases his mistake was about the world in which we live, and not about himself.

CHAPTER NINE

Beyond the Pale

————

Let us reconsider one kind of debate between the solitary interpreter and his critic. (For ease of exposition, feminine pronouns will be used for the critic, masculine pronouns for the solitary interpreter.) While the solitary interpreter could not find a private condition grounding his interpretive choice, the critic claimed that there was such a condition. His inability to see that condition is due to either error or self-deception. The critic may even concede that she partially agrees with the solitary interpreter's findings: viewed from within the narrow limits of his experiences concerning this matter, he thinks himself free of either error or self-deception. Yet as soon as we enlarge the boundaries of his world, it will be evident that he was a victim of one or the other. The limits of his world can be expanded by taking into account a larger unit within a given social world or a historical development subsequent to his interpretive choice. Interpretations arrived at within the limits of local interests are questioned from the viewpoint of regional, national, or global interests. Similarly, interpretations accredited at one time are discredited at a later time. Interpretations rooted in a given time, place, and relatively small social contexts seem to be free of private conditions. As soon as a critic sees what is beyond the limited horizon of such an interpretation, a choice that seemed to be free of private conditions is seen as grounded on such conditions.

1. Relativism

Some of our ancestors considered themselves at the center of a geocentric universe. Others believed that slavery was a condition for the functioning of their society. It can be argued that with the help of an adequately understood relativism we can account for their views. In their own ways, they searched for what was true and strived for what was good; given their limited view of the world, they did as well as they could. Their concepts were the same as their successors', which ultimately were the same as ours are today. By our lights, they had the right concepts at their disposal. Only their conceptions of these concepts distinguished them from their successors. At this stage, relativists invoke different paradigms and incommensurable views at the background of seemingly identical concepts. To be sure, relativism deserves to be understood as a serious philosophical view. It can be defended against the charge of inconsistency, and it can be shown to be compatible with the facts, as they are known to us. Nevertheless, even if it is admitted as a serious philosophical view, philosophers suggested good reasons for its rejection, for the question arises: can we attribute understanding of our concepts to our ancestors? Davidson answered that we cannot, and so did Hegel.

Davidson questions beliefs about the earth in a geocentric universe; Hegel questions conceptions of *man* (*Mensch*) in a society where slavery is tolerated. Davidson asks:

> . . . how clear are we that the ancients—some ancients—believed that the earth was flat? *This* earth? Well, this earth of ours is part of the solar system, a system partly identified by the fact that it is a gaggle of large, cool, solid bodies circling around a very hot star. If someone believes *none* of this about the earth, is it certain that it is the earth that he is thinking about?[*]

Davidson argues against relativism. According to his unsympathetic readers, his question also reveals an ahistorical view of our concepts. They are mistaken, for other examples show that such questions arise even for philosophers who insist on the historical character of our concepts. Hegel writes:

> *So z.B. wäre für das römische Recht keine Definition vom Menschen möglich, denn der Sklave ließe sich nicht darunter subsumieren, in seinem Stand ist jener Begriff vielmehr verletzt.* . . . (In Roman Law, for example, no definition of a *human being* would be possible, for the slave could not be subsumed under it; indeed, the status of the slave does violence to that concept. . . .)[†]

---

[*] Donald Davidson, *Truth and Interpretation* (Oxford: Oxford University Press, 1984), 168.

[†] G. W. F. Hegel, *Grundlinien der Philosophie des Rechtes*, section 2; English translation by H. B. Nisbet: *Elements of the Philosophy of Right*, ed. Allen W. Wood (Cambridge: Cambridge University Press, 1991), 27.

According to Hegel, freedom is part of the real definition of the concept *Mensch*. A *Mensch* is the bearer of rights and duties. Since a slave is not free, he can have neither rights nor duties. A question arises in this context. How should we read Jefferson's line "All men are created equal"? Relativists and their opponents agree that for Jefferson part of the real definition of *man* was that only white, propertied, and male human beings exemplified this concept. Immoderate relativists may argue that Jefferson and we have different conceptions of one and the same concept. Extreme anti-relativists could claim that Jefferson did not have the same concept of *man* as we have. Moral condemnation of Jefferson or any other slaveholder is not at issue here. The anti-relativist's point is to show that slaveholders did not have a clear concept of *man*, and, further, that our remote ancestors did not have a clear concept of *earth*. The following may be a useful test for the reader's intuitions about this matter. Late-eighteenth-century politicians successfully argued for counting a slave as three-fifths of a man in the United States census.[*] Did these politicians have the concept of *man*? Even if they did not have such a concept, they are not free from blame.

Relativists, and especially relativists who have a historical view of our concepts, may wish to exonerate our ancestors who were slaveholders. It could be argued that these ancestors could not even imagine the organization of their societies without slaves. Seen from within the limits of their world, Plato and Aristotle found slavery just as indispensable for the continuing welfare of their society as the courts of law. Accordingly, it would not make sense to blame them for not arguing against the institution of slavery. Such arguments became available only to those who could at least imagine the organization of their society without slavery. Relativists and anti-relativists may suggest that within the narrow boundaries of their world, contemporaries of Plato and Aristotle could indeed support the institution of slavery by appealing to Universalizability. Only their successors and critics could argue that the narrow limits of their view of the world vitiated such an appeal.

According to their successors, it seems as if the contemporaries of Plato and Aristotle were entitled to appeal only to the Restrictive Principle concerning slavery, and not to the Universalizability Principle. If this were the case, then the debate between relativists and anti-relativists would offer only two quite unattractive choices. The anti-relativist would argue that contemporaries of Plato and Aristotle did not have a clear concept of *man*. The relativist would argue that the appeal to Universalizability must be

---

[*] For details, see Garry Wills, *"Negro President": Jefferson and the Slave Power* (New York: Houghton Mifflin, 2003).

understood as an appeal within the pale of a given world. Taken literally, the relativist's appeal to Universalizability collapses into an appeal to the Restrictive Principle. Concerning the past, both agree that an appeal to Universalizability reaches beyond the pale of a given world. But relativists agree to the legitimacy of such an appeal only if it is restricted to the limits of that world. Concerning the present, we are all confined to the limits of our world. Accordingly, the difference between relativism and anti-relativism tends to be obliterated. (I suppose both relativists and anti-relativists among opponents of female genital mutilation would reject the legitimacy of an appeal to Universalizability concerning this practice. It may be even controversial whether the defenders of this practice are sufficiently reasonable and knowledgeable about the issue for an appeal to the Restrictive Principle.) Concerning the future, we must conceive it not only possible, but also probable that many of our interpretations grounded on appeals to Universalizability will be rejected by our successors because they were acceptable to us only within the pale of our world. It may seem as if the two principles offered only unattractive choices. Appearances must not dictate the last word in this matter.

2. Reaching Beyond the Pale

It must be conceded that in appealing to Universalizability we always attempt to reach beyond the pale of our world. Even if the solitary interpreter cannot find a private condition supporting his interpretation, his contemporary and future critics can both object by pointing to the limitations of his perspective grounded on his gender, class, race, or any other limitation imposed by the limits of his world. The private conditions he could not discover from his own viewpoint are revealed by his critics, who thereby undermine his interpretation supported by an appeal to Universalizability. Let us assume that both the interpreter and his critics are sincere; we will see at the end of this section that this proviso is quite important. What objections can the critics raise when they reject the solitary interpreter's appeal to Universalizability?

Their most general objection is that the interpreter was mistaken. It is conceivable that he could not help being mistaken. If Plato or Aristotle could not conceive of a society's organization without slavery, their critics must concede that although they were mistaken, nonetheless they could appeal to Universalizability in support of the institution of slavery. There were private conditions grounding their appeal, but from within the world in which they lived, they were blind to these conditions. In contrast to Plato and Aristotle, Jefferson and his contemporaries could appeal only to the Restrictive Principle in support of the institution of slavery—for they surely knew of societies that flourished without slavery. They had the opportunity to be informed about the evils of slavery by Benjamin Franklin's widely circulated pamphlet "Observations Concerning the Increase of Mankind" (written in 1751 and made available to readers beginning that year, published in 1755) or Hume's essay "Of the Populousness of Ancient Nations" (1752).

Critics of Jefferson and his slaveholding contemporaries can even raise the question: is it really the case that they were entitled to appeal to the Restrictive Principle in support of their views on slavery? Is it really the case that all those who agreed with them were reasonable and knowledgeable about what was at issue? If many of their critics hold that in a conflict between greed and reason, they followed the dictates of greed rather than of reason, then even the appeal to the Restrictive Principle merely serves to hide what in their critics' view is naked greed. Seen in the light of our two principles, the mistake of Plato and his contemporaries appears to be different from the fault of Jefferson and his contemporaries. Moreover, the force of the two principles becomes clear if we examine their successors' beliefs and attitudes concerning these two mistakes.

Let us shift our focus from the contemporaries of Plato, Aristotle, and Jefferson to their critics—our contemporaries. Seen in the light of our contemporaries, Plato and Aristotle were mistaken in supporting the institution of slavery, yet, they would argue, they could not help being mistaken. Our contemporaries can support their judgment with an appeal to Universalizability. Note that the critics' appeal to this principle about their ancestors supports a further claim: had the concept of an appeal to Universalizability been available to Plato and Aristotle, they could have appealed to that principle. No doubt, they were mistaken, no matter what principle they appealed to. But their being mistaken does not vitiate such an appeal. Since all qualified interpreters about this topic agree that they could not help being mistaken, the appeal to Universalizability—about the judgment that they could not help being mistaken—supports the claim that Universalizability would have supported their defense of slavery.

Jefferson and his contemporaries were also mistaken in supporting the institution of slavery. But their successors and modern critics cannot appeal to Universalizability in supporting the judgment that Jefferson and his contemporaries could not help being mistaken about the institution of slavery. In support of such a judgment about Jefferson's contemporaries the successors and modern critics can appeal only to the Restrictive Principle. However, even if all those who agree with them are reasonable and knowledgeable about the issues, this does not support an appeal to Universalizability by Jefferson's contemporaries about the institution of slavery. At best, it supports an appeal to the Restrictive Principle: all those who agreed with Jefferson's contemporaries about slavery were reasonable and knowledgeable about that issue. Accordingly, the appeal to Universalizability is not vitiated by the mere fact that it is invoked on behalf of an interpretation that later turns out to be mistaken. But it is invalidated if it cannot be reinforced later by a judgment grounded on Universalizability.

The same considerations emerge when we examine our beliefs and attitudes concerning brute facts that were at one time matters of interpretation rather than of fact. Some of our ancestors believed that the earth was at the center of the universe. Had they appealed to Universalizability in supporting that belief, we would concede the validity of their appeal regardless of our views about their concept *earth*. Relativists would argue that our ancestors' conceptions of *earth* were different from our conceptions, and that whatever principle they appealed to in support of their conceptions must be understood within the pale of their world. Anti-relativists would argue that they did not have a clear concept *earth*, but that this does not invalidate their appeal to Universalizability as long as their critics' judgment that they did not have a clear concept *earth* is itself grounded on Universalizability. Note that a relativist critic need not specify what principle her ancestors appealed to. From the relativist's viewpoint the specification merely introduces a distinction without a difference, for she cannot admit that the appeal to Universalizability is an attempt to reach beyond the pale of a given world. Successful attempts of reaching beyond the pale of a given world would undermine one of the basic tenets of relativism, for relativists hold that there are no universal truths about the world. But if an appeal to Universalizability by our remote ancestors can find support from an appeal to Universalizability by our contemporaries, then there is at least one universal truth about the world. We are successful in reaching beyond the pale of our world through a chain of appeals to Universalizability that is not vitiated by the fact that the interpretation grounded on Universalizability happens to be mistaken.

I have assumed at the beginning of this section that both the interpreter and his critics are sincere. This was not a trivial assumption. Suppose an interpreter supports his judgment about Jefferson's contemporaries with an appeal to the Restrictive Principle. In his judgment, Jefferson's contemporaries were entitled to appeal to the Restrictive Principle. If we spell out the conditions of the two appeals, we find that every appeal to the Restrictive Principle motivates mistrust about the interpretation and suspicion about the interpreter. Interpretations that cannot be supported by an appeal to Universalizability are controversial, or temporary—until an interpretation is found that satisfies the two constraints on interpreting and can be supported by an appeal to Universalizability. Interpreters defending those who agree with their interpretations by appealing to the Restrictive Principle are suspected of supporting their interpretations *sotto voce* with an appeal to Universalizability.

3. Psychological Limitations

Within the limits of his social world, the solitary interpreter was unable to see the private condition grounding his interpretative choice. Psychological limits—such as the content of his belief box #1 or a partially mistaken or inadequate self-understanding—create another barrier undermining his ability to notice these private conditions. Attitudes toward slavery in classical antiquity will again serve as an example. Aristotle argued against some who "maintain[ed] that for one man to be another man's master is contrary to nature, because it is only law that makes one a slave and the other a free man and there is no difference between them in nature and therefore it is unjust, for it is based on force."[*] Aristotle may have argued against opponents who believed that his views on slavery were mistaken or he may have argued against straw men. Either way, there could have been an individual slaveholder in classical antiquity who asked: is it right to treat another human being as an animated tool? Was Aristotle right in holding that slavery is a natural condition? M. I. Finley could not find evidence to prove that Aristotle's contemporaries who were slaveholders had a guilty conscience concerning the institution of slavery. This need not deter us from imagining that such a slaveholder who argued against Aristotle existed. Let us call Aristotle's opponent on this matter AO.

Voices contrary to Aristotle's views on slavery could be heard at a later time in classical antiquity. The statement "God has left all men free; nature has made no one a slave" is attributed to Alcidamas (*c.* 360 B.C.); and the comic poet Philemon (*c.* 368–264 B.C.) wrote that "no one was ever born a slave by nature, but chance enslaves the body." Let us assume that AO, a prosperous Athenian slaveholder in the third century B.C., well versed in both biology and jurisprudence, heard about these views contradicting Aristotle. He is thinking about writing his last will and testament, and he must decide whether upon his death he should free all his slaves or bequeath them to his relatives. According to AO, if slaves are men who are

* Aristotle, *Politics* 1253b, 20–25.

slaves by nature, as Aristotle claimed, then it is right to free only those who became slaves because of an unfortunate accident. If slaves are not men who are slaves by nature, as Philemon wrote, then all must be freed. He is aware that his judgment about these views is clouded by his desire to bestow his possessions on his relatives. For this reason, he decides to examine each case separately, and he is especially careful about putting aside his desire when deliberating on this matter. About each slave he asks: is this particular slave a free man in the body of a slave, is he capable of deliberate choice as any other free man, or is he a slave by nature? If he were not more than what Aristotle called "an animated tool," then freeing him would be a mistake. Having examined each case on its merits and to his own satisfaction, he decides that none of his slaves deserve to be freed. As a solitary interpreter he may even add that he conscientiously excluded all private conditions grounding his interpretive choice. He is certain that all reasonable persons who know his slaves would agree with him.

AO's critic, a resident of his household, disagrees. Let us call her RC—resident critic. It is irrelevant whether RC accepts AO's premise that only those who became slaves because of an accident deserve to be freed. AO claimed to have been guided by certain rules in his deliberations. Guided by her knowledge of these rules and the facts of the matter, RC has come to the conclusion that AO was mistaken when he decided not to free any of his slaves. Adopting his rules entails that at least some deserve to be freed. In examining each slave, he may have been completely blind to the possibility that some are not slaves by nature; in that case his interpretive choice was mistaken. However, if RC accepts AO's complete blindness in this matter, then she must also reject his examination of each slave as a sham. And vice versa: if she does not reject his examination of the slaves as a sham, then she cannot maintain that he was completely blind in this matter, and she must hold that his appeal to Universalizability was mistaken. She may fault both his interpretive choice and his appeal to Universalizability. Or she may argue that his interpretive choice was grounded on the Restrictive Principle. At issue here is only one further claim: his interpretive choice can be grounded on the Restrictive Principle if he is self-deceived, and only if his interpretive choice is based on a minor mistake or he is self-deceived. (We will allow for the possibility that he is a fully qualified interpreter but his interpretive choice is based on a trivial mistake.) The necessary condition will require additional explanation. But first, a few words of caution.

The conditions that are necessary and sufficient for the suggestion that someone is a victim of self-deception are not at the center of my interests, and I claim no originality about identifying these conditions. They have been discussed in the literature on this topic.* My concern here is only the connection between self-deception and the appeal to the Restrictive Principle. If it turns out that the conditions derived from the appeal to the Restrictive Principle are consistent with the necessary and sufficient conditions for the claim that another person is a victim of self-deception that are discussed in the literature, then the account defended here will have gained additional support.

From RC's viewpoint, AO's interpretive choice can be grounded on the Restrictive Principle only if she believes him to be a reasonable person who is knowledgeable about what is at issue. But if she grounds her interpretive choice on Universalizability, she would find it embarrassing to concede without further explanation that her opponent grounded his contrary choice on either of the two principles. Unless she can show that she and her opponent pursue different interpretive goals or she can provide another explanation of their incompatible interpretive choices, she cannot claim that all qualified interpreters agree with her and at the same time admit that all who agree with her opponent are also qualified interpreters. According to her, he was as informed as she about each slave and about the rule guiding his deliberations. She asks: why did he arrive at a result that was at variance with her conclusion? They shared the same information and she accepted his rule guiding his deliberations. They were at odds only in one respect: he desired to enrich his relatives, but she was not concerned about this matter. He was neither completely blind to his desire nor sufficiently vigilant about it. His desire to enrich his relatives was certainly not his reason for his decision in each case. Had it been *his* reason, then the examination of each slave would have been a sham. It was a *cause* of his adverse decision about the individual cases that she judged favorably. While he was in a good position to recognize that his desire causally determined his decision, he failed to discover it. His failure implies that there was something that he did not know about himself.

Occasional lack of self-knowledge can be dismissed as one of many trivial mistakes that each of us makes about ourselves. Interpretive choices based on such lack of self-knowledge need not imply that the interpreter was self-deceived. Recurrent lack of self-knowledge cannot be so easily dismissed. For example, faux experts are often convinced that they are entitled to make interpretive choices based on what they mistakenly believe is their mastery of a given field. As long as they are lucky and their interpretive choices agree with the choices of genuine experts, they will not be

---

* For example, see Alfred R. Mele, *Self-Deception Unmasked* (Princeton: Princeton University Press, 2001).

found wanting. They will be charged with self-deception, if their lack of self-knowledge causally determines their interpretive choices, and only if their interpretive choices are considered to be mistaken.

Since RC believes that AO's interpretive choice is mistaken and that he is a reasonable person who is knowledgeable about what is at issue, he has satisfied the necessary condition for being self-deceived. She also believes that his lack of self-knowledge led to his self-deception, for it enabled him to restrain his vigilance about wanting to enrich his relatives, and his lack of vigilance causally determined his interpretive choices. Provided that she can discredit alternative explanations—as we will see, this is not an easy task—she also believes that he has satisfied a sufficient condition for being self-deceived. Now, if RC believed that AO was neither reasonable nor knowledgeable about what is at issue, she would dismiss his interpretive choices as mistaken, off-the-wall, or irrelevant. In this case, she would not admit that his interpretive choices could be grounded on either of the two principles. So if she claims that he is self-deceived, then she must admit that he is sufficiently reasonable and knowledgeable about the issues for grounding his interpretive choices on the Restrictive Principle. Her claim that he is self-deceived establishes a sufficient condition for grounding his interpretive choices on the Restrictive Principle. It is more difficult to establish self-deception as a necessary condition for grounding his interpretive choices on the Restrictive Principle. Even if she succeeds in this task, she has a good reason to expect further controversy. Her charge of self-deception rests on unstable ground: it is for want of a better explanation that she is charging him with self-deception.

A critic may admit in many uncontroversial cases that an interpreter was both reasonable and knowledgeable about what is at issue, yet insist that his interpretation was mistaken and cannot be grounded on the Universalizability Principle. In supporting her judgment, she may rely on one disjunct of a very long disjunction: his interpretation was based on a minor mistake, or he was not a good observer, or he was narrow-minded, or he was deficient in some respect, or . . . , or he was self-deceived. The controversial character of the charge of self-deception emerges if we imagine such a long disjunction whose last element is the claim that the interpreter was self-deceived. Each disjunct disqualifies the interpretation from being grounded on Universalizability. Can it be grounded on the Restrictive Principle? The answer is that it can be so grounded. In the case of each disqualifying disjunct, the critic cannot do better than dismiss or explain away the interpretation that is incompatible with the interpretation that she claims is grounded on Universalizability. In admitting the interpretation's grounding on the Restrictive Principle, the critic shifts the focus of the debate from what is interpreted to the interpreter who proposed such an incompatible interpretation. This shift of focus makes sense only if the critic wants to argue with the interpreter who proposed the incompatible interpretation.

In arguing that the interpreter was self-deceived and that this is the necessary condition for its support by the Restrictive Principle, the critic claims that all other disjuncts are either false or irrelevant. The charge that the interpreter was self-deceived appears for want of a better explanation. The critic asks: what else explains that only the Restrictive Principle can support his interpretation? Since all other explanations have been defeated, what remains is the explanation of last resort: he was self-deceived. Charges of self-deception are always controversial. The controversy can be easily generated by a second critic who rejects the charge of self-deception and supports a less controversial disjunct.

Even if a second critic claimed explicitly that interpretive statements are not either true or false, from her viewpoint RC and AO can both be right only if a trivial explanation for their incompatible interpretive choices is available. (For example, they pursue divergent interpretive goals.) Without such an additional explanation a second critic would find it awkward to agree with RC that all qualified interpreters agree with her interpretation, and at the same time hold that all who agree with her opponent's incompatible interpretation are also qualified interpreters. Accordingly, a second critic must examine only three cases. (1) RC's interpretation is correct, while AO's interpretive choice is mistaken. In this case, she can support her interpretation by appealing to Universalizability. All those who disagree with her are either not reasonable, or not knowledgeable, or at least partially mistaken, or victims of self-deception. (2) Her interpretation is mistaken, while his interpretive choice is correct. In this case, he can support his choice by appealing to Universalizability. Since he is right about the matter, he is now in the same position as she was in the previously mentioned case. (3) Both were mistaken, for they were either insufficiently reasonable or insufficiently knowledgeable about the matter, or each was partially mistaken, or self-deceived in his or her own way.

If we support with Universalizability our own interpretive choices, we must argue that those who oppose our choices were either mistaken or self-deceived. If they were mistaken, then they cannot ground their alternative interpretations on Universalizability, unless we have evidence that they were completely blind to their mistake and—for good reasons—could not help being blind to their mistake. So if they were mistaken, not irredeemably blind to their mistake, and not mistaken on account of a less controversial reason, then they were self-deceived. An appeal to the Restrictive

Principle is the best support for their interpretive choices if they are self-deceived. Self-deception appears now as a sufficient condition for an appeal to the Restrictive Principle. Provided that less controversial explanations in the previously mentioned long disjunction are rejected, self-deception also appears as a necessary condition for grounding an interpretive choice on the Restrictive Principle. Three remarks must be added.

(1) If by our own lights another person's interpretive choice is mistaken, we are seldom called to decide whether he is entitled to appeal to Universalizability or only to the Restrictive Principle. But the usefulness of the Universalizability Principle would be greatly diminished if we did not concede the possibility that another person may be mistaken, yet he may be right in appealing to Universalizability. We are just as fallible as our ancestors, and if history provides some guidance, it can be safely predicted that in some cases our successors will identify as interpretations what we call facts. We agree that our remote ancestors were mistaken about slavery being a natural condition, yet we are willing to concede the validity of an appeal to Universalizability to our ancestors. There are no good reasons for expecting less generosity from our successors. After all, we, too, satisfy the foundation of such generosity. We, too, search for what is true and strive for what is good, and within the limited view that we have of the world, we, too, do as well as we can. The appeal to Universalizability would be useless if we did not detach the judgment about the validity of such an appeal from the fact that such an appeal often supports mistaken views.

(2) Except in circumstances that require additional justification—such as when trying to secure hearing for a new theory in the sciences or a novel interpretation in the arts—if we agree with another person's interpretive choice, we do not ordinarily suggest that only the Restrictive Principle can support this choice. Such a suggestion implies that the interpretive choice is faulted for containing an element that invalidates its support by the Universalizability Principle. If it were merely mistaken, we could simply dismiss it without adverting to the Restrictive Principle. The suggestion that the Restrictive Principle should support it implies that we do not agree with the interpretive choice and consider it mistaken, yet admit that those who agree with it are reasonable and knowledgeable about what is at issue.

(3) Contemporaries of Plato and Aristotle cannot be faulted for being self-deceived if they believed that slavery was a natural condition. No doubt, they had a mistaken belief and they satisfied the necessary condition for being self-deceived. But since their mistaken belief was not causally determined by a lack of self-knowledge, they have not satisfied a sufficient condition for being self-deceived. Their mistake was not about a minor

matter. It was about a fundamental issue touching their lives. By comparison, we fault our contemporaries for minor mistakes or self-deception in the context of less important interpretive choices. We admit the validity of our remote ancestors' appeal to Universalizability, yet at the same time we claim that if our contemporaries' interpretive choices are based on minor mistakes or self-deception, they can be grounded only on the Restrictive Principle. Why must our contemporaries satisfy higher standards than our remote ancestors? The answer will suggest itself, if we compare three available responses to the mistaken belief about natural slavery. If one of our contemporaries would argue that slavery is a natural condition, we would dismiss his views as neither reasonable nor knowledgeable about what is at issue. We would not dismiss the views of either Plato's and Aristotle's contemporaries or AO's and RC's contemporaries. If Plato's and Aristotle's contemporaries could not help being mistaken about natural slavery, then the decision that they could ground their beliefs on the Universalizability Principle rather than the Restrictive Principle, or the other way around, seems arbitrary. Appearances must not be trusted, for the choice is no longer arbitrary if the same belief is held by contemporaries of AO and RC. Both AO and RC asked: were all, or some, or none of the slaves they examined natural slaves? If RC could validly ground her interpretive choice on Universalizability, AO could not ground his incompatible interpretive choice on the same principle, or the other way around. Or one could ground his choice on one principle, while the other could ground her choice on the other principle. Or both could ground their incompatible choices on the Restrictive Principle. We must have good reasons for claiming in all these cases that an interpretive choice can be grounded only on the Restrictive Principle and not on the Universalizability Principle. Such reasons are available about the views of AO's, RC's, and our contemporaries, but not about the views of Plato's and Aristotle's, or their contemporaries. Accordingly, Plato, Aristotle, and their contemporaries could ground their mistaken belief only on the Universalizability Principle.

4. The Sincerity Condition

I have stipulated that both the solitary interpreter and his critic are sincere—here I must spell out the point. If a critic disagrees with an interpretation because it is incompatible with the facts known to her or to the interpretations adopted by her, she must choose among a limited number of available alternatives. She can reject it—without additional comment—as an off-the-wall interpretation, or consider it irrelevant for her purposes, or dismiss it as mistaken. From her viewpoint, further scrutiny and explanation are warranted only if the interpretation presented is incompatible with her own interpretation that is supported by the Universalizability Principle. No further explanation is required if she can show that the interpreter she is criticizing is simply mistaken. If this cannot be shown, and she cannot dismiss his competing interpretation as off-the-wall or irrelevant, then she must defend her own interpretation, provided that it is grounded on Universalizability. (Other problems arise if she can support her interpretation only with the much weaker Restrictive Principle: she must deal with the mistrust and suspicion inspired by her appeal to this principle.)

While she is defending her interpretation, when all other choices in confronting an incompatible interpretation have been found wanting, the focus of attention shifts from what is at issue to the interpreters who have presented incompatible interpretations. Charges of insincerity or self-deception arise at this stage. Religious or political disputes exemplify this point. Antagonists of fundamentalist religious or radical antireligious beliefs change their focus from the issues to real or imagined adversaries. They denounce their adversaries as insincere or self-deceived. Those who are so denounced attribute the same failings to their opponents. Charges of insincerity or self-deception also arise in the context of disputes about legislative or judicial decisions. If ideological bias is attributed to some legislators and judges in their decision-making process, their critics often suggest that bias was either a reason or a cause for a given decision. If it was a reason, and legislators or judges were aware that ideological bias rather than the facts or the laws guided their decisions, then they must be charged with dishonesty. If their decisions were determined by a cause of which they were unaware, then they can be charged with self-deception. Strong as these charges are, they can be answered to the satisfaction of these legislators' and judges' defenders: they wanted to avoid a greater evil by their decisions, even at the cost of their integrity. To be sure, this defense will be unacceptable to their opponents and critics.

5. The Shift of Focus in Interpreting

We will better understand the role of Universalizability in interpreting if we recapitulate what has been said so far about the variety of available responses to a given interpretation. In the large majority of cases we accept the interpretation of what has been said or done without further questions. When the occasion presents itself, we transmit that interpretation to others. As long as the interpretive chain connecting the speaker or agent with a given audience remains uninterrupted, the interpretation becomes a hereditary property of what has been said or done. The interpretive chain can be interrupted at any time or place by an interpreter who cannot reconcile the interpretation presented with the accepted facts or with the interpretations supported by the Universalizability Principle. The interpreter challenging that interpretation can reject it without further comment as a mistaken, irrelevant, or off-the-wall interpretation. In rejecting it without comment, the interpreter implies that those who hold the challenged interpretation pursue interpretive goals different from his own, or are not reasonable or not knowledgeable about what is at issue. He can suggest that the challenged interpretation be replaced by another, starting thereby another interpretive chain. If successful, the new interpretation will become a hereditary property connecting with its new audience. As long as facts and interpretations are at the interpreter's center of attention, topics connected with other interpreters of what is at issue need not arise.

When the rejection of the available alternative interpretations without additional comment is considered to be insufficient, the interpreter must provide reasons for dismissing them and for replacing them with his own interpretive choices. Detailed criticism of the available alternative interpretations is required if the suggestion that they pursue goals different from his own is seen as nothing more than a dodge for avoiding further discussion. Explanations are also required if those who hold the available alternative interpretations are generally acknowledged to be both reasonable and knowledgeable about the issues. As soon as an account for rejecting the incompatible interpretations seems either necessary or useful in supporting a new interpretation, the interpreter's focus shifts from what is at issue to the interpreters who hold the incompatible interpretations. It would be useless to support his views by stating explicitly that those who hold the incompatible interpretations are either not reasonable or not knowledgeable about the issues, for this explicit claim has the same force as the rejection of the incompatible interpretations without further comment. But he can suggest that although all reasonable and knowledgeable persons would agree with his interpretive choice, there are such persons who claim to hold an incompatible interpretation. Surely, such an odd suggestion requires further explanation! Assuming that the incompatible interpretation is mistaken, and it is defended by reasonable interpreters who are at least partially knowledgeable about what is at issue, one of three explanations can be fitted to this odd suggestion: those who claim to hold the incompatible interpretation are insincere, or they are completely blind to one aspect of what is at issue through no fault of their own, or they are victims of self-deception.

Interpretations grounded on Universalizability are certainly not damaged—maybe they are even provided with additional support—if it turns out that those who claim to hold incompatible interpretations are insincere. Accordingly, the first explanation is not interesting for our purposes. The second explanation suggests itself when an interpreter appeals to Universalizability in support of his own interpretation and at the same admits that an incompatible interpretation of his predecessors was in its own time and place validly grounded on Universalizability. Plato's and Aristotle's contemporaries who could not even imagine the organization of society without slaves believed that some men were natural slaves. Some of their successors no longer believed that there were natural slaves, while others accepted this as a fact. Contemporaries of Plato and Aristotle were entitled to appeal to Universalizability in support of the claim that there were in their time and place natural slaves. Their successors' belief that there are no natural slaves was also grounded on Universalizability, before it was considered as fact. The third explanation paves the way for suggesting that even if self-deceived interpreters are not entitled to rely on Universalizability, they can ground their interpretations on the Restrictive Principle.

The force of the Universalizability Principle and the Restrictive Principle emerges in the context of the second explanation. If the critic of a discredited view believes that those who held that view were completely blind to one aspect of what was at issue, through no fault of their own, and she is prepared to appeal to Universalizability in support of her judgment on this matter, then she will also admit that those who held the discredited view were entitled to appeal to Universalizability in support of their own view. Moreover, if those who held the discredited view were only partially blind to an aspect of what was at issue, she will also suggest that—as long as the blindness was not their own fault—they were also entitled to ground their view on Universalizability. But if their blindness were their own fault, then she would suggest that they were entitled to appeal only to the Restrictive Principle. To the extent that they were reasonable and at least partially knowledgeable about the issues, they would have satisfied the sufficient condition for an appeal to the Restrictive Principle. To the extent that their blindness was their own fault, they were self-deceived. Since they were self-deceived, they could ground their views at most on the Restrictive Principle.

The two principles provide standards of judgment in confronting discredited interpretations. We need not yield to the call of relativism when judging such interpretations. Not all mistaken interpretations need to be judged by the same standards. Some who held mistaken interpretations were entitled to ground their interpretation on Universalizability, while others—the self-deceived—could appeal only to the Restrictive Principle.

6. Alternative Interpretive Goals

Are two competing interpretations, proposed at different times and places, both entitled to be supported by the Universalizability Principle? Or must we admit that one of the two can be supported only by the Restrictive Principle? These questions arise only if an interpreter's focus shifts from the issues discussed to those who hold competing interpretations. For good reasons, interpreters and their critics ordinarily resist such a shift of focus. As long as a competing interpretation can be dismissed without further comment, or simply rejected as an alternative proposed by those who pursue goals different from his own, there is no need for further debates. Interpreters successful in avoiding such debates are not necessarily more tolerant than others who engage in them. Their choice is often limited to entering or avoiding an interminable debate, for it is indeed an interminable debate that can be glimpsed on the horizon of debates about conflicting interpretations.

An interpreter may pursue interpretive goals different from those who hold an incompatible interpretation. He may support his own interpretation by appealing to the Universalizability Principle and dismiss the incompatible interpretations without comment or explain them away by reference to the different interpretive goals. Relativists may seem to be more tolerant in these circumstances than anti-relativists. Appearances must not be trusted in these cases, for the anti-relativist can always argue that other interpreters' tolerance merely shows that they do not care for one interpretation more than for another. The claim that the interpreter pursues goals different from those who maintain incompatible interpretations is often suggested in the contexts of art and religion. Even if such claims have their place in these contexts, they must not be accepted in other interpretive contexts, for even in the contexts of art and religion, it is questionable whether such claims should be considered more than a dodge for avoiding further discussion.

In the context of the arts, the claim that two incompatible interpretations are both valid is based on a false analogy. More than a thousand literary artworks have been written about the Don Juan theme since Tirso de Molina wrote his *El burlador de Sevilla* in 1635. It would be a mistake to claim that these artworks are interpretations of one and the same myth. Molière's play is not an interpretation that is either in agreement or incompatible with Tirso's play or Da Ponte's libretto. Each deserves to be evaluated on its own merit, and each has its own interpretive career, independently of all the others. Actors are commonly said to provide interpretations of characters in a play. But just as it is a mistake to raise questions about the compatibility or incompatibility of two plays on the same theme, it is also a mistake to raise such questions about two actors playing the same role in two different performances of a play. Similarly, just because we speak about Herbert von Karajan's and Georg Solti's different interpretations of Wagner's *Der Ring des Niebelungen*, we cannot assume that it always makes sense to ask whether their interpretations are compatible or incompatible. Initially, we may ask whether their interpretations of a certain passage in the score are compatible. This question loses its point as soon as we speak about the two performance artworks containing these two different interpretations. No doubt, the different performance artworks are based on a common score. But as a performance artwork each is unique: they cannot be judged as either compatible or incompatible. An actor creating a role or a conductor directing an orchestra is creating artworks and not interpretations. We may prefer the creation of one actor or one conductor rather than that of another. At different times we may prefer different performance artworks. Each of these is based on a very large number of interpretations of well-defined short segments of a literary or musical work of art. Although they are based on interpretations, they are incommensurable artworks and not interpretations. Their incommensurability does not provide support for relativism, and it certainly does not create obstacles for anti-relativism.

Arguments for relativism are sometimes advanced in support of a plea for tolerating beliefs held by others. The desire to diminish the threat of violence against the outsider who holds views divergent from the insider deserves support. But we have no good reasons for believing that religious, racial, or ethnic strife could be avoided if we admitted the relative merit of beliefs that are incompatible with our own. The ethnocentric critic who suggests that the outsiders' incompatible interpretations be considered incommensurable in order to diminish the threat of violence overestimates the power of interpretations and misidentifies the cause of violence. Interpretations of texts and legal or religious documents do not cause violence. Ethnic groups may dislike each other, followers of different religions may be suspicious of each other, and members of one ill-defined racial group may even hate the members of another such group. Yet the dislike, the suspicion, the hatred, and any other negative sentiment are insufficient for provoking violence against the other for purely ideological reasons. Self-interest or the prospects of improving an agent's own condition motivates his (or her) violence against another. Purely ideological violence is motivated by the conviction that the elimination of the other contributes not only to improvements in the agent's own condition, but also to a better world.[*]

---

[*] For a detailed discussion, see Saul Friedländer, *Nazi Germany and the Jews*, vol. 1 (New York: HarperCollins, 1997), 73–112.

7. Individual or Social Viewpoints

Our concepts are innate, or inherited from others within our community, or created by us for specific purposes. Regardless of their origin, social interactions prompt our awareness of most of our concepts. At the time we become aware of them, each of them already has had its own history. A social and historical viewpoint seems to recommend itself when we speak about our concepts. But in an account about our reaching an understanding, interpretation, and application of these concepts, we must adopt the viewpoint of a single individual. The intellectual work required in becoming aware of concepts that are hard-wired in us or in reaching the understanding of the concepts we inherit is not a gift that we can receive from or transmit to others. Each of us is alone in performing the required intellectual work. No doubt, two or more persons can share the same understanding of a concept, accept the same interpretation of what was said or done, and apply that interpretation for a common purpose. Communication among them relies on the understanding they share. In the large majority of cases we are satisfied with the understanding, interpretation, and application we share with others. We adopt the role of a solitary interpreter only if we question what we have inherited from others. However, if I engage in such questioning by playing the role of a solitary interpreter who is trying to discover whether there are any private conditions influencing my interpretive choices, then my critic will suggest that I am engaged in a self-defeating activity. The unique characteristics of each interpreter and of each of his critics guarantee that there are always private conditions influencing their interpretive choices. Accordingly, my effort to discover whether there are such private conditions is either futile or a sham. This objection would be sufficient for defeating all appeals to the Universalizability Principle if we could not distinguish between relevant and irrelevant private conditions. Can we distinguish between these two kinds of private conditions?

When AO asked whether each slave was a natural slave or a free man in the body of a slave, he was using concepts that he had received in interaction with his social world. When RC asked the same question and later criticized AO's answers, she was also using concepts that she had learned from others in the world in which she lived. Both may have believed that they were solitary interpreters trying to discover whether there were any private conditions influencing their interpretive choices. But isn't the understanding of the concepts AO had inherited different from RC's understanding of the concepts she had inherited? They may have had different conceptions of the same or of different concepts. Either way, their having different conceptions already burdened them with different private conditions. Granted, private conditions undermine and ultimately defeat appeals to the Universalizability Principle. However, private conditions that are irrelevant to a given interpretive choice will not be regarded as obstacles to Universalizability. For example, depending on the specific circumstances, the fact that RC is a better observer than AO may be a relevant or irrelevant obstacle to Universalizability. The question arises: on what grounds do we judge that a given fact or interpretation is relevant or irrelevant in appealing to Universalizability? Since such judgments are based on interpretations, the answer is not surprising. Whenever interpretations are at issue, the question arises whether the Universalizability or the Restrictive Principle supports a given interpretation.

The force of an appeal to the Universalizability Principle emerges whenever one interpretation grounded on Universalizability is supported by another that is also grounded on Universalizability. It will be useful to recall a previously discussed example. If our claim that contemporaries of Plato and Aristotle could not help being mistaken in supporting the institution of slavery finds support through an appeal to Universalizability, then Universalizability would have also supported their defense of slavery. They were mistaken in defending slavery, yet their mistake would not have invalidated their appeal to Universalizability, as long as it was supported by our claim grounded on Universalizability. Our successful second-level appeal to Universalizability supports their first-level appeal to this principle. Similarly, if our second-level claim about the irrelevance of a private condition finds support from the Universalizability Principle, then this principle provides further support for the first-level interpretation containing that irrelevant private condition.

Finally, a question must be answered: do we really need to adopt the role of a solitary interpreter who is trying to discover whether there are any private conditions influencing his interpretive choices? Couldn't we find a more direct way to a right understanding or interpretation of a topic, if we asked about the consensus of professionals within a given field? The answer is that we ordinarily ask about such a consensus and accept whatever answer we are offered. We accept the answers as we accept the large majority of interpretations, as long as we do not have good reasons to raise questions about them. As mentioned before, we adopt the role of a solitary interpreter if we are not satisfied with the answers provided by others. We defend our own alternative interpretation and support it with the Universalizability Principle in order to establish it as part of a new consensus of professionals within a domain of competing interpretations.

CHAPTER TEN

Critique of Interpretive Reasoning

We are now in the position of understanding a major problem in interpretive reasoning. Let us retrace our steps. I have argued that we defend our interpretations by showing that they are consistent with the facts known to us and that they are the best available for our purposes. We are entitled to appeal to the Universalizability Principle if and only if we have satisfied these two constraints on interpreting. We appeal to the Universalizability Principle concerning a natural interpretation in the indicative or subjunctive mood and to the Restrictive Principle about an essentially contestable interpretation. An unresolved problem remains in the context of alternative interpretations: can we satisfy the call for both tolerance and sincerity? Earlier I suggested that sincerity is the price of tolerance and the other way around; here I will discuss this problem within the general framework of a principle-driven interpretive reasoning.

1. Principles

Ordinarily interpretations are self-confirmed until they are challenged. We accept them and pass them on to others without questions. They are scrutinized only when they do not seem to satisfy the factual or normative constraints on interpreting. If an interpreter has satisfied both constraints for a given interpretation, he has reached the highest standard. Accordingly, he can claim with considerable confidence that all qualified interpreters agree with his interpretation. The close connection between his satisfying the two constraints and the appeal to Universalizability explains an often-heard reply, when a well-defended interpretation is challenged. The interpreter's critic asks: "Do you really believe that all qualified interpreters agree with your interpretation?" He answers: "No, but they *ought* to agree!" His answer transforms an easily falsifiable statement expressed by an application of the Universalizability Principle into a recommendation that is not truth-valued.

Advocates of incompatible interpretations can both appeal to Universalizability, and if such an appeal could decide between two incompatible interpretations, we would easily reach the end of interminable controversies. The principles governing interpretation must be sufficiently flexible so that they do not provide exclusive support to one side of an interminable controversy or to one contestable religious or political view. So what is their use?

To answer this question we must focus on an interpreter who adverts to an appeal to Universalizability when he believes he has satisfied the two constraints on interpreting. If another qualified interpreter who holds an incompatible interpretation challenges him, he can withdraw his interpretation or hold on to it against any opposition. If he holds on to it and retreats to safer ground, he must choose between more or less tolerant responses. Even if he offers the most tolerant response to his opponents, he cannot claim that he has satisfied the two constraints on interpreting. He may even admit that not all reasonable and knowledgeable persons agree with his interpretation, but as soon as he adds that they *ought* to agree with him, he casts doubt on his facile admission. The recommendation that they ought to agree with him is grounded on three firmly held beliefs. (1) His interpretation satisfies both constraints on an interpretation. (2) He is sincere: he is recommending to others only what he himself believes. (3) All qualified interpreters agree with his interpretation because it satisfies both constraints on an interpretation.

The most tolerant response rests on his taking away with one hand what he is willing to grant with the other. Charges of self-contradiction, deception, or self-deception arise at this stage, for he cannot spell out the conditions for holding the three firmly held beliefs and at the same time admit that *not* all qualified interpreters agree with his interpretation. If he further retreats to an appeal to the Restrictive Principle in order to defend all interpreters who agree with him, then he advances beyond reach down the path of deception or self-deception. He cannot hold on to a contested interpretation unless he believes that it satisfies the two constraints on interpreting, but if this is the case then he is entitled to appeal to Universalizability. In essence, he professes tolerance and with a loud voice appeals only to the Restrictive Principle, but in a whisper he appeals to Universalizability. From center stage he proclaims that all who agree with his interpretation are reasonable and knowledgeable about what is at issue, while from the backstage area he adds that all reasonable and knowledgeable interpreters agree with his interpretation. Jointly these two claims imply that all and only reasonable and knowledgeable interpreters agree with his interpretation. The point of his pronouncement on center stage to an appeal to the Restrictive Principle is to show that he is tolerant of interpreters who do not agree with him. The show of tolerance is empty if no qualified interpreter disagrees with him. It yields a logical contradiction if there is at least one such interpreter. If he is fully aware of this contradiction, he will admit that sincerity is the price of tolerance. He can maintain speaking with both center-stage and backstage voices only at the cost of giving up the belief that he is recommending to others what he himself believes. If he is aware of the contradiction, he deceives others for the sake of tolerance. If he is unaware of the contradiction, tolerance is purchased at the cost of self-deception or incoherence. If we disregard the possibility of incoherence, we must admit that either way insincerity is the price of tolerance.

I have argued that essentially contestable or deep interpretations are appropriate only when the subjects we are interpreting not only do not, but also cannot, agree with the interpretation offered. We defend interpreters offering a deep interpretation with an appeal to the Restrictive Principle, thereby leaving the door open for alternative interpretations. What was said about the retreat to the Restrictive Principle for the sake of tolerance also holds true for the defense of interpreters offering a deep interpretation: insincerity is the price for admitting deep interpretations. At the same time, deep interpretations, together with the theories supporting them, have a moral dimension. This dimension is the most neglected aspect of deep interpretations and their supporting theories. No doubt, the views of Marx, Nietzsche, and Freud have been found wanting. But as I suggested (chapter 3, section 8), even if most of their contributions to philosophical speculation have been disproved, the moral aspect of their thinking deserves to be preserved. Deep interpretations, together with their supporting theories, deserve to be discredited if their moral import is removed.

We must face the predicament of deep interpretations. The predicament leads to a dilemma. We can avoid deep interpretations and reject deep interpretation theories. The price of such a choice is high. If this is our choice, the moral dimension of the interpreting activity becomes lost to sight. Equally high is the price of a second choice in response to the predicament. Its price is insincerity. Supporters of deep interpretation opt for this choice. Some interpreters are fully aware of the insincerity required for supporting deep interpretations, and at least temporarily accept its high cost. Others are unaware of the high cost or deny that hypocrisy is required for preserving the moral dimension of interpreting. Many other interpreters hold views between the extremes on this topic.

So we avoid deep interpretation altogether or accept it for the sake of its moral import. The second horn of the dilemma leads to a paradox. Having accepted deep interpretation in order to preserve the moral dimension of interpreting, we find that deep interpretation trades on insincerity. Its center-stage voice proclaims that all who agree with the findings of deep interpretation are qualified interpreters. This seems to leave the door open for the claim that even those who disagree with these findings are qualified interpreters. But this door is carefully closed by its backstage voice telling us that all qualified interpreters agree with those findings. The incompatibility between the two voices does not remain hidden for long, and practitioners of deep interpretation surrender the defense of their views hitherto provided by an appeal to the Restrictive Principle. They reaffirm their claim that all reasonable and knowledgeable interpreters agree with their interpretation. At this stage, deep interpretation yields to natural interpretation in the subjunctive mood at a high cost to the interpreter. Since he grounds his interpretation on the agreement with all qualified interpreters and not of those persons he is interpreting, he risks being considered a dogmatic or authoritarian interpreter.

We have come full circle. We started with opting for the second horn of the dilemma and admitted deep interpretations and their supporting theories for the sake of their moral import. Since we were prepared to argue with the speakers and agents whose words and deeds were subject to deep interpretation, we left the door open for the claim that they were also reasonable and knowledgeable about what is at issue. Hence, publicly we grounded our deep interpretation on the Restrictive Principle, while privately we maintained that it was grounded on the Universalizability Principle. As soon as we noticed that we were trading on insincerity, we rejected our interpretation grounded on the Restrictive Principle and opted for grounding it on the Universalizability Principle in the subjunctive mood. We ended with opting for the first horn of the dilemma. But the same considerations that originally moved us to choose the second horn of the dilemma could reappear at any time and motivate us again to admit deep interpretations and their supporting theories for the sake of their moral import.

Deep interpretations introduce an element of instability in the interpreting situation. Practitioners of deep interpretation become vulnerable themselves to the charge of deception or self-deception. Did the theoreticians of deep interpretation see this point? Are Nietzsche's lines in defense of the unconditional will to truth intended as a way out of the deep interpreter's predicament? (Detailed arguments in support of an affirmative answer to both questions are beyond the scope of this work.) Nietzsche wrote in *The Gay Science:*

> ... "will to truth" does *not* mean "I will not let myself be deceived" but—there is no choice—"I will not deceive, not even myself"; *and with this we are on the ground of morality.**

If we accept Nietzsche's way out of the deep interpreter's predicament, we must consider the Restrictive Principle a defective principle that is useful only as a temporary expedient. As before, we defend what we called deep interpretations by showing that they satisfy both constraints on interpreting, permitting an appeal to Universalizability. According to our revised vocabulary, deep interpretations are understood as natural interpretations in the subjunctive mood that have a moral dimension, in contrast to other natural interpretations in the subjunctive mood that do not have a moral dimension. The proposed revision of our vocabulary does not have untoward consequences and does not change our understanding of the interpreting activity—at least until the interpreter argues about an essentially contestable interpretation with the speaker or agent whose words or deeds he is interpreting. (To save words, I will continue using "deep interpretation" rather than more roundabout expressions.)

2. Validity of the Principles

The usefulness of the two principles cannot be shown within the context of an interpretive controversy. They show their validity when we are speaking about such controversies. I do not claim that interpreters actually appeal to these principles in speaking about the interpreting activity. Yet if a principle guiding an activity is considered to be a valid principle, it must be considered to be valid even if it is not formulated, and even before it is formulated. Anecdotal evidence gathered from interpreters who may have appealed to one of the two principles in support of their interpretations does not provide sufficient support for accepting their validity. Nor is it sufficient to claim that since these principles rely on interpretations of our interpretive practices, they must be consistent with the facts; they must

---

* Friedrich Nietzsche, *The Gay Science,* Book 5, [344] trans. Walter Kaufmann (New York: Viking Penguin, 1982), 449.

be guided by facts, but they do not suggest factual claims about our interpretive practices. If the principles were merely interpretations, then they
would be together with all other interpretations on a segment of a line
between misinterpretations and factual descriptions. Whatever is on that
line requires support by one of the two principles. If the two principles
were on that line, we would be moving in a very small circle. Alternatively,
we would be inconsistent if we exempted them from support by one of
these principles. Provided that the principles can be defended independently of both alternatives, the alternatives may be ignored. The principles
will be defended as either guiding the interpreting activity or in accordance with that activity.

It may be argued that interpreting does not have any rules, and that
interpretations are merely results of arbitrary decisions; in deciding to
defend or to accept an interpretation, we follow our intuitions, the dictates
of fashion, or the teachings of a guru. Such views require as much defense
as their denial. In defending them or denying them, we are engaged in
interpreting the interpreting activity. Moreover, we rely on reasoning in
order to convince our opponents. Reasoning suggests that while engaged
in interpreting, we are engaged in a rational enterprise. Interpreting may
not have rules, in the same sense that chess or baseball has constitutive
rules, but it has principles that can be formulated. These principles must
satisfy certain desiderata. Good models for these desiderata are provided
by what we know about reasoning in other fields. With adjustments to be
added later, what must be said about interpretive reasoning fits well with
what Paul Grice said about reasoning *tout court:*

> The discrimination and systematization of acceptable principles of inference
> provide for us a model, or rather, perhaps, an infinite set of models, by ref-
> erence to which we may understand actual reasonings (an ideal construction
> to which actual reasonings approximate). Such models or ideal construc-
> tions are models in three ways: (1) they are *analytic* models, since it is an ade-
> quate degree of approximation to them which confers on certain sequences
> of thought the title Reasoning; (2) they are *explanatory* models, in that they
> provide (or play a central part in providing) accounts of how actual reason-
> ing proceeds, and why it so proceeds; (3) they are *normative* models, in that
> they provide patterns of the ways in which actual reasoning *should* (ought to)
> proceed.[*]

Even if the actual reasoning of a subject does not necessarily improve after
learning the rules of reasoning, the spelling out of these rules is useful.
Their explicit statement permits us to rely on them as explanatory and

---

[*] Paul Grice, *Aspects of Reason* (Oxford: Oxford University Press, 2001), 7–8.

normative models. The following are examples of principles of logical reasoning. It is a guiding principle of logical reasoning that from true premises we cannot derive validly a false conclusion. Valid inferences have a valid logical form; invalid inferences have no valid logical form. The logical principles and theorems are trivially true, and their addition among the premises of an inference is irrelevant to the validity of that inference. Interpretive reasoning relies on trivial principles, but they cannot be shown to be trivially true in the sense in which the guiding principles of logical reasoning are trivially true. If this is considered to be sufficient for dismissing the principles of interpretive reasoning, then we ought to dismiss also the principles guiding moral reasoning. Alternatively, if this is insufficient for dismissing the principles of interpreting reasoning, then we must show how they satisfy our desiderata in interpreting.

Since interpretive conflicts are common, we expect that all principles guiding interpretations must accommodate conflicting interpretations. This does not imply that two interpreters holding incompatible interpretations are both entitled to appeal to Universalizability. This may be the case in the specific circumstances previously discussed. But it may also happen that each of the two interpreters dismisses the interpretation of the other as mistaken, irrelevant, or off-the-wall. The principle guiding the interpretive reasoning is not subject to criticism in these cases. Only the interpretations presented are dismissed. They are dismissed because they do not satisfy the two constraints on interpretations, and they cannot be supported by appealing to the Universalizability Principle or to the Restrictive Principle. Interpreters supporting incompatible interpretations will argue in these cases that their opponent's appeal is a misapplication of a principle guiding interpretive reasoning. With respect to such misapplications, we must remember a parallel with invalid logical reasoning. When we reject an invalid logical inference, we do not do so because it is an instance of an invalid logical form. We reject it because it is not an instance of a valid logical form or because it is a misapplication of valid logical reasoning. Similarly, we need not search for invalid principles of interpretive reasoning in order to claim that a given interpretation is invalid. It is sufficient to show that valid principles of interpretive reasoning do not warrant that interpretation or that the interpretation is a misapplication of a valid interpretive principle.

The idea behind an appeal to a principle of interpretive reasoning is the following: an interpreter may adopt or defend an interpretation if and only if in that interpreter's judgment all or some persons who are reasonable and knowledgeable about what is at issue do so as well or ought to do so as well. If the appeal to a principle is formulated in this way, an objection can be answered. Critics of the views presented here ask: instead of engaging in a solitary interpretive inquiry, why don't we pursue an empirical investigation or a sociological survey to find out what interpretations are adopted or defended by all or some reasonable and knowledgeable persons? The answer has been suggested earlier: we would have to evaluate the interpretations prior to counting them among the acceptable interpretations for our purposes. Even the fact that a compact majority supports a given interpretation cannot serve as an explanation of our adopting that interpretation. Moreover, we would not want to enter a normative claim that interpretive reasoning should proceed in this manner. After all, the fact that a compact majority has adopted an interpretation does not imply that it is the best available interpretation for our purposes. I have mentioned in chapter 8 Heidegger's views about what "people say." More illuminating here is what Hegel wrote about public opinion:

> Public opinion therefore deserves to be *respected* as well as *despised*—despised for its concrete consciousness of expression, and respected for its essential basis, which appears in that concrete consciousness only in a more or less obscure manner. Since it contains no criterion of discrimination and lacks the ability to raise its own substantial aspect [to the level of] determinate knowledge, the first formal condition of achieving anything great or rational, either in actuality or in science, is to be independent of public opinion. Great achievement may in turn be assured that public opinion will subsequently accept it, recognize it, and adopt it as one of its prejudices.

Hegel added the following note to the above:

> "Every kind of falsehood and truth is present in public opinion, but it is the prerogative [*Sache*] of the great man to discover the truth within it. He who expresses the will of his age, tells it what its will is, and accomplishes this will, is the great man of the age. What he does is the essence and inner content of the age, and he gives the latter actuality; and no one can achieve anything great unless he is able to despise public opinion as he here and there encounters it."*

Even if we had great men of the age among our contemporaries, we would have much less confidence in them than our early nineteenth-century predecessors. We may acknowledge the competence or expertise of an interpreter in a restricted field, but even in these cases we are suspicious about that interpreter's motives. For example, we recognize the need for professional critics in the arts: we expect each of them to tell us about their understanding of individual artworks in their field of competence. Yet

---

* Hegel, *Elements of the Philosophy of Right,* 355.

guided by what we have learned from theories of deep interpretation, we have become suspicious even about professional art, literary, or music critics. Their pretension is that they know something about a given art form that their audiences do not know. Do they in fact know what they claim to know? Are they entitled to speak with a universal voice about their area of specialty?

We must note that Hegel did not restrict his remarks about public opinion to criticism in the arts. The great men of the age or the "world-historical individuals"—so-called in *Reason in History*—"are those who were the first to formulate the desires of their fellows explicitly." They are not only interpreters of what is needed for their age, but also agents who help to bring about what is needed in their age. We may disregard the fanfare about great men or world-historical individuals, and speak more modestly about professional interpreters. As interpreters, their task is to engage in a solitary inquiry and apply the principles of interpretive reasoning. Very few of them will be short-listed for becoming world-historical individuals, but even Hegel's list of such individuals was not extensive.

To avoid confusion, it may be useful to understand "great man of the age" or "world-historical individual" as technical terms. Hegel applied these terms to persons who successfully formulated the desires of their contemporaries and who had sufficient insight for finding the truth in public opinion. Similarly, my use of "professional critic" or "professional interpreter" is restricted to persons who are entitled to speak with a universal voice about matters requiring interpretation. The use of such terms implies success in matters of interpretation. If persons designated by these labels disappoint us for insufficient insight or mistaken judgment, then we can no longer apply these labels to them. To be sure, not much harm can be done by persons who have been designated by others (or in the past, by us) as professional art, music, or literary critics. If their judgments about individual artworks turn out to be mistaken, then their views will be discredited, and sooner or later they will be consigned to oblivion. But harm can be done (and has been done) by persons who are considered professional interpreters in social and political contexts. Skepticism is the best defense against the claim that they know what their contemporaries need. In arguing for the principles of interpretive reasoning, we must be mindful of the skeptical rejoinder: those who are claimed by others to be professional interpreters and professional critics do not know more than their contemporaries about what is needed for their age. I expect that occasionally each of us will find the skeptical rejoinder more persuasive than the interpretations of last Tuesday's professionals in interpreting the arts or in formulating the desires of our contemporaries. But the reader must not expect the customary conclusion that there are good arguments on both sides of this issue, and whoever opts for either skepticism or interpretive reasoning supported by an appeal to Universalizability finds herself in good company. No doubt, since we are engaged in interpreting the interpreting activity, we cannot expect to find facts or arguments serving to establish definitively one of the two sides. However, the preponderance of the evidence points to the advantage of interpretive reasoning supported by Universalizability over the endorsement of skepticism. The reason for this is that each of us is a solitary interpreter who relies on interpretive reasoning supported by Universalizability even while deciding to reject someone else's interpretive claims on skeptical grounds. Skepticism is subsumed under interpretive reasoning supported by Universalizability, and not the other way around.

3. Professional Interpreters

It would be useless to question the credentials of interpreters we consider reasonable and knowledgeable about what is at issue by telling them that they are merely self-appointed.

Regardless of whether we are professionals, amateurs, or illiterates in a given field, each of us is a self-appointed interpreter—and we cannot escape being self-appointed interpreters—every time we rely on our own authority for accepting or rejecting someone else's interpretation. Of course, we may ask someone else's counsel as to whether to accept a given interpretation, but it is up to us whether we accept that counsel; hence, it is up to us whether we accept that interpretation. Accordingly, it is not only the case that each of us is capable of having an individual voice; we are in fact exercising our individual voices whenever we accept or reject a given interpretation. Anyone who has an individual voice is capable of having a universal voice; hence, each of us is capable of having a universal voice. Since we cannot escape from exercising our individual voices in accepting or rejecting at least some interpretations, we are all in possession of a universal voice. Although each of us is entitled to appeal to Universalizability in support of an interpretation, some of us prefer to appeal to the Restrictive Principle. The risks of such a strategy will be shown by an example.

You support your interpretation on the grounds that your guru suggested it; I happen to be skeptical of such sources of received wisdom. So if I have no other reasons for accepting the interpretation that you offer, I reject your interpretation. In this case, skepticism about the evidence you have provided is sufficient for its rejection. But I could just as well add: all reasonable persons who are knowledgeable about what is at issue support my rejection of your interpretation. My skeptical rejoinder is supported by an appeal to Universalizability. In telling me that your guru supports your interpretation, you claim that it is reasonable to accept guidance from a reasonable person, and you certainly argue that your guru is reasonable. I agree that both you and your guru are reasonable—I wouldn't wish to argue with you if I didn't consider you reasonable—but isn't it rather odd that you have selected a well-defined subset of persons (those who agree with you and your guru) and then tell me that they are all reasonable and knowledgeable about what is at issue? You are appealing to the Restrictive Principle. You invite criticism by avoiding an appeal to Universalizability. You rely on your own authority as a self-appointed interpreter for accepting your guru's guidance. All reasonable and knowledgeable persons agree that you have that authority. They also agree that as long as you are a student in a given field or a novice in a given profession, it is prudent to listen to the advice provided by others. They also agree that there is an indefinite number of other good reasons for accepting the interpretations provided by others. But these good reasons share one common feature: they can be grounded on an appeal to Universalizability. However, if your reason for accepting the interpretation suggested by your guru cannot be grounded on Universalizability, then your reason does not validate your acceptance of your guru's interpretation. If you happen to think that it does validate it, then you must also believe that the deliverances of public opinion or of what "people say" also validate interpretations just as much as your guru's suggestions.

A pattern emerges here that we have encountered previously. An interpretation is supported by appealing to one of the two principles. In addition, the appeal itself can be also supported by one of the two principles. In some cases, appealing to Universalizability can reinforce an interpretation supported by the Restrictive Principle. (All persons who are reasonable and knowledgeable about the issues agree that a novice in a given profession should listen to the advice of his teachers.) In some other cases, an interpretation supported by the Restrictive Principle can be reinforced only by appealing again to the Restrictive Principle. (All persons who accept a given guru's interpretation on a certain topic are reasonable and knowledgeable about what is at issue.) But this is a rather weak support for accepting that interpretation; in fact, it opens the door for questioning its acceptance.

You are capable of having a universal voice. But instead of appealing to Universalizability in support of the interpretation you accept (or reject), you withdraw to an apparently safer ground and appeal only to the Restrictive

Principle. Since you act on your own authority in accepting (or rejecting) that interpretation, you are fully responsible for your choice. You cannot diminish your responsibility for your choice by appealing to the Restrictive Principle rather than to the Universalizability Principle. No doubt, in some circumstances an appeal to Universalizability will support your appeal to the Restrictive Principle. But if an appeal to Universalizability does not support your appeal to the Restrictive Principle, your critic has good reasons for believing that your choice of accepting or rejecting that interpretation is at least contestable. After all, even misinterpretations or discredited interpretations can be and have been supported by an appeal to the Restrictive Principle.

4. The Voice of Professional Interpreters

We are now in the position to understand and appreciate the difference between professional interpreters or critics in a given field and their non-professional counterparts. Earlier I designated the solitary interpreters speaking with a universal voice as professionals in criticism or interpretation. We must now note that professionals cannot advert to other interpreters' agreement about an interpretive choice as a reason for accepting that choice. As solitary interpreters they must rely exclusively on their own experiences in reaching an interpretation. They would undermine their standing as professionals in their own fields if they admitted that in reaching their interpretations they followed common sense, public opinion, their colleagues' recommendations, or the dictates of what has been adopted by all reasonable and knowledgeable persons. By relying on the interpretive decision of others in adopting an interpretation they would cast doubt on their exercising their own individual voices within their field of competence. Their interpreting activity must be in accordance with Universalizability in the sense that they can demand the agreement of others; but it cannot be guided by Universalizability in the sense that they rely on the agreement of others. Nonprofessional interpreters or critics may advert to Universalizability as a reason for adopting or defending an interpretation. They may claim that they have adopted or defended a given interpretation because all persons who are reasonable and knowledgeable about what is at issue agreed with that interpretation. They need not rely exclusively on their own experiences as solitary inquirers in reaching an interpretation.

An important difference emerges here between interpretive reasoning and logical reasoning. If questioned why we accept the conclusion of an inference, we advert to its logical form. We accept it because the logical form of that inference guarantees that we cannot derive a false conclusion from true premises. Professionals and nonprofessionals in logic or mathematics may—but do not always—appeal to the same considerations in accepting or rejecting the conclusion of an inference. Matters are different in the context of interpretive reasoning.

Professional interpreters or critics are expected to lead rather than follow others in formulating their critical judgment or interpretive choices. A nonprofessional need not formulate his own interpretive choice; he may rely on a consensus in adopting such a choice. When we accept or reject a given interpretation, we are all self-appointed interpreters. Professional interpreters and critics among us are also self-appointed as professionals in their fields, exercising their universal voice, when they formulate a given interpretation or critical judgment.

5. Consensus among Interpreters

I have derived from what Kant wrote about a pure judgment of taste the professional or solitary interpreter's ground for an interpretive choice (chapter 8). I have accepted as the ground for an aesthetic judgment what Kant has described as the subject's ground for a pure judgment of taste. Moreover, I have suggested—in a context larger than pure judgments of taste or aesthetic judgments—the solitary or professional interpreter's ground for adopting and defending an interpretation. Such an interpreter could not discover as grounds of the interpretive choice "any private conditions, pertaining to his subject alone, and must therefore regard it as grounded in those that he can also presuppose in everyone else." Confronted with what was being interpreted, the professional interpreter was not influenced by what he had learned from others. He did not rely on the authority of other professional interpreters or on an agreement with all reasonable and knowledgeable persons. Moreover, as far as he knew, he was not biased by some private conditions that were unique to him or to his social circle. His interpretive choice was prompted by what was interpreted, and it was presented for adoption by all persons who were reasonable and knowledgeable about the issues.

The professional interpreter's demand that others adopt his interpretation can succeed only with the nonprofessional segment of his audience. Other professional interpreters must reach their own interpretations in a solitary confrontation with what is being interpreted—independently of any prompting by others. Yet there is a consensus among professional interpreters—how is this possible? We must not be satisfied with the suggestion that a common cultural or social background explains the consensus. Even if the professional interpreters share the same background, this does not explain their agreement on a given interpretation. The sociological explanation is vacuous at best: we would get the same answer if professional interpreters had adopted any other interpretation, and this includes interpretations that are inconsistent with what has been adopted.

Professional interpreters may reexamine their views upon learning of an interpretation that is incompatible with their own views. Many strategies are available to them on encountering such an incompatible interpretation. They may ignore it, dismiss it as a misinterpretation or an off-the-wall interpretation, or explain it away by arguing that there was some private condition pertaining to the interpreters defending the competing interpretation. They may even prefer the interpretation that is incompatible with their own interpretation. (The roles of teacher and student are occasionally reversed, and the teacher adopts the student's interpretation.) Such strategies are infrequently needed. There is a widespread consensus among professional or solitary interpreters—how is that possible? I have recommended a philosopher's confrontation with the problem of skepticism as a paradigm of the solitary inquiry in interpreting (chapter 8). The agreement among philosophers in their answers to the most radical formulation of skepticism could be understood as the result of each philosopher's success in finding—until the next skeptical challenge—a right answer to the problem of skepticism. Similarly, the consensus among professional interpreters could be grounded on each interpreter finding, temporarily, the right interpretation of what is at issue.

Since all of us are self-appointed interpreters capable of having a universal voice, and the professional interpreters and critics among us are also self-appointed as professionals in a given field, we can all try to establish ourselves in the role of a professional interpreter or critic. Few of us will succeed in that role. Many are called to speak with a universal voice and to argue for a given interpretation, but few are chosen. Some will convince only themselves that they are professional interpreters or critics, a few will be recognized only by their friends, and even fewer will be recognized by those who know them only in their role as professional interpreters. Art critics, artists, or philosophers find themselves in a similar situation. Many rely on large doses of self-deception in considering themselves professionals in these fields, a few gain recognition within their own coterie, and even fewer are recognized by others for the role they are playing as professionals in criticism, art, or philosophy. Is there a correlation between the role they are playing as professionals in these fields and the recognition they receive? It would be incredible, if there were none or if it were perfect. We expect a correlation and hope for a strong correlation. The solitary and professional interpreter or critic formulates her own interpretation of what is at issue. Occasionally, her nonprofessional counterpart also tries to rely only on himself. Confronted with an object of interpretation or an artwork, he tries to emulate the professional interpreter or critic, and to speak with a universal voice. He may succeed, and then he too will become a professional interpreter or critic with respect to that object or artwork. Or he may fail. Since he is self-appointed as a professional interpreter or critic, the judgment whether he is a success or failure may be left safely in his own hands. No harm is done in the context of artworks if an amateur falsely believes that he is a professional critic—he risks only ridicule. Harm can be and has been done in social and political contexts by incompetent interpreters who insist on formulating their own interpretations. Ridicule or the charge of insincerity will not discourage demagogues and spokespersons for sectarian groups. They do not have an individual voice; hence, they are not entitled to speak with a universal voice—such critical claims will be accepted only by their opponents.

6. The Concept of Interpretation

A philosophical topic remains to be discussed. Is there only one concept of interpretation? Do we use the same concept when we speak about interpretation in such different fields as the sciences, the social sciences, the human sciences, and the arts? Alternatively, are there different concepts of interpretation that are dependent on the topic that is being interpreted? I do not know how to argue directly either for or against the view that we have only one concept of interpretation. Guided by the hypothesis that we have only one such concept, I approach the problems of interpreting from its goal: understanding. The verdict on this hypothesis depends on its usefulness for a discussion of interpretive reasoning. The reader may prefer to argue for the usefulness of the opposite hypothesis: we have many different concepts of interpretation. The decision about accepting one hypothesis rather than another depends on other views about the interpreting activity that we may wish to defend.

Contrary to the views accepted by Nietzsche, Heidegger, and many of their followers, I suggest that interpreting is not a prerequisite for understanding. We interpret only when interpretations are needed. Such a need arises when we cannot grasp immediately what was said or done. The interpreter cannot grasp it, because from his viewpoint there is a gap between what was said and his understanding of what was said. Guided by common sense, he attributes reasons to the speaker's or agent's words or deeds. Interpreting may be an art, but there is no science of interpretation. If there were such a science, then its understanding would have to be supported either by commonsense considerations or by another science. The second alternative must be rejected, since it opens the door for infinite regress. The first alternative has an important consequence. Interpretation rests on commonsense considerations, and this holds not only for surface- but also for deep-level interpretations. In the context of deep-level interpretation, we can at best speak about an extension of commonsense considerations, but not about applications of scientific theories. Contrary to what some of their followers may have thought, Freudian or Marxist interpretive practices are supported only by extensions of commonsense considerations. They are not supported by scientific theories.

Common sense urges a trivial claim in guiding interpretations: all speakers and agents want us to understand their words and deeds as they wish we should understand them. If they are sincere, they want us to understand them either as they understand them or better than they understand them. This provides us with a criterion for success in natural or surface-level interpretation in the indicative mood. As soon as we realize that some speakers or agents occasionally have a deficient understanding of their own words and deeds, the distinction between interpreting in the indicative and in the subjunctive mood is forced on us. We want to understand them either as they understand themselves or as they would understand themselves if they were in their interpreters' place. Caregivers or physicians want to understand their charges or patients as they would understand themselves if they had the expertise of their interpreters. Interpretation in the subjunctive mood—without the additional qualification that it is an interpretation that has a moral dimension—is insufficient whenever a qualified speaker or agent can reach only a deficient self-understanding. Because of his distorted self-understanding, the speaker or agent cannot in principle agree with his interpreter's understanding of his words and deeds. He cannot confirm or disconfirm the deep-level interpretation of these words and deeds. Deep-level interpretations are essentially contested interpretations, and they rely on the overt or covert claim that the speaker or agent is self-deceived.

Interpretive reasoning on any level requires that we simultaneously satisfy two demands that are mistakenly believed to be at loggerheads. The interpreter may adopt or defend an interpretation if and only if all or some persons who are reasonable and knowledgeable about what is at issue do so as well. At the same time the interpreter must often rely only on his own judgment in formulating an interpretation. He formulates his interpretation without asking for the opinion of others. Yet unless he is in the position to add that all reasonable persons who are knowledgeable about the issues agree with his judgment or—in essentially contested cases—all who agree with his judgment are reasonable, he will not receive a hearing. The two demands do not contradict each other. Such demands must be satisfied also by reasoners in other contexts. (Creative work on the cutting edge of a discipline often requires that the solitary inquirer formulate his own proof of the claims presented; at the same time, they are presented with the understanding that all reasonable and knowledgeable persons would agree with the results obtained.) As soon as we admit that an interpreter cannot ground his interpretation on his unique characteristics, the two demands can be seen as dependent on each other. Even the most talented interpreter in a given field must formulate his interpretive claims so that interpreters lacking his talent can adopt the interpretations he recommended. Just as a laboratory experiment leading to a discovery in the sciences must be repeatable by different scientists, reasonable and informed interpreters must be able to reproduce the interpreting activity leading to a given interpretation.

There are successful interpretations—how are they possible? Kant did not formulate this question, but he can be understood as providing a model for its answer. We must have a standard of correctness for our interpretations if we wish to avoid the major pitfall of interpreting: the projection of our own beliefs, desires, and understanding of what is at issue onto the object of interpretation. Such a projection merely succeeds in superimposing what is in the interpreter onto what is being interpreted. The Universalizability Principle and to a lesser degree the Restrictive Principle provide the standards we seek. The demand that the solitary interpreter be free of private conditions grounding his interpretative choice yields a constant reminder of the demarcation line separating interpretive liberty from the abuse of that liberty. He must first convince himself that he is free of private conditions before he is in the position of convincing others about this matter. The possibility of self-deception arises in this context. Unless he is self-deceived about being free from private conditions, he has an individual voice and he is entitled to speak with a universal voice. Interpretations presented with a universal voice are deemed to be successful interpretations.

Three remarks must be added. First, it merely seems paradoxical that the solitary interpreter must free himself of private conditions in order to have an individual voice. At issue are only the relevant private conditions; "relevant" carries the burden of removing the absurdity from this claim.

For example, the commission that the older connoisseur received for paintings sold with his attributions (chapter 1, section 3) or AO's desire to enrich his relatives (chapter 9, section 3) was seen by their critics as a relevant private condition while many of their other characteristics were considered irrelevant. The solitary interpreter's focus must be what is interpreted, and at issue is his own understanding of what is interpreted. Whatever cannot be traced to his own contribution to the interpretive situation will be understood as originating from an anonymous source of public opinion or of what "people say." For example, the residue of prejudices against a class, gender, or race will be understood as distorting his individual voice, since it does not originate with that voice.

Secondly, the ever-present possibility of self-deception concerning the solitary interpreter's individual voice cannot be overestimated. Does this imply that there is such a phenomenon as self-deception? We may hold such a view on grounds that are independent of this discussion, but suspicions about the solitary interpreter's individual voice do not provide decisive evidence on this topic. Two cases must be distinguished. First is the solitary interpreter's self-examination: "Do I speak about my own experiences, or am I deceiving myself about what is being interpreted?" (See chapter 8, section 5.) Second is his critic's claim that because of self-deception the solitary interpreter was indeed blind to some aspect of his experiences (chapter 9, section 5). In the first case, the self-examination can proceed regardless of the solitary interpreter's views about self-deception. Even if he believes that there is such a phenomenon, he cannot answer that he is self-deceived, for such an answer would be self-defeating. The point of the self-examination is merely to convince himself that he has an individual voice and accordingly that he is entitled to be speaking with a universal voice. In the second case, the claim that there is such a phenomenon as self-deception does not add anything to the critic's charge that the solitary interpreter was self-deceived (chapter 1, section 6). The critic may understand and use the charge of self-deception as a way of speaking, as a *façon de parler* without implying that there is such a phenomenon. After all, what is needed to substantiate her charge is only the claim that the interpreter was blind to a private condition grounding his interpretive choice (chapter 8, section 9, and chapter 9, section 5). Readers committed to rejecting the assumption that there is such a phenomenon as self-deception may do so while proceeding with a self-examination or when criticizing others.

Thirdly, the interpreting activity does not have a theoretically satisfactory beginning or ending. Based on the need for an interpretation, each interpreter must decide on the limits of interpreting. One interpreter may grasp directly what was said or done without the intermediary of an interpretation, while another may require an interpretation. Where one interpreter comes to an end, another may choose to give continuity to interpreting. The limits of interpreting are dependent on the interpreter's beliefs, desires, and understanding.

7. Alternatives

Objections may be raised—and I expect they will be raised—against some of the views on interpreting presented here. Readers concerned with the philosophical debate that I have traced to the views of Wittgenstein and Heidegger about the relation between understanding and interpreting may question my views. Is there a sharp distinction between understanding and interpreting, and is interpreting only seldom a prerequisite for understanding? Or is interpreting always a prerequisite for understanding, such that the two notions cannot be separated in isolation from each other? I have suggested that the redescription of interpreting presented here can be adjusted to agree with either side of this debate (chapter 3, section 5). What were the reasons for this rather confident suggestion?

If this is indeed a philosophical debate, then the views of both sides must be compatible with the facts and our practices. If either side of a philosophical debate becomes incompatible with the facts, then that side must be discredited. What was mistakenly believed to be a philosophical debate becomes a debate among philosophers. I have assumed that this debate is a philosophical debate and within this framework I have tried to offer a redescription of the interpreting activity, while endorsing one side of the debate. The task of showing how to adjust this redescription in order to make it compatible with the other side could be left to those who are willing to endorse that side of the debate. I may have been mistaken on one or both of two grounds: (1) the debate is only a debate among philosophers, and the side that I have endorsed deserves to be discredited, or (2) the views presented here are mistaken about the facts and do not provide an adequate account of the interpreting activity. If the critical reader's alternative account succeeds only in convicting me of being mistaken about the facts, then my confident suggestion will turn out to be irrelevant. And if the alternative account shows that the debate is only a debate among philosophers, then it still must be shown in order to discredit the views presented here that I did not do justice to the facts and the interpreting activity. Either way, the facts of the matter and the understanding of the interpreting activity will prove to be decisive in accepting or rejecting the views presented here. Commitment to one or the other side of the philosophical debate will turn out to be of little importance.

8. Preparing the Ground for Others

What I have said about the constraints on an interpretation is also applicable to the views presented here. This is a trivial claim, but it must be spelled out. If in the reader's considered judgment my views have not satisfied the two constraints, he will reject them or consign them to oblivion. Alternatively, even if he opts for accepting some or all of my views, he must build on them, thereby destroying at least some of what has been presented. Either way, he will be acting as an interpreter who must make up his own mind about these matters in solitary confrontation with what has been presented. Writers on the interpreting activity must acknowledge the prospect that their contributions will make way for those of their readers and critics. The author's role is merely offering a ground where others can build. This is especially important in the context of writing about deep interpretation. The founders of deep-interpretation theories provided tools for a critical understanding of what has been said or done. Their followers and disciples can avoid dogmatism only if they refuse to regard these tools as established verities that need no further development. The tools are useful only as long as they prepare the ground for others to create and to build on their intellectual heritage. Dogmatism resulting from their acceptance as verities blunts their point, thereby undermining the critical purpose for which they were created. As tools of criticism, they serve to criticize ideologies; as established verities, they themselves become ideologies.

Asked to highlight the road leading from the beginning to the end of this work, I would point to the role of the solitary inquirer interpreting from its inception, and to the moral considerations that arise within the interpreting activity at its end. To secure a foothold for the solitary inquirer I started my account of interpreting with our earliest attempts at understanding others. At that time we could not ask what the consensus was about what others had said or done. Yet the little we did know about the world around us prepared us for a critical attitude about what we were told. We understood that our task was not finding, but making sense of what we were told. Understanding is not only a goal, but also a product of interpretation. There is a lesson in this insight that could have made us impervious to the attraction of all consensus-driven interpretation theories. It could have done so, and it should have done so, but it did not, for at the end of the line we are confronted with a fear: maybe as a solitary inquirer I feel at home with this particular interpretation for a wrong reason, maybe even for the worst possible reason. Something is wrong with me. In extreme cases the solitary inquirer is in a similar situation as a radical skeptic. At issue is the fear that they are exceeding the bounds of reason in a totally reasonable environment, or the other way around: that they are the only reasonable inquirers in an unreasonable surrounding.

The two principles aim at securing a foothold for the solitary interpreter. If he can convince himself that all competent interpreters agree with him or that all who agree with him are competent interpreters, then the fear dissolves. Even if something is wrong with him, this need not have determined his acceptance of a given interpretation. If this is the case, he need no longer doubt that he opted for the right interpretive choice. But what if he merely thinks that he has satisfied both constraints on interpreting, and in reality did not do so? To be sure, if this were the case he would not be entitled to appeal to the Universalizability Principle. On the other hand, the appeal to the Restrictive Principle would still be available. However, what if even this principle does not alleviate his fear? Suppose he strongly suspects that he is the only interpreter who defends a given interpretation. If this is the case, then the appeal to either of the two principles is self-confirming or vacuous.

Let us return to the case in which he merely thinks that he has satisfied both constraints without actually satisfying them. What has gone wrong? Many things could have gone wrong. At issue was a minor mistake, or a momentary blindness to some detail, or . . . , or a bad judgment, or a case of self-deception. I expected to discuss the last disjunct of the very long disjunction—introduced in chapter 9, section 3—only in the penultimate chapter of this book. Contrary to my intentions, the problem of self-deception arose in the first chapter. Looking backward from the vantage point of the end of this inquiry, it is easy to see why this problem arose at such an early stage. In any interpretive conflict each interpreter asks for a reason for his disagreement with others. In trying to understand another interpreter's disagreement with me, I must focus on one of the disjuncts of that long disjunction. He must also focus on one of the disjuncts in understanding my disagreement with him. If each of us believes that he has satisfied both constraints on interpreting, then each of us could appeal to Universalizability in the subjunctive mood. Were it not for one disjunct in that long disjunction, each of us could claim that all competent interpreters agree with his interpretation.

For expository purposes let us group the disjuncts in that long disjunction under three headings. The other interpreter does not agree with my interpretation because (1) he failed to notice a significant detail, (2) he had bad judgment, or (3) he was self-deceived. In claiming that another interpreter failed to notice something, we are in effect charging him with ignorance. Ignorance can be easily remedied. We could recommend that he investigate once more what is at issue, that he read another book, and so on. For the last two groups there are no easy remedies. We shall see that in charging another interpreter with bad judgment in the context of a particular interpretation, we are in effect charging him with stupidity. Finally, in charging him with self-deception, we are recommending—with help of one of the deep-interpretation theories—that he change his life.

About the connection between bad judgment and stupidity we must start with what Kant said on this topic. (Kant's long footnote is quoted in parentheses.) For a better understanding of what follows, it is useful to keep in mind that for Kant the power of judgment is the faculty of determining whether something falls under a given rule:

> [A]lthough the understanding is certainly capable of being instructed and equipped through rules, the power of judgment is a special talent that cannot be taught but only practiced. Thus this is also what is specific to so-called mother-wit, the lack of which cannot be made good by any school; for, although such a school can provide a limited understanding with plenty of rules borrowed from the insight of others and as it were graft these onto it, nevertheless the faculty for making use of them correctly must belong to the student himself, and in the absence of such a natural gift no rule that one might prescribe to him for this aim is safe from misuse.
>
> (The lack of the power of judgment is that which is properly called stupidity, and such a failing is not to be helped. A dull or limited head, which is lacking nothing but the appropriate degree of understanding and its proper concepts, may well be trained through instruction, even to the point of becoming learned. But since it would usually still lack the power of judgment [the *secunda Petri*] it is not at all uncommon to encounter very learned men who in the use of their science frequently give glimpses of that lack, which is never to be ameliorated.)
>
> A physician therefore, a judge, or a statesman, can have many fine pathological, juridical, or political rules in his head, of which he can even be a thorough teacher, and yet can easily stumble in their application, either because he is lacking in natural power of judgment (though not in understanding), and to be sure understands the universal *in abstracto* but cannot distinguish whether a case *in concreto* belongs under it, or also because he has not received adequate training for this judgment through examples and actual business. This is also the sole and great utility of examples: that they sharpen the power of judgment. For as far as the correctness and precision of the insight of the understanding is concerned, examples more usually do it some damage, since they only seldom adequately fulfill the condition of the rule (as *casus in terminis*) and beyond this often weaken the effort of the under-

standing to gain sufficient insight into rules in the universal and independently of the particular circumstances of experience, and thus in the end accustom us to use those rules more like formulas than like principles. Thus examples are the leading-strings of the power of judgment, which he who lacks the natural talent for judgment can never do without.[*]

A slight addition to Kant's diagnosis of bad judgment will be necessary to appreciate the reasons for distinguishing cases of ignorance from cases of bad judgment. We notice cases of bad judgment in the interpretive choices of our contemporaries primarily when at issue is a subject matter that is outside their main field of interest. Within their field of expertise, they usually had sufficient training "through examples and actual business." It is outside their field that stupidity or bad judgment raises its head. And this is true not only for the professionals Kant named, but also for philosophers, including Kant himself—along with his predecessors and successors.

A case in point is what he wrote about capital punishment or the status of illegitimate children within society.[†] Insights won and rules derived from the study of metaphysics or epistemology cannot be uncritically applied when dealing with social or political issues. Respect for achievements in philosophy kept traditionalist readers from bringing to light evidence of occasional bad judgment. Such readers preferred to hide it behind a trite remark suggesting that even philosophers shared their contemporaries' prejudices. Guided by suspicion rather than by respect—I am using here a distinction introduced by Paul Ricoeur—our contemporaries are willing to forgo such platitudes and to identify stupidity wherever they find it. The theories and practices of deep interpretation paved the way for replacing respect with suspicion in interpreting. (My own bad judgment must be faulted for failing to insist sufficiently on the importance of stupidity and bad judgment in the evaluation of interpretive choices.) Nonetheless, the trite remark has a point.

When we say that a speaker or writer shared his contemporaries' prejudices, we are saying that in a given context he did not speak with his own voice. It was the conventional wisdom of his time or what others have said that spoke through him. No doubt, we are all capable of having an individual voice. But this does not mean that we always have such a voice when offering an interpretation. Our actually having an individual voice on a given occasion is our own achievement. It is only after I excluded

[*] Immanuel Kant, *Critique of Pure Reason*, ed. and trans. P. Guyer and A. W. Wood (New York: Cambridge University Press, 1998), A133–34, B172–74.
[†] Immanuel Kant, *Metaphysik der Sitten* (Hamburg: Felix Meiner, 1959), 160–65.

the possibility that I am just a mouthpiece for what "people say" that I can reach the level of speaking with my own voice. Richard Wollheim referred to this problem when he mentioned that looking at a painting is a time-consuming process. He described the first hour as being preoccupied with setting aside what he brought to that painting. Liberated from that ballast during the second hour, he could see the painting for what it was. As solitary interpreters we must take the time to set aside the ballast of received opinion, if we wish to achieve the level of having an individual voice. When we achieve that level, we are ready to examine whether our interpretation satisfies both constraints on interpreting and accordingly whether we are entitled to speak with a universal voice.

Let us now focus on a conflict with another interpreter where at issue is anything but the last disjunct of that long disjunction. (Excluded from consideration at this stage is only the hypothesis that the other is self-deceived.) If each interpreter believes the other would agree with him, if they could agree on one disjunct in that long disjunction, then each interpreter's appeal to Universalizability in the subjunctive mood is well-grounded. The available choices for each interpreter are limited. Each may opt to remain silent about his judgment that the other is not a competent interpreter of what is at issue. One may opt to talk about his interpretation but avoid a confrontation with the other. Finally, one may engage in a discussion with the other. In the last case, he cannot publicly admit that as long as the other does not agree with him, he cannot be considered a competent interpreter of the issues. So in order to show tolerance for the opinion of the other, he must maintain publicly that both appeal merely to the Restrictive Principle, while with his backstage voice he continues to appeal to Universalizability. The insincerity of appealing to one principle in public and to the other in private is a stain on tolerance in interpreting.

If we now admit to our consideration the last disjunct of that long disjunction, the three options reappear if the interpreter appeals to Universalizability in the subjunctive mood. The situation changes slightly if he decides to appeal to the Restrictive Principle on the ground that the other interpreter cannot agree with him if he wants to avoid a self-defeating claim that here and now he is deceiving himself. Again, he is insincere for maintaining in public that he supports his interpretation by appealing to the Restrictive Principle, while behind the stage he appeals to Universalizability. The judgment that the other is self-deceived makes sense only if we wish to raise a moral issue and urge the other to change his life. So his case against the other interpreter rests on insincerity, while he urges the other to mend his ways from a moral point of view. Call this the flaw of deep interpretation.

Tolerance is stained; deep interpretation is flawed. Should we give up on tolerance and/or deep interpretation? An affirmative answer would run counter to the dominant strain of philosophy that flourished within the tradition of skepticism and liberalism. A negative answer recognizes that we must accept tolerance, even if stained, and deep interpretation, even if flawed.

9. Envoy

The solitary interpreter confronted what was to be interpreted. She could not find a private condition that informed her interpretation. What she brought to her interpretation could be presupposed in everyone else. She concluded that her interpretation was grounded on what was to be interpreted. Professional interpreters approximate this model. Interpretations so reached are self-confirming. Does the professional interpreter know when she is right in accepting an interpretation? She cannot know that; she can only know what is trivially true: unless she is mistaken (about matters major or minor), or has bad judgment, or is self-deceived, she is right. If she has any competitors in her field, they are all in the same position. Having reached their interpretive decisions, they speak with a universal voice and thereby claim that all reasonable and knowledgeable persons would agree with their interpretive decisions. The appeal to Universalizability suggests an explanation of the interpretive decision and enters a normative claim—this is how interpretive reasoning should proceed.

On looking closer at what I have presented as the model of the solitary interpreter, the explanatory and normative claims accompanying the solitary interpreter's interpretation, the reader may ask: isn't there a tension between my model of the solitary interpreter and the claims accompanying that model? A self-confirming interpretation is explained by an appeal to Universalizability and is supported by the claim that this is how interpretive reasoning ought to proceed—isn't there something paradoxical about these claims? Three responses can be expected. Some readers will find the tension between the model of the solitary interpreter and the accompanying claims sufficient for rejecting the view of interpreting presented here. Others will focus on what they see as the paradoxical character of these views, will reach for an ideologically driven account of interpreting (derivative books on deconstruction are prime candidates for such exercises), and will further explore—in a book of their own—what they see as a paradox. Finally, others will not see any paradox and will come to understand and to appreciate matters as they are.

I stand with the last group.

Index

Alcidamas, 173
Aristotle, 84–85, 141, 169–71, 173–74,
    178–79, 182, 186
Authoritarianism, 10, 70, 72–74, 154

Belief box, 32–35, 37, 41–42, 106–18,
    125–26, 162, 166, 173
Beardsley, M. C., 90–91
Burge, T., 128

Cantor, G., 161
Consensus on interpretations, 24–26, 52,
    68, 79–80, 84, 121–22, 124, 147–48,
    150–51, 154, 165, 186, 199–200, 206
Constraints on interpretations, 49–53, 61–
    64, 68, 71–72, 77–78, 81–83, 86, 114,
    121, 159–60, 163–64, 187–88
Conversation terminators, 8–12, 70–73;
    derived from the Universalizability or
    the Restrictive Principle, 9–10

Da Ponte, L., 183
Davidson, D., 6, 144–45, 168
Dedekind, R., 161
Derrida, J., 99–100
Deep (-level) interpretation, introduced,
    13. *See also* Self-deception
Dogmatism, 8, 10–11, 30, 70, 72–73, 89, 206

Finley, M. I., 173
Foucault, M., 60
Franklin, B., 171
Frege, G., 130, 133
Freud, S., 15, 20, 21, 58, 60–61, 71, 189, 202
Friedländer, S., 184

Frye, N., 94

Gap between what we can and do know
    about our own words, 27, 144, 201–2
Goethe, J. W. v., 76, 164
Grice, H. P., 192

Hart, W. D., 128
Hegel, G. W. F., 43, 168–69, 194–95
Heidegger, M., 57, 97, 98–99, 151, 194, 201,
    205
Hieronymus, St., 140–41
Hirsch, E. D. Jr., 90
Homer, 102
Hume, D., 171

Interpretations, application-driven, 68–69,
    101; consensus-driven, 79–80, 121–23,
    206; principle-driven, 122–23, 187

Jefferson, T., 169, 171–72
Joyce, J., 137, 139–40

Kant, I., 34, 65, 74–75, 116, 131, 137,
    139–40, 150–52, 163, 199, 203, 208–9
Keynes, J. M., 132
Klopstock, F. G., 76
Kripke, S., 132

Luther, M., 30, 39

Marx, K., 15, 20, 21, 58–61, 71, 87, 105, 189,
    202
Meaning, 22, 128, 131, 133–34, 143–46
Mele, A. R., 175

Misinterpretation, 19, 49, 70–73, 98, 100, 103–4, 160–62, 192, 198, 200
Molière, J. B. P., 183
Montaigne, M. E. de, 28, 40
Moore, G. E., 55

Natural (surface-level) interpretation, in indicative mood, introduced 8–12; in subjunctive mood, 12–13, 19, 22, 27, 46, 53, 57–58, 61–68, 77, 82, 112–13, 120, 124, 190–91, 202, 210
Nietzsche, F., 15, 20, 61, 144–45, 189, 191, 201

Off-the-wall interpretations, 49, 70, 97–98, 100–104, 176, 179–81, 193, 200

Pascal, B., 145–46
Philemon, 173–74
Plato, 84–85, 91, 133, 141, 169, 170–71, 178–79, 182, 186

Quine, W. V. O., 144–45

Relativism, 168, 170, 172, 182, 184
Restrictive Principle, introduced, 10
Retreating to a safe position in interpreting, 2, 11, 50, 68, 73–74, 114, 121, 188–89
Ricoeur, P., 209
Rilke, R. M., 19, 61, 63
Russell, B., 42
Ryle, G., 43, 94

Schapiro, M., 98–100

Schick, F., 42–44
Schiffer, S., 2, 32
Schiller, F., 75–76
Self-deception, 2, 14–15, 17–23, 33–34, 55–56, 58–59, 62, 68, 72, 98, 106, 108–10, 112–26, 147, 174, 180, 188–90, 200, 203–4, 207–8
Self-understanding, 12, 16–17, 20, 24, 27, 32, 45–49, 52–58, 63–64, 67, 77, 123, 173, 202
Shakespeare, W., 15, 88–89, 102–3
Shift of focus in interpreting, 2, 26, 29, 41, 44, 90, 92, 113, 156, 159, 164, 176–77, 180–81, 183
Sincerity or insincerity in interpreting, 11, 14, 47, 56, 58, 77, 114, 124, 160, 180, 187, 189–90, 201, 210–11
Skepticism, 29, 60, 104, 111, 126, 145, 148, 155–58, 162, 195–196, 200, 211

Tirso, da M., 183
Tolerance, 48, 64, 66–67, 110–12, 122, 183, 187–89, 210–11

Universalizability Principle, introduced, 9; conditions for appealing to this principle 49. *See also* Constraints on interpretations

Weber, M., 165
Wilamowitz-Moellendorff, U. v., 144–46
Wills, G., 169
Wittgenstein, L., 9, 42, 57, 144–45, 205
Wollheim, R., 210